# OPERATIONS

CARRIED ON AT

# THE PYRAMIDS OF GIZEH

IN 1837:

WITH AN ACCOUNT OF

A VOYAGE INTO UPPER EGYPT,

AND

An Appendix.

<hr />

By COLONEL HOWARD VYSE.

VOL. I.

LONDON:

JAMES FRASER, REGENT STREET.

MDCCCXL.

LONDON:
PRINTED BY MOYES AND BARCLAY, CASTLE STREET, LEICESTER SQUARE.

# CONTENTS

OF

# THE FIRST VOLUME.

CONTENTS. **ix**

# LIST OF PLATES

IN

# THE FIRST VOLUME.

# PREFACE.

THE chief object of the following pages is to give a distinct account of the works carried on at the Pyramids of Gizeh, under a firmaun granted by the Pasha in the winter of 1836.

The form of a Journal has been adopted, and the daily employments, and numbers of the people, have been given, that the extent and difficulties of the various operations may be more fully understood; — difficulties not a little increased by the irregular attendance of the labourers.

Abstracts from various authors antient and modern, who have treated of the Pyramids, are inserted in the Appendix: for those taken from Arabian writers I am indebted to the labours of Dr. Sprenger. A few other subjects are, likewise, incidentally alluded to, from a supposition that

they might interest, and, perhaps, assist future travellers in Egypt, but without any idea of compe-
tition with Mr. Lane's accurate account, or with
Sir J. Gardner Wilkinson's[1] more extensive work,
—two books, with which every traveller in that
country should be supplied.

When, in consequence of Colonel Campbell's
letter, M. Caviglia withdrew from the Pyramids, I
was engaged in assisting Mr. Perring in his survey
of those monuments, and, although I had not, at
first, the slightest intention of remaining abroad, I
considered it my duty to await the completion of
the survey, and, at the same time, to pursue the
objects, for which the firmaun was obtained. The
discovery of the exterior mouth of the northern
air-channel in the Great Pyramid, and the hope of
arriving at the apartments, which were supposed
to exist in the Third, by the excavation begun in
its interior induced me to persevere; and, as is
often the case, one thing led on to another, until,
being fairly engaged in works of so much interest,
I was, of course, determined to carry them on to

---

[1] Sir J. Gardner Wilkinson has received the honour of
knighthood since the following pages were written.

a favourable result, whatever sacrifices of money or of time might be incurred.

Many of our researches proved failures, they are, however, all described, together with the reasons why they were attempted. It will also be seen that some of the discoveries were accidentally made, a circumstance, indeed, to be expected from the little analogy, which exists in the internal construction of the three larger Pyramids, although their general purposes appear to have been the same; and the following pages will clearly shew that, whatever ultimate success was obtained, it must be chiefly attributed to the zealous and able assistance of Mr. Perring and of Mr. Mash, and to the unwearied perseverance of Mr. Hill and of Mr. Raven; nor should the valuable services of two other Englishmen (Goodman and Jack) be forgotten, the latter of whom, besides being constantly employed during the day, passed every night for nearly five months, in superintending the excavations in the interior of the Third Pyramid. These details, however, it is to be feared will not be completely understood, excepting by a constant reference to Mr. Perring's plans, published in two numbers, by Mr. Fraser, of Regent Street, from which the sections and admeasure-

ments inserted in these volumes have been copied.[s]
Plans of Campbell's Tomb, and of most of the other
Pyramids, as far south as the Faiyoum, including
the ruined site of Abou-Reche, have also been received from Mr. Perring, and will compose a third
number. The whole, it is presumed, will form a
work of considerable interest; and the value of it
will be greatly increased by a number of excellent
drawings taken on the spot by Mr. Andrews, who
remained at Gizeh for a considerable time, and
who with the same disinterested kindness, which
distinguished the conduct of the other two gentlemen, was indefatigably employed in my behalf
even during the intense heat of summer. I find
it difficult to express my acknowledgments for the

[s] The plates which relate to Gizeh have been executed
from Mr. Andrews' drawings by Mr. Arundale, with the exception of the panoramic view, the well, and the tent, which together
with the other plates that gentleman has contrived to arrange
from rough and imperfect sketches attempted by myself. I take
this opportunity of remarking that the table of levels at the
bottom of the plate containing the section of the rock (see page
138, Appendix, Vol. II.) was added in this country to Mr.
Perring's drawing, and that the difference of 13 feet 10$\frac{3}{4}$ inches
is erroneously inserted, as may be seen by reference to page 150.
Another mistake in the level of high Nile of 1838, instead of
1837, has been corrected.

cheerful and valuable assistance which these gentlemen invariably afforded me. The public will
be enabled, in some degree, to estimate the extent
of my obligations by the excellence of their works;
and I beg to assure them, that I shall ever remem-
ber with pleasure the time spent with them at
the Pyramids.

It is with regret I allude to the unpleasant
detail, which the dishonourable accusations made
in the name of M. Caviglia against Colonel Campbell and myself have rendered indispensable; but
in doing so I think it particularly necessary to
mention, in reference to that gentleman's opinion,
that I never experienced any interruption, or even
had reason to suspect the slightest hostility on the
part of the French, or of any other persons, whilst
I was engaged at the Pyramids.

Could I have obtained a direct order from the
Pasha to enforce the constant attendance of a
sufficient number of people, my intention was to
have excavated the entire area round the Sphinx,
which appears, at least on the western and southern sides, to have been enclosed by a peribolus of
unburnt bricks; but my application was not forwarded to the Pasha: and, from the immense
quantity and the looseness of the sand to be

removed in order to make the operation of any real utility, without the constant attendance of a considerable number of people the undertaking would have been almost indefinite as to time and expense. I conceive that this object, and the different levels of the water in the tombs, are peculiarly worthy of further investigation.

It was understood that the antiquities discovered under the firmaun were to belong to the Pasha, and that, without his Highness's permission, nothing whatsoever could be retained by either Colonel Campbell or myself. Separate lists are in consequence subjoined of the different articles found at Gizeh since the 13th of February, distinguishing those, which we were allowed to keep in consequence of an application to Boghos Bey; and since my return to England I have sent every thing of value to the British Museum. The Sarcophagus of Mycerinus was removed with considerable trouble and expense out of the Third Pyramid for the same purpose; as I was convinced that owing to the brittle quality of the stone, of which it was composed, it would soon have been entirely destroyed had it been left in an open pyramid. I was the more confirmed in this apprehension by having found, to my great regret,

that the magnificent casing-stones discovered at
the base of the Great Pyramid were so much
defaced, even during the time that I remained
at Gizeh, that I thought it my duty, upon leaving
the place, to cover them again with a considerable
quantity of rubbish, and thereby to do all in my
power to protect from further injury one of the
most interesting features of these unrivalled monuments. I am sorry to add, that my precautions
were unsuccessful, and that I have been subsequently informed that the blocks have been
again uncovered and much injured.

The following narration is chiefly composed
from a regular journal of the daily occurrences,
as they severally happened; and I have to observe,
that it was written in 1838, notwithstanding the
great delay, which has taken place in its publica-
tion, owing to the number of plates, to my own inexperience, and to other incidental causes, which
have also unfortunately made a list of errata necessary; and the reader's attention is particularly
requested to these inaccuracies, and likewise to
lists of corrections made by hand, which are
added in order to prevent mistakes although every
copy has been carefully examined.

I cannot conclude these prefatory observations
without returning my best thanks to Mr. Birch

for his valuable notes now published, and likewise
for those on the inscriptions at Tourah, Abouseir,
&c., already prepared for a third volume, which
will contain Mr. Perring's recent discoveries, since
my return from Egypt, and one or two other
papers relating to that country. I have also
great satisfaction in expressing my acknowledgments for the kind assistance and attention, which
I have met with at the British Museum; and at
Oxford from Dr. Macbride, and Dr. Bandinel of the
Bodleian Library; likewise at Eton College, particularly from the Rev. Mr. Coleridge, an advantage, for which I was chiefly indebted to the
late Rev. Mr. Wright; whose lamented death
has deprived me of a very old and much-respected
friend, and the Church and the College of a most
virtuous and distinguished ornament; a man possessed of the soundest judgment, and of great
literary attainments; dignified by the highest sense
of honour and of moral integrity; and inspired with
an ardent love for his country, and with undaunted
resolution to secure its liberties, and to promote
its prosperity, by maintaining inviolate its antient
laws and glorious constitution:

> " Cui pudor, et justitiæ soror
>  Incorrupta fides, nudaque veritas,
>  Quando ullum invenient parem?"

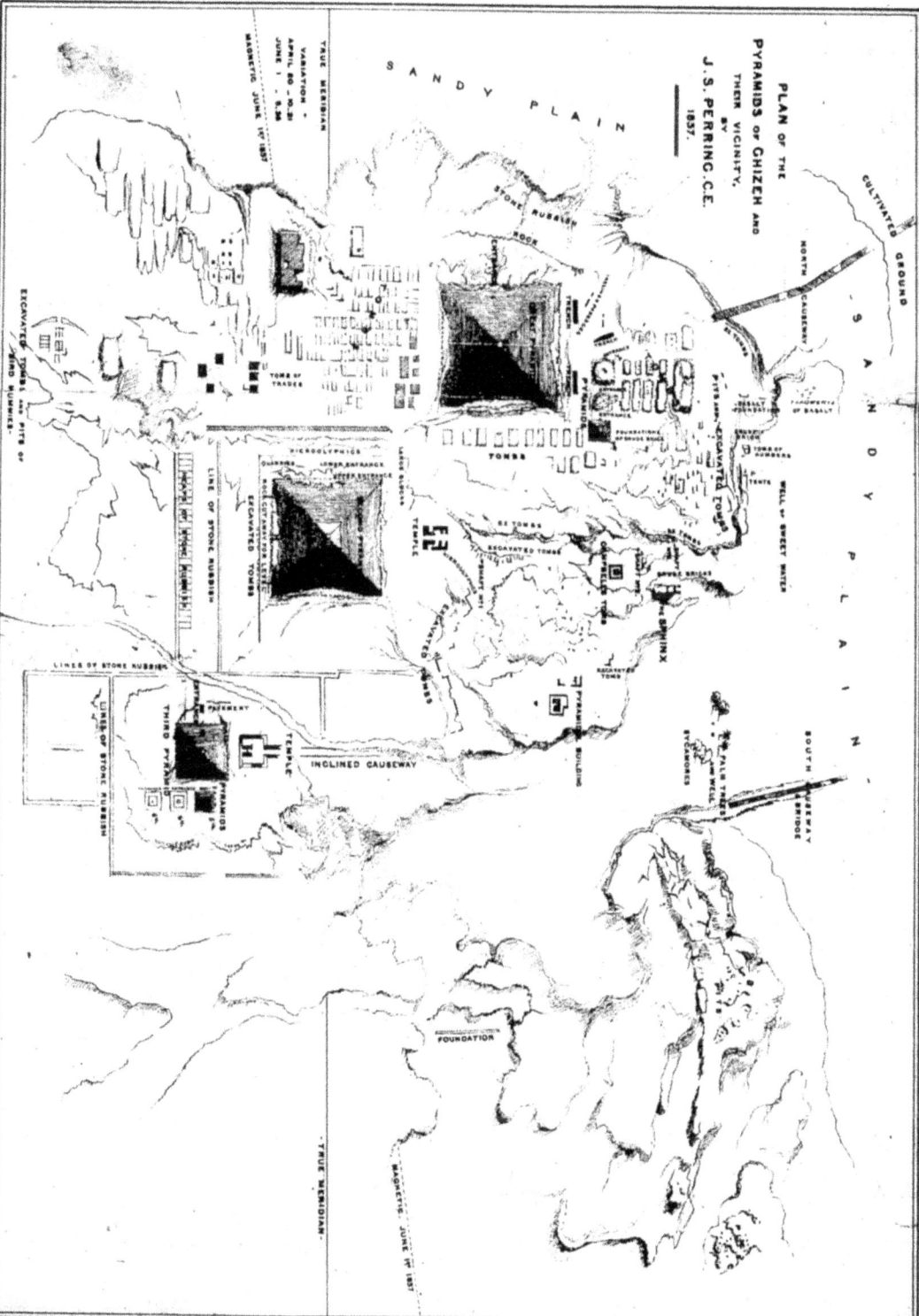

PLAN OF THE
PYRAMIDS OF GHIZEH AND
THEIR VICINITY,
BY
J. S. PERRING, C.E.
1837.

SANDY PLAIN

SANDY PLAIN

CULTIVATED GROUND

TRUE MERIDIAN
VARIATION
APRIL 60 · 10.31
JUNE 1 · 9.38
MAGNETIC JUNE 19TH 1837

INCLINED CAUSEWAY

THIRD PYRAMID
TEMPLE
PAVEMENT
LINES OF STONE RUBBISH
PYRAMIDS

EXCAVATED TOMBS
EXCAVATED TOMBS
LINE OF STONE RUBBISH

TOMB OF TRADES
TOMBS
FOUNDATIONS OF CRUDE BRICK
TOMB OF NUMBERS
WELL OF SWEET WATER
BASALT FOUNDATION
FRAGMENTS OF BASALT
NORTH CAUSEWAY

THE SPHINX
ROUGH BRICK
EX TOMBS
EXCAVATED TOMBS
TEMPLE
EXCAVATED TOMB
PYRAMID BUILDING

FOUNDATION

SOUTH CAUSEWAY
DOUM PALM WELL
FAIR TREES
SYCAMORES

PUBT BY JAS FRANCIS, 216, REGENT ST.

PRINTED BY GEO A. MANN, 11, GATE ST.

TRUE MERIDIAN
MAGNETIC JUNE 1ST 1837

# OPERATIONS CARRIED ON AT GIZEH,

## *&c. &c.*

---

BEFORE I describe the Operations carried on at the Pyramids in the spring and summer of 1837, it is necessary to state the condition, in which I found them on my first arrival in Egypt, and some other particulars, which may tend to make the Operations in question better understood.

I arrived in Alexandria on the 29th of December, 1835, with the intention of visiting Upper and Lower Egypt; but finding that an opportunity would present itself, towards the end of February, of visiting Syria with peculiar advantage, I determined to postpone till my return from that country my voyage into Upper Egypt, and to spend the time, that remained at my disposal, in Cairo.

Among the many objects of interest, which the neighbourhood of that curious and picturesque city afforded, the Pyramids, particularly those of Gizeh, attracted my attention; from the grandeur and simple majesty of their forms, from the remote antiquity and uncertainty of their origin, and also from the peculiarity of their mysterious construction; since, after the investigation of many ages, doubts were still entertained, not only as to the purpose for which the passages and chambers already discovered

were originally intended, but in a much greater degree
respecting any other passages or apartments, which
might reasonably be supposed to exist in these enormous
structures.

An additional interest arose from the great probability
that they were the mighty works of the Shepherd Kings,
whose descendants, according to Manetho, after their
expulsion from Egypt, under the denomination of Philis-
tines built in Syria Jerusalem, and also many defensive
towns, which had the same names as those they had
quitted in Egypt.[2]  This extraordinary people appear to
have been of the same race with the Cyclopes and
heroic adventurers, whose enormous structures and architectural skill, and whose wanderings and misfortunes,
have been celebrated by the antient poets.

As it had been suggested, that the inclined passages

---

[2] See Bryant's " Antient History," p. 231.  And here let me pay
a tribute to departed excellence and learning, which appear from various
causes to have been much undervalued, notwithstanding the unacknow-
ledged advantages that have been frequently derived from them, particularly as regards the Antient Chronology and Dynasties of Egypt.
Etymological researches, it must be confessed, are uncertain, and may
give rise to many fanciful conjectures; but no person can examine the
works of the author to whom I have referred, without being convinced of
the great extent of his learning, of the soundness of his conclusions, and,
above all, of his profound conviction of the truth of Revelation, and of
the unerring justice of the Almighty.  The candour and simplicity of
his character, and the benevolence of his disposition, are apparent in his
writings; and it may with justice be observed, that the chief object of
his learned inquiries, through a long and laborious life, was a zealous
and humble endeavour to " assert eternal Providence, and justify the
ways of God to men."  It is, therefore, much to be lamented that his
posthumous works have been unaccountably suppressed.

GREAT PYRAMID

VERTICAL SECTION from SOUTH to NORTH
through PASSAGES and CHAMBERS

LEVEL OF EXTERNAL BASE

were intended for astronomical observations, I endeavoured to ascertain, whether the angles of inclination were the same in the Great and Second Pyramids of Gizeh and in that of Dashoor. I was anxious, likewise, to examine more particularly the Channels [2] proceeding from the King's Chamber in the Great Pyramid, which appeared likely to conduct to other apartments: for this purpose I revisited the Pyramids of Gizeh on the 13th February, 1836, and took with me Mr. Hill, a very intelligent person, who now keeps the hotel at Cairo, but who was then employed in the Pacha's service, as superintendant of some copper mills worked by steam in the citadel.

The following is an account of the condition in which we then found the Pyramids, and, I may add, in which they remained when operations were commenced upon them in the following November.

## STATE OF THE GREAT PYRAMID AT GIZEH.

The inclined passage from the entrance to the subterraneous apartment, that apartment itself, and the unfinished passage proceeding to the southward from it, were open, although much encumbered with stones and rubbish; as were the forced and upper passages leading to the King's and Queen's Chambers. [3] These two

---

[2] As these channels were subsequently found to have been made for the ventilation of the King's Chamber, they are called Air Channels.

[3] A reference to Mr. Perring's Plans (Fraser, Regent Street, London) will fully explain the passages and chambers here alluded to.

chambers, together with Davison's, and the communication, or well, descending from the great upper passage to that of the subterraneous apartment, were also open. In the floor of the subterraneous apartment, an excavation had been made to the depth of a few feet; some stones had also been removed from behind the wall at the south-eastern corner of Davison's Chamber: one of the blocks composing the pavement had been taken up near the north-western corner of the King's Chamber, and an excavation had been carried on beneath the Sarcophagus : this last, however, was almost entirely filled up with rubbish. The mouth of the southern Air Channel had been partially enlarged, and an excavation of a few feet had been made near the portcullis, along the course of the northern Air Channel. In the Queen's Chamber a considerable passage had been forced into the solid masonry, from the niche on the eastern side. There was also a large hollow near the granite blocks at the commencement of the ascending passage, which was supposed to have been the forced entrance made by the Caliphs. These were the only excavations of any consequence. On the exterior of the Pyramid a vast heap of stones and rubbish, 50 feet in height, extended from the base to the entrance of the inclined passage.

## STATE OF THE SECOND PYRAMID.

The upper entrance, conducting to Belzoni's Chamber, and the chamber itself, with the descending passage returning to the north, were open; as were also the

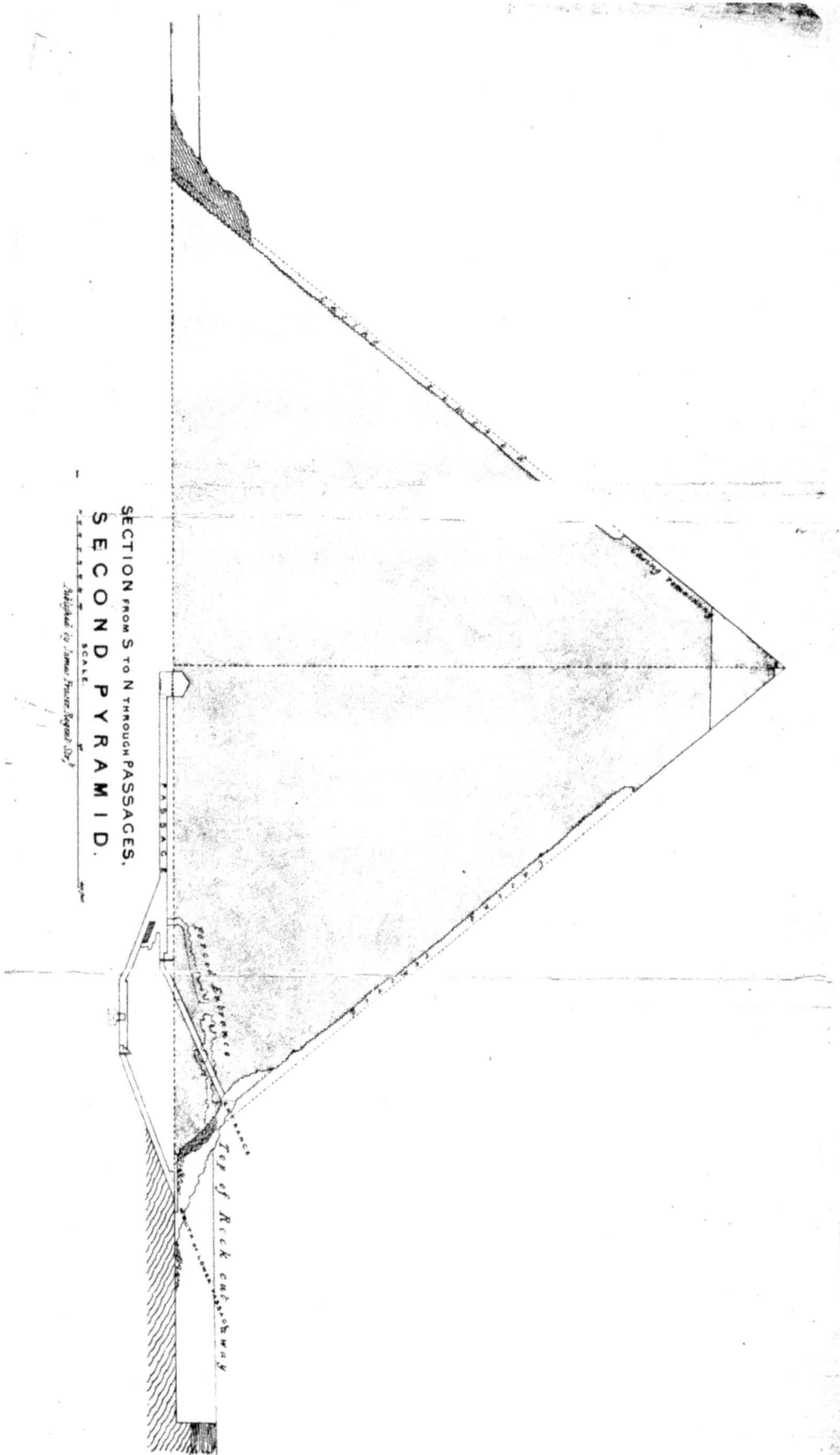

SECTION FROM S TO N THROUGH PASSAGES.

SECOND PYRAMID.

SCALE

Published by James Fraser Regent St.

PASSAGE

Forced Entrance

Top of Rock causeway

horizontal passage to the forced portcullis, and a considerable part of the re-ascending passage leading to the lower entrance. The inclined passage from the horizontal part of this communication, together with the small chamber to which it conducted, were likewise accessible. Several stones had been removed from the pavement near the Sarcophagus in Belzoni's Chamber, and a large excavation had been carried on across the upper horizontal passage to a considerable extent. A mound, similar to that on the exterior of the Great Pyramid, extended from the base to the upper entrance. The chasm in the centre of the northern front, by which the Caliphs are supposed to have entered, and in which Belzoni commenced his operations, was apparent; and there is no doubt that, before the stones had collapsed, it communicated with the excavation, already mentioned, across the horizontal passage.

## STATE OF THE THIRD PYRAMID, AND OF THE OTHERS.

In the northern front of the third Pyramid a considerable chasm had been made,* said, by Denon, to have been the work of the Mamelukes; while below it another smaller chasm had been carried on upon the level of the upper line of granite, which forms the front of the lower part of the Pyramid. A great deal of rubbish, and many large blocks of calcareous stone

* The eastern side of this excavation was in the centre of the northern front.

and of granite, were lying around it; particularly on the northern side, in which the above-mentioned excavations had been made. Some of these had been taken away at the centre; but the difficulty of removing the heavy masses without the assistance of machinery, had put a stop to the operation. Opposite the centre, and at some little distance from the base of the Pyramid, a pit about 20 or 30 feet square had been excavated in the rubbish, the sides of which had been supported by a revetment of large stones. Several blocks had been forced from a pavement at the bottom of this pit, it would seem in search of an entrance into the Pyramid, and many others yet remained there, similar to those afterwards uncovered to the eastward; but there was no appearance that the Pyramid had ever been opened.

The three smaller Pyramids south of the third, and the three east of the Great Pyramid, were more or less dilapidated, but were closed up.

We took the angles of the entrance of the Great, and of the Second, Pyramids; but, having no other instruments than a fine edge and level, and the surface of the stone being rough and uneven, notwithstanding the exquisite regularity and perfection of the masonry, our mensurations, probably, were wrong, as we afterwards found that they did not accord with those taken subsequently with a theodolite, by Mr. Perring. We carefully examined Davison's Chamber in the Great Pyramid; and the result of this examination was a conjecture, that it formed a sort of *entre-sol* between the King's Chamber and some large sepulchral apartment over it, to which the inclined ceiling of the Great Passage was, probably, an entrance. I also thought that the channels proceeding from the King's Chamber communicated with other apartments.

In the Second Pyramid it was evident that the re-ascending passage, returning to the north, led to a lower entrance.

The following remarks on the Pyramids of Saccara and Dashoor, and on those of Howara and Illahoon, may not, possibly, be altogether devoid of interest, although not immediately connected with the subject in question. I did not examine the two latter Pyramids till my second visit to Egypt.

## THE PYRAMID OF SACCARA.

This Pyramid was built in steps, or degrees, and was entered from a sort of well, or shaft, made in the sand, on the northern side. The passage, which was long and winding, and apparently in many places forced, led to a lofty chamber, in the roof of which wood had been employed. Various forced passages wound around this chamber, and conducted to openings, or windows, which looked down into it from a considerable height. These passages were much encumbered with rubbish, pieces of alabaster, and decayed wood; and in one place there was an accumulation of large blocks of polished granite, raised up by small fragments of stone sufficiently high to admit of a man's crawling beneath them. For what purpose they were so placed, we did not find out. Mr. Wilkinson mentions a chamber lined with blue tiles, but this I was unable to discover.*

---

* These buildings as well as most of the others have been recently examined by Mr. Perring, and it is intended to publish his remarks in a third volume.

## NORTHERN PYRAMID OF DASHOOR.

The entrance, like those of the Pyramids at Gizeh, is an inclined passage, commencing at a considerable height in the northern front, and leading to a spacious chamber, whence, by a forced passage in the bottom of the wall, another apartment is entered. At the height of about 28 feet, a square aperture, something like the entrance leading to Davison's Chamber in the Great Pyramid, opens into a passage about 14 feet long, which conducts to an inner chamber on a lower level, full of masses of unwrought stone, some of which are apparently intended for sarcophagi. These chambers have roofs, like that in the Great Passage of the Pyramid of Gizeh. We took the angle of the inclined passage; but, as there was reason to believe that the measurements taken at Gizeh were not correct, the result, in this instance, was not to be trusted.

## THE PYRAMID OF HOWARA.

This Pyramid is situated upon high desert land, in an obtuse angle formed by a large canal. It is at some little distance from the water; and the intermediate ground appears to have been formerly cultivated. There is a village on the opposite bank. The Pyramid stands due north and south, and is composed of large unburnt bricks, formed of the earth dug out of the canal, mixed up with a proportion of straw. They are extremely hard and well made, and put together without mortar. I examined several in the hope of finding a cartouch, by which the date and origin of this antient building, and probably, by inference, that of the canal, might be discovered. But, although many, no doubt, exist in the midst of such a quantity of materials, I could only find the usual marks of a hand having been drawn over the reverse sides. A large excavation had been made on the northern front; and several huts, apparently never inhabited, had been built with the bricks taken out of it. High mounds, which seem to be the ruins of a Peribolus, surround it on all sides; and a quantity of blocks of granite, and of other sculptured stone, appears to indicate the site of a temple at the southern front. I did not perceive any hieroglyphics; but I have been subsequently informed that some had been formerly discovered upon blocks, which may have been since removed.

The Pyramid of Illahoon is about four miles distant towards the south-east. I could not perceive any relative connexion between the situation of these two Pyramids with that of the stone ruins supposed to have belonged to a similar structure in the direction of Lake Mœris, or with that of the antient town of Arsinoe.

## THE PYRAMID OF ILLAHOON.

This Pyramid is likewise in the desert, at no great distance from the cultivated land, and is also composed of bricks; but much of its exterior has been removed, and the form is too irregular to admit of its aspect being correctly taken; the stone nucleus, around and over which it was constructed, is entirely exposed on every side of the base; as are also large spaces of stone, at equal distances in the superstructure. At each angle a column of brick-work, two courses in width, is carried up to the top.

I conceive that the entrance into this Pyramid is in the sand around its base, and that the whole of the passages and chambers are in the rock; that the Pyramid at Howara is similarly arranged; and that there are in neither of them any chambers in the superstructures of brick.

There were several natural grottoes in the adjacent rocks; but I did not observe the remains of any tombs, or of excavations, although many may lie concealed under the vast drift of desert sand, as sepulchral shafts are visible between the Pyramids and the village.

These Pyramids are to be included in Mr. Perring's Survey.

After a careful examination of the Pyramids of Gizeh, I came to the conclusion that they contained many apartments yet unopened, as well on account of their vast magnitude, as also of the small space occupied by those already discovered.

The manner in which these immense buildings were constructed, and the means by which the vast blocks of almost impenetrable stone were worked and placed at different heights with critical exactness, are even now unknown. For instance, the blocks of granite, composing the floor of the King's Chamber in the Great Pyramid of Gizeh, are laid with such precision, that not only are the joints scarcely perceptible, but the under faces and edges of the stones are so sharp and polished, that it is impossible to detect how they were lifted and placed in contact with each other, as no marks of force or of any purchase having been applied can be perceived; so that some persons imagine, that it was not until after they had been fixed in their respective places that the outward surfaces of the stones were smoothed down and finished. The blocks placed perpendicularly to the incline in the several passages have also the finest joints, and scarcely any settlings or imperfections appear. The masonry in the King's Chamber, the casing-stones, and those in the foundation and at the base, are, perhaps, unrivalled. This will be again more particularly alluded to.[5]

It appears that the Pyramids were tombs; that the inclined passages were for the purpose of assisting the conveyance of the sarcophagi, and for the better arrangement of the solid blocks with which part at least, if not the whole, of the long entrances were closed up; and also to increase the difficulty of disinterment and of violation. Having been closed with solid masonry, they could not have been used for astronomical observation, nor yet for initiation or mysterious purposes, as some have fancifully supposed.

It would indeed seem, from the great care and precautions taken to ensure the preservation of the body at an expense so vast, and by means so indestructible, that in these early ages there was a settled conviction,

[5] Mr. Perring is of opinion that the flat surfaces were obtained by working the stones level, and by afterwards rubbing a surface-plate, covered with a wet composition, over it, to ascertain the projecting irregularities, which were then cut away; applying the plate and the cutting alternately till a regular surface was obtained.

not only of an after-existence of lengthened duration, but also of the resurrection of the body, — a belief which, however obscured and mystified by imperfect tradition and by superstitious ceremonies, could only have had its origin in direct revelation.

It is also to be observed, that the subsequent discovery of the casing-stones at the base of the Great Pyramid, proves that these buildings had originally one smooth and polished exterior, which appears likewise to have actually existed in the time of Pliny. It is impossible, therefore, to imagine that their summits could have been easily attained, or conveniently occupied for astronomical observation : neither would their height, however great when compared with that of other buildings, have tended much to the advancement of scientific purposes.

Soon after these examinations (namely, on the 22d of February, 1836) I returned to Alexandria; and on the 23d I had the pleasure of being introduced to Mr. Caviglia, with whom I had a long conversation. He informed me that he had made the excavation in the Subterraneous Chamber; that to the south of Davison's Chamber, and the one also along the Northern Air Channel; and that he had attempted to force the mouth of the Southern Air Channel in the King's Chamber.[6] He stated his belief that these channels led to other apartments, which, by excavating in their direction, might be easily discovered. He also mentioned the

---

[6] It is to be remembered that Greaves, who travelled in 1638, describes the mouth of the Southern Air Channel to have been then partially forced, and blackened with smoke. He likewise alludes to excavations near the sarcophagus; but he neither mentions the Subterraneous Chamber, Davison's Chamber, nor the passage leading to it.

vertical direction he supposed the Southern Air Channel to take. He was so good as to allow me to read some papers he had written on the mystical purposes for which he believed these buildings to have been applied; together with a printed account of his discoveries some years since at the Sphinx. I proposed that he should go to the Pyramids, and carry on operations at the Air Channels at my expense, but he declined doing so; and having afterwards mentioned the subject to Mr. Sloane (the vice-consul, and Mr. Caviglia's intimate friend), that gentleman also informed me, that he knew Mr. Caviglia would not at that time engage in such an undertaking.

Accordingly, dismissing the subject from my mind, I left Alexandria for Beyroot on the 26th of February.

After a tour in Syria, Asia Minor, &c., I again arrived at Alexandria on the 25th of October, with the intention of going to Thebes and Wady Halfa, and, if an opportunity offered, of visiting also Mount Sinai, and then of returning to England by Italy and the Rhine; for, at that time, I had not the remotest idea of engaging in any operations at the Pyramids.

Soon after my arrival, however, Mr. Sloane mentioned that it was proposed to procure a firmaun for Colonel Campbell, himself, and me, who were to pay equal shares; and that Mr. Caviglia was to superintend the operations. I had several conversations with Colonel Campbell and Mr. Sloane about this business; and had subsequently frequent interviews with Mr. Caviglia, who was extremely sanguine, particularly about the apartments to which the Air Channels in the Great Pyramid were supposed to lead.

On the 2d of November I paid my first subscription

(200 dollars) to Mr. Caviglia: Colonel Campbell paid the same sum; and, I conclude, Mr. Sloane did so likewise.

The following day I left Alexandria for Cairo, Mr. Caviglia remaining behind to buy various articles, such as ropes, &c., which could there be best obtained.[7]

I embarked about three o'clock in the afternoon on the Mahmoudie, and performed my voyage with great convenience, as Colonel Campbell was so good as to send with me his Janisary Selim, whom I found of the greatest service. The voyage by this canal to Atfèe presents no objects of interest to the eye, except a few villas erected on its banks, and the sakias, or Persian water-wheels, the constant motion of which in some degree enlivens the scene, and, for a few miles, clothes the shores with verdure, soon, however, succeeded by utter sterility, which

[7] Excepting the Obelisks, the famous Pillar, the Grecian Catacombs called Cleopatra's Baths, and, possibly, one or two other foundations, Alexandria does not at present afford many objects of particular interest; but by the gradual removal of the vast mounds surrounding the new town, innumerable fragments of large columns, and other remains of antient magnificence, are continually brought to light, these massive foundations form a striking contrast to the slight and imperfect buildings erected over them. During the time I remained there, a quantity of marble slabs, broken columns, and several Corinthian capitals, of bad workmanship, had been dug up in the gardens of Mahomet El Garbi (the consul for Morocco); and soon afterwards a range of large columns of red granite, with intercolumniations of about nine feet, and likewise another row, composed of gray granite, at about seven feet distance, were discovered. Behind these columns were two parallel walls, at a considerable distance from each other, apparently Roman, and containing several arches; they had been covered with a coating of stucco, of which some patches remained, with the traces of figures coarsely painted. The whole plain beyond the Rosetta

JANISSARY SELIM.

continues, with scarcely any exceptions, on both the banks. The lake Marcotis extends along the distance to the southward; and on the opposite side a view is now and then obtained of the glorious Bay of Aboukir, beyond the intervening desert plains, interspersed with large ponds, the banks and surface of which are covered by incrustations of white salt.

*November 4th.* — We arrived about six at Atfêe; and, procuring the first boat we could find, which was, as usual, very dirty, and infested with vermin and rats, we set out about ten. The wind was favourable, but so strong, that I could not prevail upon the Janisary to keep the water even with bare poles; and we accordingly put into Fouah, a large Arab town, with a cotton

Gate is one undulating surface of ruined foundations, heaps of broken materials, pottery, &c. Several large columns of excellent workmanship had been dug up in forming the Frank Burial-grounds, where excavations, it would therefore appear, might be attempted with great success; at all events, many valuable materials, and possibly, also, interesting inscriptions, might be discovered. A lofty tumulus on the sea-shore, not far from the modern Lazaretto, is supposed to have been the tomb of Alexander the Great. The sarcophagus, at present in the British Museum, was said to have been originally found there; and also some remarkable alabaster columns, taken by Junot to Paris. The place had afterwards contained a Columbarium; and since that has been distinguished by the tomb of a Mahometan Sheik, — memorials which, although they may have confounded the original foundation, yet tend, in a certain degree, to establish the reputed sanctity of the spot. The shore, broken in upon by the waves, continually discloses, particularly near this place, fragments of columns, foundations, &c. of great extent. It is itself a commanding situation upon " the far-sounding shore," and may have formerly been, from its relative position, a fit station for the monument of the mighty hero.

manufactory, on the eastern shore. This place was once famous for its dancing girls, till the Pacha put an end to their trade, by sending considerable numbers of them to the army in Syria, and by confining the rest in the towns of Upper Egypt.[s] Fouah appears to have been the site of an antient town, and, like most other places in Egypt, much more flourishing some years since than at present. Soon after leaving this place, we were again obliged, by contrary winds, to put in shore; where I had an opportunity of observing the slovenly way in which husbandry is carried on in this once fertile country. The ground was extremely foul; and the seed, scattered by broad-cast sowing, was afterwards ploughed in, when a sort of attempt was made to clean the ground, and to break the clods. We sailed about sunset, and had some very heavy rain, with thunder and lightning. The vermin, gnats, rats, &c. were beyond all belief; and, to make matters worse, my English servant was violently ·attacked by fever.

In attempting, near Cairo, to make a short cut, the boat got a-ground, and we were obliged to return a mile or two, and then to go round, having lost the channel by the faintness of the starlight. We did not, therefore, arrive at Boulac till seven o'clock in the morning (Nov. 9th), when I was very glad to convey my servant to Mr. Hill's house, where he could have medical assistance. I called, without delay, on the consul, Mr. Piozan, respecting the firmaun necessary for the operations at Gizeh, by whom

[s] It is remarkable, that both the Crusaders and the French, in their invasions of Egypt, mistook these people for a deputation of the most considerable of the inhabitants, coming out to hail their arrival.

I was, in consequence, introduced to Habbib Effendi (the governor), and also, in the course of the morning, to Achmet Bey (the minister of war). The latter invited me to accompany him on the Wednesday following to see some battalions of infantry inspected; and also on the Friday, when the cavalry and artillery were to be under arms at Tourah.[9] In the course of the morning, I went to Ishmael Pacha's palace at Boolac, at present occupied by an establishment of cadets. The boys are taken in as early as six or seven years of age, and are instructed in mathematics, drawing, mapping, &c. They appear healthy; and I was told that the hospital did not at that time contain a single patient. They sleep in regular beds, about twenty in each room. Several of their performances were exhibited, which did them great credit. They have casts of relievos and of antient sculpture, and a large collection of prints, after the most eminent Italian and other masters, containing sacred subjects, portraits, &c., amongst which was a print of George the Third, putting an end to the riots in 1780. There were also " The Siege of Gibraltar;" Wilkie's " Village Politician ;" " Opening the Will," &c. There appeared, in short, to be no restriction as to subjects, or to the representation of men and animals, which was formerly the case in Mahometan countries.

12th.—Thermometer about 72° in the day; and 66° at night.

15th.—Mr. Caviglia arrived. I accompanied him

[9] See Appendix.

immediately to Mr. Piozan's, and we afterwards arranged matters with Mr. Hill. We dined together in the evening.

*16th.* — In consequence of Achmet Bey's invitation, I went with Mr. Piozan and Mr. Goff, attended by one of the Bey's aides-de-camp, to his house; and, after coffee, pipes, &c., we proceeded to the plain, where eight battalions were drawn up near an encampment between the town and Birket El Hadge.[1]   I was afterwards occupied in engaging a boat, and in making preparations for my voyage into Upper Egypt.   In the evening, Mr. Caviglia dined with me.

*17th.* — Mr. Caviglia set out for the Pyramids.

*18th.* — I went early in the morning with Mr. Piozan, and the aide-de-camp, to Tourah, where Achmet Bey inspected several squadrons of cavalry, and some artillery. We dined at that place with Billel Bey (the commandant); the dinner was in the European manner, and most abundant, but the room was intensely hot, and swarmed with flies. In coming back to Cairo we passed over a vast plain, covered with innumerable and beautiful tombs ; whence a number of the Pacha's hareem, having paid their devotions, were silently returning in the still hour of evening, surrounded by their numerous attendants.   The picturesque city, with its countless minarets, lay beneath the shadow of the citadel, placed on a fine promontory of the Mookattam ; and

[1] See Appendix.

beyond it, to the westward, was the ever-flowing river, with the Pyramids of Gizeh, Saccara, and Dashoor, on the distant mountains of the interminable desert. These various objects, grand and beautiful in themselves, were greatly enhanced by the fine climate and picturesque costume of the East; and many of them were of the greatest interest, from the reflections to which they gave rise. They were the mysterious records, enduring for countless ages, of mighty generations long since passed away, whose names and histories are now unknown, and whose very existence, excepting for the testimony of these unrivalled monuments, would have been lost and forgotten in the obscurity of the remotest times.

19*th*.—I signed a contract for the boat at the consul's office, and concluded my arrangements for the journey into Upper Egypt.

21*st*.—I left Cairo at eleven o'clock, with Mr. Hill, and arrived at the Pyramids about four, by a very circuitous road, on account of the waters yet remaining from the inundation. The country was rich beyond description: when the waters subsided, the surface merely required hoeing to prepare it for seed. The dykes were of considerable extent; and the Arabs were busily employed in taking quantities of fish, in large pools, left by the inundation. After dinner I went with Mr. Caviglia to the Great Pyramid, which, as well as the Second, Third, and smaller Pyramids, were in the condition before described; excepting that, at the two largest, some of the rubbish had been cleared out from the passages. We examined the Air Channels in the King's Chamber, and inserted a pliable rod to the length of about 50 feet into the southern, which appeared to pass horizontally through the wall for 5 feet, then to ascend vertically for 14, and afterwards to take an unknown direction.

22d.—We visited the subterraneous chamber in the Great Pyramid, which had partially been cleared out, and in which Mr. Caviglia had excavated, when engaged with Mr. Salt, to the depth of a few feet. He did not appear to think that there was any apartment beneath it. We then examined the ruins, supposed to have been temples, on the eastern side of the three Pyramids, and also the dykes. We awaited with great impatience the arrival of the firmaun, which was to be forwarded to us from Alexandria.

23d.—We examined the Second Pyramid, particularly with a view to a lower entrance; also the Third Pyramid, and the other ruins.

24th. — Having again gone round the several monuments, it was agreed that Mr. Caviglia should be ready to commence as soon as the firmaun arrived; and, in the meantime, should make the necessary preparations for extending the excavation he had already made on the southern side of Davison's Chamber, in order to intercept the southern Air Channel; and also for continuing the excavation he had commenced, at the entrance of the King's Chamber, along the course of the northern Air Channel. That he should remove the rubbish in search of the lower entrance of the northern front of the Second

Pyramid; and carry a gallery into the centre of the Third Pyramid, from the upper chasm in its northern front; and, likewise, that he should clear out the passages of the Great and Second Pyramids, by which operation alone many discoveries had been made. I also mentioned my intention of mapping the ground, and of taking a survey and plan of the Pyramids, as no plan, by which work could be carried on with accuracy, was to be procured. Discretionary power was also given to Mr. Caviglia to pursue, in addition to these, any other project that circumstances might seem to recommend in the Pyramids themselves, and in the temples on their eastern fronts, as regular entrances into the Pyramids, of a larger description than those already opened in their northern fronts, were believed to have been constructed, and to lie concealed below those edifices. Mr. Caviglia had a *carte blanche* with Mr. Hill, at the hotel, and in all other respects, for his own personal accommodation; and likewise for stores of every description, which he might think proper to order, for the carrying on of the work in hand.

I was extremely sanguine as to the success of our intended operations, particularly of those at the Great Pyramid; and it was with some hesitation, and much reluctance, that I set out, in the evening, for Upper Egypt. Mr. Caviglia, however, having promised that he would write if any thing important should occur, I left him with the intention of instantly returning to Gizeh, in case my presence should be required.

## VOYAGE INTO UPPER EGYPT.

The wonders of Upper Egypt, and the voyage to Wady-Halfa, have been too often described to make a detailed account necessary. I shall, therefore, confine myself to a few remarks on those objects which appear most worthy of notice, and to such general observations as may interest future travellers; and, I shall at the same time, keep connected the form of a journal, which appears best calculated to give a distinct account of the Operations at Gizeh, the principal object of this book.

Having commenced my voyage rather late in the season, I adopted the usual course of taking every advantage of the northerly winds that yet remained, in order to get to Wady-Halfa without delay, and of postponing, till my return, the examination of the various antiquities which, on every side, presented themselves to my view.

Thermometer in cabin, 68°. I sailed in the evening from Gizeh with a fair wind, which, however, soon failed; so that I did not arrive at Benisouef till November 27. The weather was like an Italian summer, and the sunsets particularly beautiful.

The general appearance of the country is that of a fertile plain, bounded by the desert on a much higher level. The barren mountains are at a considerable distance on the western side, but approach nearer on the eastern, and occasionally come down, in the form of rocky cliffs, to the edge of the stream.

The villages are situated amidst open groves of palm-trees, upon mounds of rubbish which frequently conceal

ARAB WOMAN.

Printed by C. Hullmandel

Published by James Fraser, 215, Regent St.

the foundations of antient towns; and, being sometimes embellished with lofty minarets, and with one or two considerable buildings, rendered conspicuous by white-wash and by regular windows, they produce, at a distance, a pleasing and characteristic effect; but, upon a nearer approach, nothing can be more forlorn than the flat-roofed houses, built with clay-brick of the same colour as the adjoining land, and often more dilapidated than the antient ruins amongst which they are placed. The vacant unglazed windows, instead of affording an idea of light and cheerfulness, disclose dark and dreary apartments, to which comfort and cleanliness are alike strangers.

Nor is the scenery much enlivened by the listless groups seated under the walls, to bask in the warmth of the noonday sun; by the naked children, and half-starved dogs, dispersed among the rubbish; by the cattle standing on the brink, or the buffaloes immersed in the mud, of the river; or even by the graceful forms of the Arab women, filling their jars at the all-bounteous stream.

Excepting occasional exclamations, the perpetual groanings of the unwearied sakias,[s] turned by cattle, or the splashings of the water raised by a succession of baskets worked by manual labour, are the only sounds to be heard. Nor are many objects to be seen moving along the banks. Now and then a turbaned Arab, mounted on an ass, with two or three attendant wives carrying his baggage; or a few camels, sheep, or goats, may be seen passing from village to village; or, at times, a traveller /from the adjacent desert, shrouded in the many folds of his thick bernouze, whose meagre dromedary bears ample

[s] Persian water-wheels.

testimony to the long and wearisome journey he has just performed.

Cangias, and boats of all descriptions, are constantly plying up and down the river; and innumerable flocks of wild fowl swarm on its sandy islands.

The plains teem with abundance; and it is difficult to suppose that any circumstances short of open hostility could reduce the inhabitants to the state of poverty and depression under which they labour. It may be observed, however, that in a warm climate the wants of life are few, habitations are scarcely necessary, and clothes almost an encumbrance. These circumstances, therefore, combined with many years of injustice and of oppression, will sufficiently account for the squalid penury of the inhabitants, and for the ruined state of the houses, which form as strong a contrast as the sterility of the desert itself to the surrounding abundance, and to the never-ceasing fertility of the soil. The resources, the wealth, and, consequently, the power of such a country, when properly administered, antient tradition and stupendous ruins sufficiently attest; but at present scarcely more than one-third of the land is under cultivation; and the population is yet more diminished.

28th. —We passed Abou-noor and Kom Achmar, near the village of Medil, Djebel Sheik Embarek being seen in the distance, and, on the following day, Sheik Hassan and the Convent Sittah Mariam-El-Adra, situated on lofty cliffs, which continue for some distance, and are called Djebel-Tayr, and afterwards arrived at Minyeh, and the village of Sovadee, on the opposite bank.

*30th.* — Thermometer 58°. We left Beni-Hassan, Sheikh Abadeh (Antinoopolis), and, on the opposite bank, Reramoun, near which, at Oshmounayn, were the ruins of Hermopolis Magna, now entirely destroyed. At Djebel-Toona, some miles to the westward, are several mummy pits, containing sculptures and inscriptions similar to those at Tel-El-Amarna, which will be afterwards mentioned. Melawee is supposed to be the site of Hermopolitana Philace, of which no traces remain, excepting some mounds of rubbish; and opposite are the remains of Sbayda. Beyond Sheik Saïd is the site of other buildings; and at Tel-El-Amarna may be seen the ruined mounds of Alabastron; and beyond Tanoof, in the plain on the opposite bank, is the entrance of the Bahr Yousef; at Dharoot, also, are the mounds of another antient town. El Karib (Hieracon) is situated on Djebel Abou Faydee. The cliffs continue to Abou-Hadji-Mahomet; and on the western plains is Cosseh (Cusæ).

*Dec. 1st.* — Thermometer 61°. I arrived at Manfaloot, whence there is a track to the Oasis of Daklah; and, on the opposite shore, according to Mr. Wilkinson, an old convent, called Deir-El-Bukkara.[3] The eastern shores at this, and many other parts of the river, are peculiarly picturesque; and several mounds, marking the site of considerable towns, bear testimony to the extent of the former population of the country. In this neighbourhood crocodiles are generally first observed.

[3] It will be seen, by the frequent reference I make to Mr. Wilkinson's book, how extremely useful it is to a traveller in this country.

*2nd.* — Thermometer 70°. We arrived at E-Siout (Lycopolis), the present capital of Upper Egypt. It is a flourishing town, well situated near picturesque mountains; and caravans set out from it for Darfoor. It is to be observed, that the force of the stream, which varies considerably in different parts of the river, is here very rapid.

*3d.* — According to Mr. Wilkinson, at Shodb are the mounds of Hypsele; at El-Wasta, those of Contra-Lycopolis; at Sherg-selin, of Selinon; and at Abou-teeg, those of Abutis. The mountains at Gow-el-Kebeer (Antæopolis) are very fine; and the adjacent plain is supposed to have been the scene of the contest between Isis and Typhon. In the plains on the western bank, is situated Tahta, probably the site of Hesopis. Sheik Hereedee is next passed, near which Mr. Wilkinson supposes Passalon, and another antient town, to have been situated. Itfou (Aphroditopolis) is on the western plain, near which are the Red and White Monasteries, which will be afterwards mentioned; and in the neighbourhood are the ruins of Atribis, now called Medeenet-ashaysh.

We passed Souhaaj, the site of an antient town, and afterwards Echmim (Chemmis, Panopolis), in the time of the Mamelukes, the capital of Upper Egypt. Beyond Echmim is said to be the site of Thomu. We then passed Mensheeh (Ptolemais Hermii), situated on a high bank; and, on the 4th, we arrived at Girjeh, near which is Arabet-El-Matfoun (Abydos), containing the tomb of Osiris.

Near Abou-haled is the site of Chenoboscion; and

further on, the catacombs of Quasresyad, and at Fow the remains of Bopos; also at How, those of Diospolis Parva, finely situated amongst groves of palm-trees. In this part of the stream rocks are first observed — a consideration of some importance in a navigation where boats are often aground eight or ten times a-day. We soon afterwards arrived at Kenneh.

*5th.* — Thermometer 80°. The mountains to the eastward are very magnificent; and the appearance of the Nile well justifies the appellation of the mighty river of Egypt, being navigable for above 1000 miles by boats of forty or fifty tons, without the aid of a single tributary stream, although it is just possible that it may be periodically supplied by subterraneous sources. It may, I think, well be questioned, whether the Delta be alluvial, as the water becomes clearer the higher you ascend the river; and as there are not any depositions at the Cataracts, or any where below them, whence so vast a quantity of soil could have been derived. It seems to be diluvial, and its surface to have been raised, together with the bed of the river, by gradual deposits.

The fertility of the land, although a great part of it can scarcely be cultivated during half the year, is almost equal to that of volcanic countries; whilst it is wholly exempt from the perilous visitations to which they are subject, and might be irrigated with facility in those parts which are not renewed by the annual inundation of the Nile.

The climate may be considered as healthy as any in the world, and, by the periodical rising of the stream, has the peculiar advantage of a succession of the seasons without their uncertainty.

"Besides these peculiar advantages, Egypt possessed a considerable degree of civilisation and knowledge at a very remote period; and, from various expressions in the Holy Scriptures, it may be collected, that it was a country peculiarly favoured by the Almighty.[*] It seems, also, more immediately connected with the Bible than almost any other country. From the time of Abraham to that of our Saviour the connexion is kept up, chiefly, however, as a prohibited land, in contrast to that of Judea; neither is the extreme state of corruption and of idolatry, into which it afterwards fell, at all inconsistent with the supposition that, when most other nations were immersed in darkness, and living in the most savage ignorance, Egypt, and, perhaps, some portions of the East, preserved distinct and accurate traditions of the antediluvian world, originally derived from revelation; and that the Egyptians, for especial purposes, were endowed with great wisdom and science.

A vast quantity of provision was collected at Kenneh, to be sent by Cosseir to the Hedjas. The war in that country appears likely to destroy the wealth and population of Egypt, the mortality, by the enemy and by sickness, being very great; and, besides these losses, the men, to avoid the conscription, fly to the mountains; so that the land in many districts is out of cultivation for want of hands, and it has already become necessary to import corn for home consumption into a land which was once styled the granary of Rome. The supplies, also, are subject to great waste, besides that incident to warfare, as they are first collected into magazines

---

[*] Isaiah, xix. 25.

from the villages by means of boats; thence reshipped to be conveyed to Kenneh; and, lastly, carried upon camels to Cosseir, there to be embarked for Jidda or Mocha.

The camels are pressed from the villages in the neighbourhood of Kenneh, at the price of eighteen piastres per head, and are paid for by paper, which is supposed to be deducted afterwards from the taxes.

From Kenneh to Cosseir is a journey of three or four days. After the first day there is no water, and many camels die on the road.

Opposite to Kenneh are seen the ruins of Dendera (Tentyra); and near them a high mountain projects into the plain, where the Necropolis of the antient city is supposed to have been excavated. Further on the same bank is Ballas, remarkable for the manufacture of porous jars, used for the cooling of water. In their construction, a stone, called hamr, is an ingredient; it is brought by the Ababde Arabs from the neighbourhood of the Red Sea.[5]

This evening, the mountains of Thebes were seen about twenty miles off. The banks of the stream, which here resembled a magnificent lake, were covered with luxuriant crops amidst open groves of sount and of palm-trees. The ranges of the desert hills were of the finest forms, and appeared to greater advantage from the unrivalled clearness of the atmosphere. Recollections, also, of the antient glories of the mighty capital

[5] Coft (Coptos) is on the eastern bank, and afterwards Coos (Apollinopolis Parva); Shenhoor, also, stands on the site of an antient town.

added greatly to the interest of the scene, and raised
expectation to the highest pitch on approaching its
famous plains.

*6th.* — In the morning, Thebes was eight or nine miles
distant: the land to the westward was at a considerable
height above the water, and, about eight years before,
had been the scene of an engagement between the Pacha
and the Mamelukes. But little cultivation appeared:
the fields, sown with barley, were formed into small
beds, round which the water raised from the river was
conveyed by channels on a higher level.

The walls of some of the larger houses inclined
gradually, in a pyramidal form, something like the propylæa of the antient temples, and had a border of red
and white over the doors, as also along the tops, which
gave them, at a distance, a turreted appearance — an
ornament often seen in this part of the country. But
most of the habitations were merely huts; and each,
however small, was inclosed in a yard, in which the
poultry, cattle, &c., were defended by a wall, and guarded
by dogs; whilst the whole village was surrounded by
heaps of rubbish and offal.

The scanty population appeared extremely poor, and
had a bad reputation, which they seemed to deserve, by
the precautions that had been taken to secure the little
property they possessed from mutual acts of depredation.

Thermometer 57°. As we advanced, the mountains
between the plain of Thebes and the valley of Biban-
El-Moluc appeared on the western shore; and on
the eastern, Karnac and Luxor. The great Temple at
the latter place is finely situated upon a sandy bank,

CHILDREN OF UPPER EGYPT.

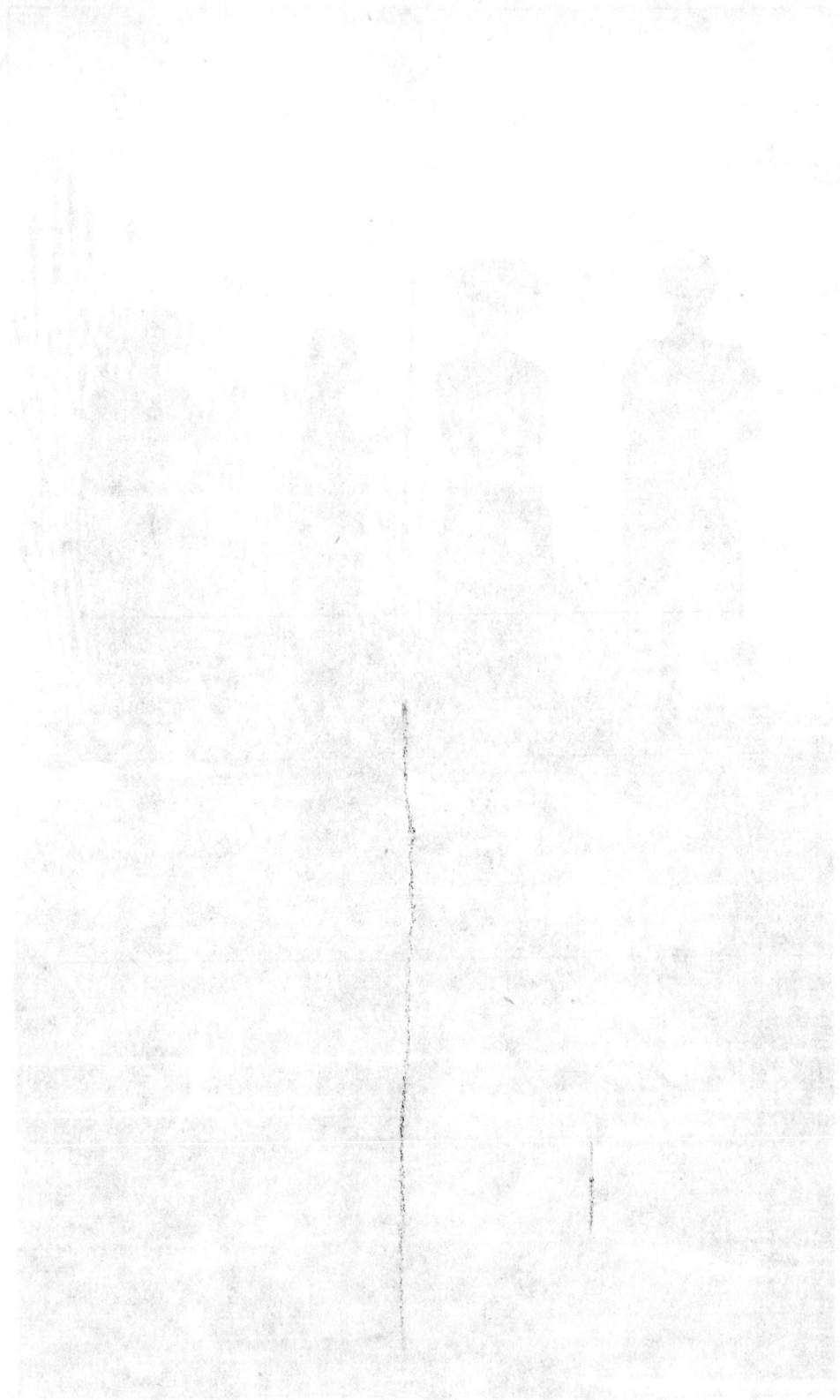

above which the river is wider, and forms a sort of harbour.

The village is, as usual, in a grove of palm-trees; and beyond it a plain, exhibiting at present but little cultivation, extends to some distance, and is bounded by desert hills. Above the village is a large and fertile island, and on the western bank of the river are likewise extensive levels in a rough and neglected state, where the well-known Colossi are seated in mournful solemnity amidst groups of ruined temples—the isolated but magnificent monuments of antient splendour. This plain is also bounded by lofty mountains, amongst which are the valleys of Biban-El-Moluc, and other recesses, full of sepulchral excavations, while the lower parts of the rocky heights facing the east are occupied by the village of Gournou. Further on towards the south, the mountains recede to the westward, and the flat country extends to Erment, being partially cultivated along the banks of the river.[6]

---

[6] Thebes was famous for chariots of iron; and both sacred and profane history record the vast power of the whole country in chariots and horsemen, and also the expeditions performed by them, and, if the accounts we have of the siege of Troy deserve credit, they penetrated even to the shores of the Hellespont. Yet it is not easy to imagine how they could have been conducted, even through Egypt, from the plains of Thebes, either over the cultivated ground, or by the desert sands. If roads were established, sufficiently permanent to resist the inundations, and to allow a passage for so many wheeled carriages, some vestiges would have probably remained. Their conveyance across the desert, and subsequent movements in a mountainous country like Syria, and where few, if any, appearances of antient roads exist, seem to be attended with still greater difficulties.

The wind being fair, I passed Erment (Hermontis).

*7th.* — Left Eilelithias and Kom Achmah on the eastern shore, and in the evening was opposite to Edfou.

*8th.* — I went through the narrow pass of Hadjar Silsilis, where the water must be exceedingly deep, as the current is not perceptibly increased; and leaving Koum Ombos, situated on a promontory on the eastern shore, I arrived in the evening at Es Souan. The island of Elephantine is covered with rubbish and broken pottery: but, with the exception of a few foundations, a wall towards the south-eastern end, and a figure in a sitting posture, nothing can be distinctly made out. Tablets of hieroglyphics have been inscribed in many places on the rocks in these islands, and also in those near the town of Es Souan. The neighbouring quarries to the eastward are very interesting, on account of the vast monuments they have furnished for so many ages, and of the peculiar nature of the stone of which they are composed. They appear to have been worked principally with a chisel, although the marks of wedges are in some places visible.[7]

The column containing the well-known inscription has been removed; but the Obelisk remains, and I

---

[7] It is to be remarked, that in the various painted representations of the sculpture of images from granite and from other stone, the instruments employed are often represented of a yellow colour, like that of brass.

observed upon it several curved rows of small square
holes, similar to those on the great stone in the quarry
at Baalbec. As neither of these blocks had been finished,
these holes were, probably, made for the convenience
of moving them, and not for the purpose of fixing
them in any particular building, as I at first conceived
to be the case, when I saw similar cuttings on the three
large stones built into the wall of the Temple at
Baalbec; and naturally concluded that they must have
belonged to some former building, as the holes did
not appear to be of any use in their present position.
In returning to the town, I passed through an extensive burial-ground, where there are many curious
inscriptions.

10*th.* — Having changed my boat, and made the
necessary arrangements, I set out for Wady Halfa at
twelve o'clock, and in about two hours I perceived,
by a considerable noise and slight ripplings of the water,
that we approached the Cataracts. As the channel was
winding and full of isolated rocks, and the stream ran
with great violence, a fair wind was absolutely necessary. This, unluckily, we had not; and, therefore, were
obliged to put into a small creek, or bend of the river,
under some high rocks of granite, on the eastern shore,
upon which various tablets of antient hieroglyphics had
been inscribed, and several figures also coarsely drawn,
probably by the French army, who were stationed in
the neighbourhood for some time. The shores on both
sides of the river were entirely barren. The weather
was cold and dreary; and, when it was almost dark,
a Nubian woman, with her clothes and a bundle upon

her head, swam through the foaming waters from the western shore, and climbing up the rocky cliffs, dressed herself, took up her bundle, and pursued her solitary journey.

*11th.*—We were enabled, by a fair wind, to proceed about eleven o'clock; and were hauled by a rope through the first cataract, or, rather, rapid. The boat was full of Nubians, who were extremely active, and, when occasion required, swam from rock to rock with great dexterity: they were remarkably well made, and, from their dark glowing colour, had the appearance of bronzed statues. We had ascended two strong eddies, or rapids, without encountering any fall or cataract, and seemed to be in a fair way of getting through our difficulties, when the wind lulled, and the people, probably for the sake of another day's pay, took advantage of a sudden turn in the river, where the passage was rather difficult, and, after much altercation and noise, finally moored the boat to the eastern shore. As no further progress could be made, I set out for Philæ, over sandy hillocks interspersed with patches of cultivation wherever the inundation had left any alluvial deposit, and passing a village of scattered clay huts in a grove of palm-trees, and afterwards some cultivated ground, I arrived at a promontory, composed of large masses of black granite, on the brink of the river opposite the island of Bigge, which is also formed of enormous blocks of the same material, of the most extraordinary and picturesque shapes. The inhabitants resembled Negroes rather than Arabs, and appeared tolerably well off.

Beyond the promontory lay a desert plain of considerable extent, with a few houses collected together under the lofty rocks where the road branches off to Es Souan,[8] and on the high bank near the stream a number of Jaloups were hutted, with a few slaves and a quantity of dates, and other goods, upon which an import duty is levied at Es Souan. The river sweeps in a majestic curve round the island of Philæ, which is separated by a smaller branch of the stream from Bigge, and is adorned with most beautiful ruins, seen to great effect amongst trees and verdure. The whole of the island appears to have been covered formerly with temples, and surrounded by a wall; and even now there are but few spots capable of cultivation: after visiting this interesting spot, I returned to the boat.

12th.—The wind being fair, we passed the only fall which could be termed a cataract. No danger can occur with good cordage; but if the tow-lines gave way, the boat would probably be dashed to pieces, by the rapidity and force of the stream, against the numerous rocks above and below the water. We were nearly twenty minutes in getting through this place, as the rudder broke just in the critical moment. Having paid the people and the pilot, we again proceeded, passed Philæ, and the temple of Debode and arrived at Gertassee.

The Nubians are tributary to the Pacha, and formerly paid for each sakia two slaves; they procured

---

[8] This place, and also the Cataracts, are called Sehayl; a name by which this part of Nubia is also sometimes distinguished.

them by sending parties into Dongola, and the adjacent
countries, who, concealing themselves near the river,
seized the people when they came for water: at present,
however, two hundred and twenty-five piastres (about
forty-five shillings) are paid by half-yearly instalments
for each machine. In addition to this tax, duties of
one piastre for every palm-tree, of ten per cent upon
dates, and of sixty-five piastres on every slave exported
from Es Souan to Cairo, are also demanded. The
Nubians seem proud of their country. They are a handsome people, excepting that the lower parts of their faces
often project like those of Negroes; they have, like the
Arabs, very fine teeth and eyes; their hair, generally
woolly, is cut short, excepting one tuft on the top of the
head, according to the Mahometan custom. Their clothing is composed of white cotton, and consists of a shirt,
short trowsers, and a long folded scarf passing over the left
shoulder, and confined round the waist by a narrow girdle
with long ends. They wear a white cotton cap, and a
knife or dagger, fastened in a case to the inner part of
the left arm above the elbow. They have generally ear-
rings, carry spears and large daggers, long straight swords,
and invariably nabouts four or five feet long.[9] The women
are chiefly clothed in coarse brown garments, but in
some places in gowns of blue cotton, with a quantity
of necklaces and bracelets composed of courie shells,
armlets above the elbow, ear-rings, and also nose-rings,
which are likewise frequently used by the Bedouins.
Their thick hair plaited in ringlets, and often adorned
with fetichies and ornaments composed of shells and

9 Nabouts are thick sticks, of a very hard wood.

of beads, is arranged in a straight line across their fore-
heads and round their heads, something in the style of
the head-dress of the Sphinx, and is copiously anointed
with castor oil, or with grease. I saw in one of the
villages a little child, apparently the daughter of a sheik,
and evidently proud of her appearance, carrying milk in
an inlaid basin, and adorned with a profusion of bracelets,
ear-rings, necklaces, &c., and with her hair dressed with
coloured stones, but without any clothing excepting a
leathern girdle round her waist, ornamented with silver
in various devices.

13th.—Thermometer 81°. I arrived at Kalabshee,
and afterwards at Dendoor (within the tropics). We then
passed Sabagoora, a large ruined village on the eastern
bank, where a battle had been fought between a Nubian
chief and Ishmael Pacha; and on a chain of barren hills,
on the opposite shore, we noticed the ruined temple of
Gerf Hossein, formerly Thosh, the abode of Pthah.
Mr. Wilkinson observes, that the Coptic name, Thosh,
greatly resembles Ethaush, signifying Ethiopia; and that
Kush, the old Egyptian name for Ethiopia, is retained in
the Nubian name of this antient place, which is now
called Kish. The cultivation is here confined to the
immediate banks of the river. The remains of two
antient watch-towers are to be seen towards the north,
and the ruins of the temple are finely situated above the
modern village. I sometimes fancied that in this country
the evenings were accompanied by a longer twilight than
in Italy.

14th.—I came to Maharaka and Korosko, and, proceeding up the stream to the north-west, landed on the western bank at the ruins of Sabooa. A few huts, and some patches of cultivated ground, occupy the western bank of the stream, where twenty or thirty black Arabs exist in the greatest misery and want. Nothing can exceed the utter desolation of this forlorn place, which may formerly have been thronged with unnumbered multitudes, pressing forward with prayers and offerings, in all the pomp of idolatrous worship. According to Mr. Wilkinson, this Temple, which has a very grand and antient appearance, was built in the time of Remeses the Second, about 1355 B.C. It was approached from the river by an avenue of Sphinxes, amongst which are two colossal figures. Two similar statues guard each side of the entrance of the Propylæon, which, as well as the Temple, has been covered with sculpture and hieroglyphics. The interior is hypæthral, and is surrounded by columns cut into the shape of Colossi, similar in style to those at Abou Simbel. The immense blocks which form the architraves, bring to the recollection of the English traveller those of Stonehenge. The adytum appears to have been an excavation in a ledge of rock, which may probably also contain many antient sepulchres; but the whole is at present nearly overwhelmed by desert sand.

*15th.*—Thermometer 63°. The boat was tracked up the Wady-el-Kharib. The shore was hilly, with here and there a little cultivation near the river, and a few sheep and goats grazing among the bushes. A road branches off from Korosko, through Wady-Halfa, to Dongola. The journey is performed in eight days, and is the usual route for the slave koffles, although it affords little or no water

THE TEMPLE OF SABOOA.

Published by James Fraser, Regent Street.

Printed by C. Hullmandel.

TEMPLE OF AMADA.

Published by James Fraser Regent St.

Printed by C. Hullmandel.

by the way. These desert roads are called Agaba (probably the same as Akaba). On the opposite western
bank a few huts are occasionally to be seen amongst
the groves of palm-trees.[1]

16th. — Thermometer 57°. While the boat passed
slowly along against the stream, I took an opportunity
of examining several extensive mounds of pottery, nearly
opposite the temple of Amada, and which seem to mark
the situation of an ancient town. I observed on several of
the squared stones the remains of red plaster, and also
traces of foundations that had been cut in the rock,
with cavities for the fastening of stone doors. In many
places, excavations had been made; but when, and by
whom, I could not discover.

The temple of Amada, situated in an extensive desert
plain, is said by Mr. Wilkinson to have been built in the
time of Thothmes the Third, 1490 years B.C. Like that
at Sabooa, it has an appearance of great antiquity. It
is composed of large squared stones laid in mortar. The
apartments are small, and, as far as can be seen from
the sand, not above ten or twelve feet in height. The
roof consists of immense slabs, and is surmounted by a
cupola, for it has been used as a church, or a mosque.
The chambers and the rest of the interior have been
painted with hieroglyphics, and the whole is a most
venerable and curious specimen of antient skill. The
colours yet remain perfectly fresh and brilliant, and the

---

[1] When the Nubians marry, a separate hut is made of mats for the
happy couple at a little distance from the village, where they remain for
three days, and then return to their former occupations.

cattle, birds, and other figures, are executed in a masterly style. Many tombs are said to be in the adjacent rocks.

Derr is situated advantageously in a grove of palm-trees on the eastern bank, which is cultivated to a considerable extent: it is supported chiefly by the slave-trade, and is tolerably populous.

The house of Hassan Catchief, the Nubian mutzellum, looks extremely well from the river. The people seem, upon the whole, in a better condition than those in Egypt; but their welfare depends entirely upon the conduct of the Catchief, who has almost unlimited power. The contrast of extreme fertility with the yellow sands of the desert is at this place very striking. On the opposite shore are several ruins, apparently Roman.

17th. — Thermometer 70°. I arrived at Ibrim, a town built upon some high cliffs, that extend for some distance along the margin of the road. Not far to the northward is an extensive burial-ground, held in great estimation by the natives, probably on account of some antient tradition. It contains, amongst other tombs, those of the Mamelukes who fell some years ago in a great battle with the Pacha. The remains of Roman buildings are to be seen in the citadel, and some remarkable tombs have been excavated in the cliffs, which will be afterwards described. This part of the country is called Wadi Guanee. The eastern bank of the river is fertile; but on the western there are no signs of cultivation. Several antient tombs have been discovered near the mountains of Tosco, at some distance inland. At Aboufertig I saw a man paddle himself across the river on a bundle of rushes; and I was informed, that two or three people often pass over together in this way.

18*th.*—Thermometer 68°. We left Abou Simbel on the western bank, and, soon after, Faras, containing several antient remains, on the eastern, which is well cultivated; and, having passed some ruins and the village of Ougaguin on the western shore, arrived at Wady Halfa.

19*th.*— Thermometer 79°. Early in the morning, I went up in a small boat for three or four miles; and, disembarking on the western bank, walked to Abouseir, through desert plains of yellow sand, here and there varied by mountain ranges of different colours, composed of red, white, and black rocks. We passed two small brick buildings, intended probably for khans; and near them killed a very large snake, of which the people were much afraid. They said, that it was extremely venomous, and had the power of springing forward, when attacked, to a great distance. Abousier is a rocky promontory, about one hundred feet high, immediately over the rapids. They are composed of black rocks, with patches of white sand, interspersed with a few trees and bushes, and extend to some distance up the river, which is here very broad. The promontory is inscribed with the names of many travellers; and affords a very extensive view to the southward over Batn El Hadjar, and to the northward, beyond Wady Halfa. The country is entirely desolate, excepting about the village of Wady Halfa, which is situated in a plain, and contains a barrack and a large magazine or storehouse. A

cultivated island, called Muogis, upon which are the ruins
of a church, is to the southward of it. Very little at
present exists of the ruins, mentioned by Mr. Wilkinson, on the western shore. Wady Halfa is eight days'
journey from Dongola, thirty from Kordovan, sixty from
Habesh (Abyssinia), and forty-six from Darfour. The
western shore is said to be uninhabitable for want of
water; but a few Ababde Arabs are enabled to inhabit
the Eastern Desert by means of reservoirs, which are
filled with a considerable quantity of rain water in the
winter season. An Oasis, or Wah, is at the distance of
ten or twelve days' journey to the westward; but I could
not obtain any particular information respecting it.

The boat was now prepared for our return, by taking
down the larger mast and sail; and it was with some
satisfaction that I began to proceed homewards.

20th.—Thermometer 78°. I landed at Faras, and
went up a sloping bank covered with palm-trees, dou-
rah, and lupines, to some sandy hillocks, which possibly
conceal the remains of an antient town. They were
partly overgrown with bushes, and abounded with the
recent tracks of leopards, lynxes, wolves, gazelles, &c.
I then crossed a sandy plain, containing a Turkish burial-
ground, to some antient tombs: they had been excavated
in the rocks, furnished with stone doors turning upon
pivots, and contained vestibules, which, in general, conducted to a large apartment; whence passages, leading
to various chambers, branched off in different directions.
They appeared of great antiquity, and had probably been
used for concealment in the early ages of Christianity.
I did not see the inscriptions, nor the Egyptian cavern

mentioned by Mr. Wilkinson; but observed, at some little distance, two large buildings of unburnt bricks upon foundations of stone, which seemed to have been churches. There were Roman arches in both of these structures; and in one of them, two pillars of coarse red stone, about eight or nine inches in diameter, with capitals, apparently the work of the lower ages.

To the south of the village, there were remains of unburnt brick walls, and several fragments of small columns of granite; also, some figures roughly sculptured, and others painted upon plaster, evidently of Christian workmanship, and placed there to conceal the decorations of an antient Egyptian building. The northern side of the village did not afford any thing worthy of notice; but on the adjacent heights were several ruins, apparently of churches — proofs of the former prevalence of Christianity in this country. The rocks and the tops of the neighbouring mountains bore so close a resemblance to pyramids, that I should have stopped to examine them, had I not been assured by Ignowe (an intelligent Arab, who had accompanied M. Champollion in this country) that it was their natural shape. Between Kosco and Adda, on the eastern shore, and considerably above the level of the river, which at this place turns to the westward, are a number of remarkable hillocks on a sandy plain, bounded to the eastward and northward by barren mountains, and by isolated conical rocks, and through which the road from Kosco to Ferradj passes. These hillocks, of various sizes, are about thirty-seven in number (besides several apparently destroyed), and are nearly in straight lines.

Each of them stands in an hollow; from which it would seem that the sand and stones, used for their construction, had been taken. They have precisely the appearance of the tumuli in northern countries, and of having been raised as monuments after some great battle; for which the plain, it may be added, would have afforded a proper arena. The adjacent ground is strewed with a quantity of broken pottery. These remarkable mounds are inserted in Colonel Leake's Map, and have been supposed by some people to be volcanic; at all events, from the regularity of their positions, they can scarcely have been occasioned by the wind. I opened one of them across the centre to the foundation, and found it to be composed of sand and stones, without any indication of an artificial construction.

Ferradj is situated on a high rock, and must have been a considerable place. It contains walls of unburnt bricks, and the ruins of towers, and of a fort, which seems to have been Roman, or of the lower ages. Vast quantities of pottery, of burnt and unburnt bricks, and a few fragments of small granite columns, are scattered about; likewise part of an Egyptian cornice, with the protecting bird, &c., but of indifferent workmanship. A party of men were employed in taking away the materials for other buildings. There is a Turkish burial-ground below the mountains. The road passes through this place to Korosko, Dongola, &c. An antient excavation in the cliff, supported by four columns, is said, by Mr. Wilkinson, to be of the time of Amenoph the Third; it contains a remarkable hollow and several groovings, the object of which it is difficult to understand. This grotto had been used as a church; the antient sculpture and hieroglyphics had, in many places, been effaced, and the legend of St. George and the Dragon, and other sacred figures, had been painted on the ceiling and on the walls. The apartments, which were very elegant, had been closed by stone doors, opening inwards; the face of the cliff had been levelled for a certain distance near the entrance, and a row of holes, about three inches square, had been cut into it. The high land at this place recedes to some little distance from the river. The western bank was here partially cultivated, and Abou Simbel lay before us. I arrived there in the afternoon; and, having passed the two tablets engraved on the rock near the larger temple, moored the boat before the façade of the small one, which faces the east, whilst that of the Great Temple is not opposite any of the cardinal points, but is inclined to the north-eastward. The river seems to have gained at this place considerably upon the land, which formerly was, in all probability, cultivated, and a station of commercial importance, and of extensive communication with the interior of the country.

Many antient remains may yet be concealed under the sand, which fills up the valley between the two temples, and which would soon have entirely hidden the larger one, had it not been for the perseverance and exertions of Sig. Belzoni, and of Captains Irby and Mangles. The complete removal of this sand would be a work of considerable labour, but of little difficulty, as the situation is favourable, and as the river is at hand to carry off any quantity which might be thrown into it. The operation would possibly lead to discoveries of great interest, and, at all events, would exhibit the Great Temple to considerable advantage.[2]

Both of the temples are said to bear, in many respects, a striking resemblance to the excavations in India. They are, certainly, wonderful specimens of antient industry and science; the carving being very fine, and much of the detail, consisting of birds, animals, &c., is described with great truth and spirit, and painted with colours, yet preserving their freshness and brilliancy, after a probable lapse of above 3000 years. Their preservation, however, is in a great degree owing to the dryness of the atmosphere, and, also, to the protection afforded by the accumulated sands. It may be observed, that although great labour has been bestowed upon the colossi and portals, the surrounding face of the rock has been left in its natural state, excepting that near the entrance of the Great Temple there are some square holes, like those at Ferradj, possibly intended as guides to the work. The colossal figures, as seen at present, lose much of their effect from their oblique position, for they are inclined backwards like a buttress; and, although it is difficult to imagine how they would appear when seen from a proper distance, yet their features and proportions are not only extremely broad for their height, but coarse and ill-defined, and reminded me, in a great degree, of the Metopes at Selinus. These statues are of an enormous size, being six feet from the ground to the

[2] In the following cursory remarks, it is not intended to enter into any detailed account of these monuments, which have been not only repeatedly described, but accurately drawn.

knee; the countenances are placid, the features those of Negroes, the mouths prodigiously wide, and altogether out of proportion. Over the portal of the Great Temple, a row of grotesque Typhons form an upper cornice. Mr. Wilkinson has justly remarked, that the doorways of both the temples gradually diminish towards the sanctum, in order, probably, to assist the general effect by increasing the perspective. The doors themselves must have been of vast size, extremely heavy, and, probably, made of metal; they seem to have been folding, and to have turned on pummels, like the stone doors belonging to tombs. It is obviously impossible, in their present state, and by the light of a wax candle, to determine precisely the original effect, which these mighty temples may have produced: the Colossi do not, certainly, at present, appear to advantage; but I am inclined to believe that the Egyptians, like their pupils the Greeks, well understood the principles of effect and of proportion, and that the simplicity and immense size of these gigantic figures, the grandeur of the door-ways, with their enormous architraves and mouldings, assisted by the beauty and variety of the coloured inscriptions, which must have had the effect of tapestry, together with the great size of the heroic figures, and the solemnity of the four deities, seated in the obscurity of the adytum, must have produced an effect more splendid and finished than that displayed by any smaller buildings of plain uncoloured stone, however beautiful their proportions and exquisite the sculpture might have been.[5]

[5] It cannot escape observation that a great similarity exists between the coloured stucco, with which the interiors of these temples have

The interiors of the temples have been plastered and painted; and as the same battle is recorded here and at Thebes, Kalabsha, Sabooa, Derr, and in several other places, it must have been an event of paramount importance; and, from the resemblance of the different representations, it is evident that they were executed by the same persons, or, at least, according to conventional forms. There appears a propriety in describing the wars and exploits of the king in the largest apartments, and the sacred offerings, the ark and the symbolical representations near the adytum, where the hero is represented

been covered, and that yet adhering to the pavement of the cella and to many other parts of the temple at Egina, particularly the red, which is the colour of porphyry: and, as painted stucco may yet be seen on the Parthenon, it is to be concluded that the whole of these beautiful edifices were plastered and painted, notwithstanding the fine material and exquisite sculpture with which they were adorned. It cannot be supposed that a people of so refined a taste as the Greeks undoubtedly were, would have adopted this practice, had they not, together with other arts, originally received it from those who may have used it on account of the inferior materials with which they built, for it is not possible, according to modern opinion, that any colouring, much less a covering of stucco, could add to the exquisite beauty of Grecian sculpture. It would seem that the Greeks followed the example of the Egyptians in this instance, as, I think, it will afterwards be proved they did in some others, especially in regard to the Doric order; and it is, therefore, the more extraordinary, that the arch (which was constructed in Egypt 800 years before Christ) should have been unknown to them. These considerations make it probable that the rough surfaces of the temples, at Pæstum, and at Selinus, were either covered with plaster, or intended to be so; for, notwithstanding the imposing grandeur of these noble structures, particularly of the former, they by no means equal the magnificent and finished appearance of several of the Egyptian temples, particularly that of Karnac.

making his offerings to the gods, with a sceptre, which has, it is to be remarked, at the end of it an extended hand, like that adopted as an ensign by the Roman armies, and afterwards by Napoleon, as king of Italy. The figures are executed with great spirit and observation of nature, although not in exact proportion or drawing; and there is evidently a national distinction preserved amongst the groups of prisoners, some of whom appear to have been Negroes. The likenesses of the hero and heroine are well preserved throughout the different scenes, and they are also like each other, whether as portraits, or as family or national likenesses, or symbolical of marriage, or of the text, " male and female created he them," it is difficult to determine. The hero is handsome, and has certainly, as has been remarked, a likeness to Napoleon. The queen, as far as the formality of the sculpture will allow of an opinion, has beautiful features, well-formed limbs, and a fine figure, her complexion seems to have been of that golden hue so often to be seen amongst the common people, and which, with care and cosmetics, must have shone with increased lustre: for even many of the common boatmen have a fine tone of colour, and their muscles are well developed from the thinness of their skins. To judge by these representations, a great similarity appears to exist between the antient Egyptians and the modern Nubians.

One of the smaller chambers in the Great Temple is furnished with a stone shelf, or dresser, in the same way as an apartment in the tomb opened by Mr. Belzoni at Thebes; and I imagined that I had discovered in it the remains of an iron fastening.

The difference of the proportions of the smaller temple to those of the larger seemed to agree with its supposed feminine dedication to Isis, or Athor. On each side of the entrance are colossal Atlantides in the usual position of advancing with the left-leg foremost, accompanied by two smaller figures, the one also advancing, the other the reverse : these gigantic statues, like those in the façade of the other temple, are seen to disadvantage from their inclined positions. There are several cartouches in this temple, which I did not observe in Mr. Wilkinson's list, and a slight difference in that of Remeses the Second. It has a crypt, or subterraneous apartment, beneath it about five feet high. To the northward of these temples there is a figure of Isis remarkably well carved in the rock; and at some little distance are the remains of a wall, and of an old building apparently a church. On the sloping bank of sand between the temples a stove yet remains, that was used by Mr. Hay in taking casts of plaster. This gentleman seems to have done more than any other person to preserve from oblivion the venerable antiquities of this interesting country ; therein presenting a striking and honourable contrast to the wanton and barbarous devastation, which has marked the progress of many other noted antiquarians, particularly at Thebes and Karnac.

I left Abou-Simbel with great regret, but as I expected great discoveries to have been made by Mr. Caviglia at Gizeh I set out in the afternoon of the 21st, and proceeded to Tosko, a picturesque village surrounded by fields in a tolerable degree of cultivation; but the people were apparently extremely poor. The antient tombs are excavations in isolated rocks, and at a distance have the appearance of buildings; the roofs were supported by square pillars, but they are nearly destroyed, and the hieroglyphics almost entirely effaced. Channels and reservoirs of water had been cut in the rocks, and there were also the remains of quarries. The high-road, or communication from one part of the country to another runs at the back of these villages. The people manufacture for their own use a coarse sort of cotton-cloth, and cultivate dates, cotton, Indian corn, a small kind of doura, lupins, and the other usual crops. I was informed there were ruins at Shebash, as mentioned in Colonel Leake's map, but I did not visit them. I arrived at Ibrim at ten o'clock, and as it was a moonlight night I examined by means of a rope the tombs excavated at various heights in the face of the cliff. The first I entered had three sitting figures cut out of the rock in a kind of niche, or sanctum at the further end of the apartment; they were greatly mutilated, and the hieroglyphics nearly destroyed.[4] The sides of the excavation had been plastered and painted, and parts of the colouring yet remained, particularly on the wall to the right of the door, where two ostriches, some cattle in pairs, a panther, or leopard, and a few other figures, might be made out. The apartment was ventilated by an air-channel. The second excavation contained four figures, and the remains of painted stucco were visible upon the ceiling. The third had three sitting figures like the first, and amongst the hieroglyphics some cartouches had been inscribed, but they were no longer legible: this tomb had likewise a spiraculum, or air-channel. In a

---

[4] Some of these hieroglyphics are published in M. Champollion's works.

fourth the three figures were repeated, and many hieroglyphics inscribed, but they were in so bad a state of preservation, that I could only make out one cartouche.

22d.—I went on shore at Derr. The town is clean, and tolerably well built, and surrounded as usual by groves of date-trees and cultivated grounds. The houses were of clay, with flat roofs; that of the Catchief was larger than the rest, and had rows of red and white bricks round the doors and windows, and along the top. I found him surrounded by a number of his attendants, sitting on an earthen divan near an immense sycamore-tree in the middle of the village. He was very tall, of a swarthy complexion, and dressed in a dark-blue shirt, red slippers, and turban, with a number of strings of beads and fetichies around his neck. He received me very civilly, and made me several presents consisting of sheep and dates, of a nabout from Kostam, an iron hatchet from Sennaar, and of a small stick curved at the end, and used in riding camels, called an assar; it comes from Cordofan, and is supposed to be described in the antient hieroglyphics. I bought several mats, which are here manufactured in considerable quantities. They cost about seven piastres each, are well made, but when new have a most disagreeable smell. I went to the house of a slave-dealer to buy some courbashes. It was built of mud, about eight or nine feet high, and stood in a court-yard, in which were a few hovels, an earthen bed-place, and a mill for grinding corn by means of a stone turned by a handle, which was thrown round alternately by two women who sat opposite to each other on the ground. This must be the kind of mill alluded to in the New Testament.

CATCHEIF'S HOUSE AT DERR.

London, James Fraser Regent Street.

Printed by C. Hullmandel

In the yard a handsome young woman was employed in making a mat; she had the peculiar complexion so often described in the paintings at Abou Simbel, and was dressed in the usual manner, but wore a number of white and red necklaces, fetichies, and other ornaments formed of beads and shells. The temple is an excavation in a low rock near a burial-ground at the back of the town; it is completely ruined, and half full of stones; the foundations of eight square columns might be traced in the vestibule, and the interior was supported by others. The usual heroic exploits had been described on the walls, and a few of the hieroglyphics might still be made out; but the idols in the adytum had been destroyed. From Derr roads branch off to Korosko, Dongola, &c.; and on the western shore, Elwah may be reached by a journey of twenty days.

23d.—Thermometer 71°. I arrived at a temple nearly opposite to Maharaka, in which place I was informed that no ruins existed. This temple is in tolerable preservation, and does not appear of very great antiquity. According to Mr. Wilkinson, it was dedicated to Isis and Serapis. That it has since been used as a church appears from the remains of Christian figures still to be seen upon the walls. It stands in a court surrounded by a colonnade, with a staircase leading up to the roof. It contains also several Greek inscriptions, which have no doubt been copied. The approach from the river has been constructed with masonry, and is now covered with a collection of huts, which compose the modern village. Thence I proceeded to the temple at Dakke, which is situated in a plain, and fronts the north, with a handsome propylæon, and staircases, by which the top may be attained. It is well built, but the stones have been only finished off round the edges. Beneath it is a subterraneous apartment roofed with slabs of stone eighteen or twenty feet long, and at present nearly full of rubbish, but the figures of a lion, and the offering of a sphinx are well cut in the walls. Many excavations have been made in the plain, which seems to have been formerly cultivated; and in the rocky hills, at some little distance, there are said to be antient tombs. This temple is the most southern built by the Ptolemies between Philæ and Wady Halfa, with the exception of that of Ibrim, which with those at Derr and at Ferradj are the only three on the eastern bank of the Nile. The country at Dakke is tolerably well cultivated, but the village itself consists of a few huts covered with reeds. On the eastern shore there is a large ruin of unburnt bricks, which is supposed by Mr. Wilkinson to be the site of Metacompso.

I next visited Gerf Hossein (the antient Tutzis). The temple is an excavation in a ridge of rocky hills, and before it is an hypæthral court surrounded with gigantic figures in nearly the same style as those at Abou Simbel, but composed of different layers of stones, which are now so decayed, that the continuity of the hieroglyphics inscribed upon them is lost. The massive architraves placed upon the top of these figures reminded me, like those at Sabooa, of Stonehenge; and it is not improbable that together with religious traditions the art of building temples may have even reached that place from Egypt. The warlike exploits described at Abou Simbel are here also recorded in the interior, which has been painted.

A large architrave had been taken away from one of the doorways, but the Pacha had, I was informed, prevented any further spoliation. There are probably catacombs in the adjacent mountains; and in the plain, which no doubt was formerly productive, there are vestiges of other antient foundations, amongst which are those of a church; there has also been an extensive burial-ground, and a considerable village. The Reis had pretended for some reason or other that there was a shoal near Gerf Hossein, which would not allow of the boat being brought to the shore, so that I had a considerable distance to walk; and did not therefore arrive at Dandoor till the evening. This small temple faces the east, and is handsomely built of large stones finished round the edges, but it cannot be compared with the massive structures of more antient times, and is already much dilapidated although supposed to have been built during the reign of Augustus, whilst temples coeval with the Exodus are comparatively in good preservation. It is now surrounded by heaps of squared stones, but was originally adorned by a peribolus, with a propylæon, and was highly ornamented with hieroglyphics. The roof is destroyed; behind it is a small grotto with an Egyptian portal, and near it are some quarries, The pommels of the doors had turned in sockets let into squared stones, which does not appear to have been the case in more antient buildings.

24*th.*—Between this place and Kalabshèe, there are one or two reefs of sunken rocks across the river, which may have been cataracts in former times when the water was at a lower level. The temple at Kalabshèe, fronts the east, has been of a considerable size, and has had an extensive peribolus, but is at present much dilapidated, and surrounded on all sides by the village. The approach to it was by a handsome quay and raised road, which led to a propylæon. The interior has been covered with painted hieroglyphics, and adorned with gilding, and a staircase led to the summit. The stones with which it was built, were only finished round the edges, and the doors had been of the same construction as those of Dandoor. There are vestiges of tombs in the adjacent hills; and at some little distance a considerable accumulation of rubbish and pottery, most probably marks the site of a Roman town. The most interesting object however is an excavated temple called Beit El Walid; the interior as well as the vestibule of which had been inscribed with hieroglyphics painted on plaster, and adorned with sculptures representing the battles before mentioned. Hieroglyphics had been also inserted on the inner sides of the columns, which are of the same kind as those at Thebes, Benihassen, &c., so greatly resembling those of the Doric order. The whole had been executed with much care, and as at Gerf Hossein the imperfections in the rocks had been closed up with masonry.

The plain appeared very fertile, and well cultivated, the village as usual dirty and ruinous, but the inhabitants, comparatively speaking, were well off, they have

Printed by C. Hulmandel.

NUBIAN WOMEN.

Published by James Fraser Regent Street

the character of being turbulent, and gave the French
a good deal of trouble. The Sheik pays a duty to the
Pacha, but has hitherto contrived to prevent the admission of any troops, and to avoid the conscription.
Strangers however at present are well received. Besides
the usual crops of cotton and doura, &c., henna grows
here in abundance; it is a shrub about four feet high,
and has a small red flower, the dye is produced from
the leaves when dried and pulverised.

The women were dressed in the usual manner, but
their heads were covered with an extraordinary quantity
of castor oil, they wore very large ear and nose rings,
and a long leathern strap round their necks, to which
were attached the wooden keys of their houses, amulets,
and a small bag for money, and other valuables. I
bought several scarabæi, and other trifling antiquities,
which were strung on their necklaces. The children
were entirely naked, excepting a leathern strap round
their waists, and some of them had their hair tied up
in small bunches with strings of coloured beads. One
of the men was picturesquely dressed in a long robe,
with a scarf over his shoulder; a round shield, made of
a thick hide with a knob in the centre hung round his
neck; and he carried in his hand a straight sword similar
to those used by the Christian knights in the crusades.

The ruins at Wady Taffa are situated on a stony
plain elevated about twenty feet above the river, to
which it gradually descends in sloping banks covered
with verdure. The plain is surrounded by barren hills,
and on an eminence to the southward the house of the
Sheik seems to occupy the site of an antient building.

A raised causeway of masonry has formed the approach from the river; and amongst accumulations of rubbish, of ruined walls and foundations, upon which the huts of a few miserable savages are erected, the remains of a temple supposed to have been built in the time of the Romans may be traced, as also those of another edifice in a different direction, with Egyptian columns in the interior. They had been constructed with stones finished round the edges, and with the usual stone doors; and holes apparently for metallic fastenings may still be seen at the angles of the stones. The courses in some of the walls are, as Mr. Wilkinson has observed, in curved, and not in horizontal lines; and a doorway has been constructed in one place many feet above the level of the ground.

Not far from the village of Gertassee is a large quadrangular enclosure, the walls of which are about twenty or thirty feet high, and of considerable breadth, and externally composed of large squared stones, but the middle is filled up with rubble-work. The masonry is not of the best workmanship, and it is to be observed very inferior to that of a similar building, called Ramah, near Hebron, in Syria; which appears, like this, to have been intended for a place of security for cattle, goods, &c. Several of the courses on the western side from settling or some other cause are curved like those at Wady Taffa. I did not observe any hieroglyphics, but the remains of sculpture are visible over a lofty gateway in the centre of one of the faces of the building fronting north-east half north. The adjoining plain had but little cultivation. Towards the north were extensive stone-quarries, which contained the Greek inscriptions mentioned by Mr. Wilkinson, also a Roman bust, and a most beautiful doorway decorated with the winged globe, sacred serpents, &c., in the finest taste.[5]

An hypæthral building, apparently unfinished, is finely situated on an adjacent eminence, with its front towards the river facing east-south-east. It is ornamented with many hieroglyphics, and the four columns towards the northern and southern sides are quadriform, and decorated with the head of Isis; while, towards the eastern and western, they have Egyptian capitals. The advantage of a slight breeze enabled us to proceed, we passed several buildings of burnt brick, and arrived at the Temple of Debode (the antient Parembole) in the evening. The river is here a noble stream, and on the eastern side a

[5] The Greeks, and also the Romans appear in many instances to have followed the example of the antient Egyptians in their numerous inscriptions; and it is extraordinary with what care and expense the latter have recorded upon stone, and even upon granite occurrences apparently of small importance — such as the individual circumstances of private funerals, the excavation of stones from a quarry, the offerings of private individuals, &c.; and amongst other instances the successful petition of the priests at Philæ to obtain exemption from military contributions was even thought worthy of being inscribed upon the pedestal of an obelisk. If such trifles as these were handed down to posterity, it does not seem probable that the important events of history would have been forgotten, particularly by a people, who boasted of their accuracy in these matters. This, however, can only be ascertained by a much more extensive and accurate knowledge of hieroglyphics than has at present been acquired. It may here be remarked, that several of the tombs, temples, and other monuments appear to have been inscribed by degrees, and at different times after their erection, probably as the events recorded successively took place.

chain of picturesque mountains comes down nearly to
the water. On the western the hills are more distant, and
up on the intermediate plain the temple is finely situated
with the remains of an extensive peribolus, and an approach by a raised causeway from the river, through
three handsome propylæa. The view of the stream with
the adjacent mountains through these lofty gateways is
very striking from the building itself, which must have
been extremely magnificent, although it does not bear
the appearance of remote antiquity, indeed it is ascribed
by Mr. Wilkinson to the time of Ptolemy Philometor.
It has been built of the same materials as the temples
at Wady Taffa; and the sockets for the stone doors have
been cut in squared blocks. The apartments have been
ceiled with flat slabs, and covered with hieroglyphics, but
they do not appear to have been plastered or painted.
A few isolated ruins, probably of Roman forts, are to be
seen to the northward, together with several Nubian huts
amidst patches of cultivated ground; these habitations
are six or seven feet high, situated in small yards surrounded by walls, are built of unburnt bricks or clay,
and covered with reeds. The inhabitants are extremely poor, but appear very healthy. The boys are
naked, excepting a leathern girdle, but have a noble and
independent air, and are extremely well set up.

I soon afterwards arrived at Philæ, which was seen
to great advantage in the clear light of a still evening.
The boat was moored under a high bank opposite the
northern end of the island, along which the river sweeps
finely to the south-westward. The moon shone with
uncommon splendour, and gave a mysterious and solemn

effect to the ruined temples of the sacred island, which, surrounded by palm-trees and vegetation, formed a singular contrast to the portentous and grotesque masses of granite on the island of Bigge, and on the adjacent shores.

The river here presented the appearance of a vast lake, nor was it possible to contemplate unmoved that mighty and wonderful stream, the sources of whose periodical visitations are veiled in the same obscurity which still involves the history of those powerful nations whose industry once clothed its banks with fertility; and whose science, called into action by superstitious enthusiasm, ennobled them with buildings of such matchless grandeur and beauty, that the very ruins have for successive ages commanded universal admiration. Nor can it be recollected without increased interest, that many of those noble monuments, evincing in their construction so much power and skill, and decorated with so many elaborate devices, were raised in very early ages, certainly at no long time after the deluge; and that they therefore not only afford convincing proofs of the refinement, to which mankind had attained before that great event, but also testify that Egypt was the source from which Greece first, Rome next, and subsequently through them the rest of Europe derived the chief part of their civilisation, and knowledge.

25*th.* — I sent the boat to Es Souan, and went early in the morning to Philæ. The hypæthral temple near which I landed is extremely lofty, and, if intended for effect, must have been constructed upon principles totally different from those, which directed the works at Abou-

Simbel, and at other places. The edifices on this island
were however the productions of a much later period;
they are exceedingly beautiful, are decorated in every part
with hieroglyphics, and, together with their propylæa,
colonnades, obelisks, and ascents from the water have
a very striking effect notwithstanding their ruined condition, and their comparatively new appearance; indeed
the island is nearly covered with them, and with mounds
of rubbish. These noble objects have been so fully and
minutely described by preceding travellers, that I shall
not enter into any detailed account, which from the
short visit I paid them I am by no means quali-
fied to offer, but I shall conclude with a few cursory
observations.

The Great Temple and the principal propylæa* front
the south-east; the other propylæa, south-south-east.
The colonnade and steps leading from the water are also
in another direction, which the form of the island most
probably determined. The masonry of these edifices is
very fine, and in many places holes apparently for
metallic fastenings may be observed at the angles of the
blocks. The hieroglyphics in the interior of the temple
have been painted upon plaster. In the chamber, where
the apotheosis of Osiris is supposed to be represented,
the left leg of the principal figure, laid on his back for
the purpose of embalmment, is stretched out in the same
position, as that in which the Colossi are frequently
sculptured; and the protecting genius appears in a

---

* The lofty portals seem to have been intended for treasuries or for
places of security, as their internal construction is well adapted for
defence.

human shape, and not in that of a bird. In the chamber, where the birth of Horus is delineated, there is a curious representation of a bird encircled by the flowers of the lotus, having on the one side a serpent, and on the other

two priests in the act of worshipping a serpent suspended upon a cross, which has a great resemblance to the usual representation of the Brazen Serpent in the Wilderness.

I was informed that Mr. Hay had discovered a passage under the water, composed of solid masonry, between this island and that of Bigge, and that the entrance was from a shaft amongst the ruins of the Great Temple.

The island of Bigge is singularly composed of high mountains of granite interspersed with fields of doura, and with the huts of a few inhabitants built amongst foundations, mounds of rubbish, and ruined walls, in such a manner that no building of any consequence can be examined without previously destroying them. I saw the remains of a Roman arch, and a block in one of the huts inscribed with hieroglyphics, and no doubt many antient memorials have in like manner been consigned to temporary or perpetual oblivion. It was a romantic, and in many respects interesting place, from the strong contrast of the fantastic masses of barren stone with the luxuriant vegetation around them, and from the perfect seclusion and stillness of the scene, interrupted only by the indistinct noise of the water-wheels, which sounded, particularly as it happened to be Sunday, like the distant harmony of church-bells, whilst some yellow stones on the fertile bank reflected in the water had the appearance of primroses—a resemblance not a little heightened by the warmth and serenity of the air; but at present neither the incense of praise, nor the fragrance of Spring exist in this desert.

Being obliged to proceed to Es Souan without delay, I returned to the shore, under which the boat had been moored during the previous night, in order to proceed by land to that place. The bank was nearly semicircular, and about twenty or thirty feet above the water; a sandy plain extended towards the north totally devoid of cultivation, and bounded at various distances by ranges of mountains. In the most inaccessible parts of the masses of granite opposite to Bigge tablets of hieroglyphics had been inscribed, and a few huts formed a village near their base, but not a vestige of cultivation was to be seen excepting on the islands, whilst Philæ, with its magnificent ruins and waving palm-trees, universal emblems of victory, appeared above the stream with a dignity and pre-eminence scarcely inferior to that of the Parthenon over the plain of Athens.

On proceeding to Es Souan I passed a wall of unburnt brick, apparently intended as a defence to the road which wound through a narrow valley amongst lofty mountains, and on either side the ruins of buildings, probably Roman guard-houses, and afterwards several Sheik's tombs, and also a fountain reported to have been formed by Abd-el-Catchief, who died of the plague in the year 1836; and who is said to have built a tower not far distant. The road thence goes through the Turkish burial-ground, which I have already mentioned, and shortly after enters Es Souan. The baggage having been replaced in the boat I brought from Cairo, and the necessary arrangements made, I proceeded immediately to Koum Ombos, where I remained for the night, during which some rain fell.

26*th.*—Thermometer 76°.[7] The ruins are well situated on a high bank on the eastern and concave side of a bend in the river. The stream has already swept away great part of these interesting monuments, and will eventually destroy the remainder; whilst from the land the sands of the desert have drifted over them in immense quantities. The peribolus was composed of a very high wall, of unburnt bricks, and on its south-eastern side a doorway seems to have been originally intended, but never completed. The cartouche of Thothmes the Third is inscribed upon it, but, from the manner in which the fastenings for the door have been formed, it would appear to have been of a later date. The temples have been covered with hieroglyphics painted upon stucco. Some of the slabs of which the flat ceilings were composed, are twenty-seven feet long. I searched without success for the unfinished figures inscribed in squares, mentioned by Mr. Wilkinson. The catacombs appear to have been excavated in a ridge of hills to the northward.

[7] The thermometrical observations were always taken in the cabin, but at different times of the day.

At Hadjar Silsilis the rocks are higher, and the quarries much more extensive on the eastern, than on the western shore. The antient town was also on the former side to the northward of the quarries, which are most wonderful instances of industry and skill. It is difficult to determine whether the excellence of the workmanship, or the fine and continuous texture of the stone of which the lofty cliffs are composed, is most to be admired. In many places winding roads have been carried into the heart of the mountain, and extensive excavations made with the utmost exactness, apparently by the chisel, although in many places the marks of wedges are visible. Several ranges of squared holes may likewise be observed, similar to those on the great stone in the quarry at Baalbec; and on the perpendicular face of the lofty rocks rows of small cavities have been cut in slanting directions, apparently for the insertion of wooden supports to serve as staircases or means of ascent. Horizontal and perpendicular lines, and occasionally hieroglyphics, have also been drawn on the face of the stone, and the projecting angles in the perpendicular sides of the winding roads have been perforated, either for the insertion of ropes or pulleys, or to afford a view of the road through them.

A great deal of work has also been carried on on the western side, and several curious tablets, containing figures and hieroglyphics, have been inscribed on the rocks; and the bright colours with which they have been painted are, in many instances, distinct and fresh. There are, likewise, niches about four feet deep, with a variety of figures and inscriptions; and grottoes, like those at Ibrim, in which the ceilings have been chequered with a red and white pattern. The most remarkable of these

excavations is towards the north : it consists of an apartment adorned with hieroglyphics, and of a painted cor-
ridor, in which four large columns, or piers have been
left to support the roof. Mr. Wilkinson states that it
was begun by the successor of Amenoph the Third, and
that it contains the representation of a battle; but this
I could not discover, and conclude therefore that it has
been lately destroyed.[8]

There are many other excavations at this interesting
place, described by Mr. Hamilton and other travellers,
which for want of time I did not examine.

*27th.* — Thermometer 65°. I arrived at Edfou. The
temple, surrounded by the huts of the modern village, is
situated on an extensive plain, naturally fertile, but at
present only partially cultivated, and bounded by a distant range of mountains, where the antient Necropolis
was placed. The entrance is by a most magnificent propylæa, which appears to be a more recent structure than
the rest of the edifice. It is built with the greatest
solidity, and contains many apartments that have been
closed with stone doors, and lighted by apertures worked
in the masonry. They are connected by a staircase extending to the top of the building, and likewise to a
variety of similar chambers in the foundation. The gates
of the great entrance, probably of metal, must have been
of an enormous height, and exceedingly heavy. They
seem however to have been hung in the usual manner,
upon pommels which turned in sockets.

The temple itself, one of the most imposing in Egypt,

---

[8] Mr. Hay is said to have taken copies of these inscriptions, and
many of them have been published by M. Champollion.

affords a striking contrast to the miserable hovels, many
of which are built upon it, and others on vast mounds
of rubbish, with which it is surrounded.   The interior
covered with painted hieroglyphics has been divided by
earthen walls, to form a magazine for corn; and beneath
it are enormous substructions, which I entered by a hole
from an Arab house.   They were full of dirt and filth of
every description, but had been built in the most solid
manner, and had been adorned with highly finished
sculptures.   Several of the blocks had had fastenings
let into hollows, cut in the shape of a double wedge,
like those at Karnac.   At some little distance were the
remains of a smaller temple of equally fine workmanship,
but even more dilapidated than the larger one.   The
modern village is tolerably extensive, and contains a
small Coptic convent, and about sixty Christians.

After passing the island of Damanieh, I arrived at
El Kab, the antient Eilithias, so called from Eilitheia
(Lucina); and also named Beni-Lail, (Sons of the Moon).[9]
A large space, in which several excavations had been
made, is surrounded by a high and thick wall of unburnt bricks, constructed with ramps, by which it might
have been ascended; the bricks in several parts of it
were, as is frequently the case in Etruscan architecture,
placed endways, and lengthways in alternate courses.   It
contained a quantity of rubbish and broken pottery, and
also mounds of brick buildings; of these the most considerable was towards the northward, and appeared to
have been the citadel.   This town is supposed to have
been of great mercantile importance, and to have been

9 Neale Lail, the site of Hierocompolis according to Colonel Leake's
map is on the western shore of the river.

situated at the termination of one of the principal roads
from the Red Sea. I could not find the ruins mentioned by Mr. Wilkinson, nor the cartouche of Rameses
the Second; neither did I observe any reservoir, or collection of water, excepting a pond beyond the enclosure,
encrusted with a considerable quantity of natron. The
adjacent plain is surrounded by mountains, which approach the enclosure on the northern side, and contains
the antient Necropolis, which must have been very extensive. The intervening space between the boundary
wall and the hills is covered with broken pottery, sarcophagi, bones, fragments of mummy cloth, and other
indications of antient tombs. But the objects most worthy
of notice are excavations in the rocks, containing deep
shafts, and mummy pits, and on their walls various interesting details and hieroglyphics painted upon stucco.
Most of them have in all probability been opened many
centuries ago, and are every day losing somewhat of their
original character, it is therefore fortunate that many of
these interesting inscriptions have been preserved, and
some of them already published by M. Champollion.

Beyond these tombs, and near the river are the
remains of a ruined temple mentioned by Mr. Wilkinson; who has also described three others to the eastward, and at the entrance of the valley, through which
the communication with the Red Sea most probably lay.
They are three or four miles from the river. The small
chapel of Ra stands in the middle of the valley, and
fronts the east-north-east. It seems to have had neither
a peribolus nor portal, but is decorated with painted hieroglyphics, and with several cartouches, one of which is
that of Thothmes the Fourth. Near it at the foot of

the mountains is a temple, supposed to have been dedicated to Lucina, and built in the reign of the Ptolemies. It is partly an excavation, and is approached by a ramp with a handsome balustrade. The stones employed in the masonry had only been worked round the edges. Further on upon the hills on the opposite side of the valley is another temple, attributed to Amenoph the Third, and which contained his cartouche, and also that of Thothmes the Fourth. This building fronting west-south-west had doors at each end, a small court enclosed by a peribolus, and was painted with hieroglyphics. Higher up the mountain are appearances of extensive quarries, which may be worth examination; and further to the southward in the plain, is a considerable Arab village. In returning through the cultivated ground to the boat, which had gone down the stream, I found that the harvest of Doura had commenced. The ruins at Kom Achmah were said to have been entirely destroyed. I passed the remains of the pyramid El Koofa, which, according to Mr. Wilkinson's excellent book, was built in stages, and at present does not exceed thirty-five feet in height, and arrived in the evening at Esneh (Latopolis). The boat was moored under a high bank, in which are to be traced the remains of an antient pier, and on its summit a large school has been established for boys. Similar institutions are to be met with in all the principal towns, and sufficiently prove the Pacha's anxiety to ameliorate by education the condition of his people. Little however can be effected, unless instruction is likewise extended to the females; which, it would appear, can only be accomplished by the introduction of Christianity.

*28th.*—Thermometer 58°. I went on shore early in the morning. The town is extensive; it contains magazines, and manufactories of cotton and of indigo, and particularly of the caps that are universally worn under the red tarbouses. The various public buildings, the factories, barracks, the hareems of the principal officers, and a palace belonging to the Pacha without the town, have at a distance a clean and respectable appearance, owing to the constant renewal of whitewash; but it is to be regretted that they are erected with the materials of antient temples, and that any attempt at improvement in the different towns is at the expense of these noble monuments, highly interesting on account of their architecture, but infinitely more so from the valuable records of antiquity contained in the inscriptions. The population is Arab, and as usual in a state of abject misery. I observed here, and at other places, that the children's eyes were actually devoured by flies without any care being taken to prevent it; indeed, a woman to whom my janissary mentioned the subject, laughed at the idea of precaution. I afterwards found the Arabs at Gizeh unaccountably indifferent about loss of sight.

The temple had evidently been upon a very grand scale, but the vestibule only remains; for the ground on the inner side is occupied by Arab houses on a level with the floor. As it has been converted into a magazine for cotton, it may, it is to be hoped, for a time at least escape further spoliation. The roof was composed of enormous slabs, and supported by twenty-four columns in four rows, each of which was more than six yards in circumference, within twenty feet of the ceiling. I could not measure them below that height, as the place was full of rubbish.

The door, that formerly opened into the interior, was entirely stopped up.[1]

The temple of Contra Laton seen by Mr. Hamilton in 1801 has been removed for the sake of the materials. The site of it upon the eastern bank, whence Esneh is seen to great advantage, is however yet distinguished by part of a brick wall, one or two stones inscribed with hieroglyphics, some fragments of broken pottery, and a quantity of rubbish near El Hallam, two villages on an extensive plain, bounded in the distance by desert mountains, in which the Necropolis of the antient city may possibly be found. It may here be remarked that scarcely in any country do the tombs, which have been discovered, bear any proportion to the immense population that have successively passed away.

I did not visit Asfoon, Asphinis, nor Tofnees, supposed by Mr. Wilkinson to be the site of Aphroditopolis, as the temple at that place was entirely destroyed; nor did I go to the convent Edeir, where according to Mr. Hamilton a small temple existed upon the site of that antient town.[2]

---

[1] I was informed that Mr. Hay, and also M. Champollion, had examined several tombs and excavations at Isla, a place in the mountains about two days' journey from Edfou; and that the latter gentleman had continued his researches to Erment, and had found several grottoes, containing hieroglyphics and inscriptions, and also a sarcophagus formed of alabaster; but that the whole of these sepulchres had been previously opened.

[2] I had already heard a tradition that a considerable treasure near Koum Ombos was guarded by a dragon, which occasionally came down to drink at the river; and had at that time the power of blinding by a glance those who beheld him. A report existed at Esneh that a cliff had actually fallen down in that neighbourhood, and that a quantity of money was discovered, of which a party of soldiers had been sent to take possession. Traditions, however fabulous, are often founded upon fact.

The tombs in the mountains of Gebelein had been entirely destroyed, and nothing remained to mark the site of the antient town of Crocodilopolis, excepting a few mounds of rubbish, and the ruins of some brick huts on the side of the rocky heights, and a few cottages inhabited by the men, who work for the Pacha in the adjacent quarries. It is surprising that the sacred Crocodiles were not interred at Crocodilopolis instead of Erment, as the people of the latter place are represented to have been hostile to them.

Eight columns and some walling, included in a building adjoining the Sheik's house are all the remains of the Great Temple at Ermont (Hermontis), which is said to have been built by Cleopatra. The principal part has been taken down for the sake of the materials, and the rest will be probably soon disposed of in the same manner. The hieroglyphics had been well executed in stucco, but had not been painted. The church, which appears to have been an extensive building, is entirely destroyed, a few stones, and some broken columns of granite alone marking its former site. The ruins of a brick building, apparently those of a church, are to be seen on an adjacent eminence near an antient tank. The surrounding plain is extremely fertile, and the village was formerly rich and populous, and the inhabitants, consequently, very turbulent. They have however, within a few years past, been reduced by conscriptions and other causes to extreme poverty, and are no longer, as they once were, the terror of unprotected travellers.[3] I found vast quantities of cattle collected for the Pacha at this place, and

[3] Selim, the janissary, accompanied Mr. Leigh when the Arab was suffocated in the mummy-pit at the northern end of the island, opposite to Erment. He informed me, that when that unfortunate accident hap-

considerable manufactories of indigo and of bricks. In
the latter it was curious to observe that the apertures
in the kilns were covered over by horizontal courses,
exactly as they were in antient buildings before the arch
was adopted. I had an opportunity of purchasing several
scarabæi, and other small antiques, at this place.

The road to Elwah branches off from Erment. After
crossing the plain, it ascends the mountains to a stony
desert on a much higher level than the valley of the
Nile. As no water is to be had, and the heat very
oppressive, the journey is attended with considerable
fatigue, and was formerly also with some degree of
danger, owing to the savage disposition of the Arabs.
Their predatory habits however are, as has been stated,
at present controlled by the authority of the Pacha, and
the journey may be performed now with comparative
security. It is probable that many oases exist yet undiscovered in these wild scenes of desolation, which
appear to have been but imperfectly explored.

I proceeded to Luxor, where I found Dr. Cummings,
who had been obliged by a violent illness to return from
Esneh, and Mr. Baillie, another gentleman, whom I had
also met at Cairo, soon after arrived. Thermometer 66°.
The Great Temple is a most magnificent structure, and
stands in a very advantageous situation, but is much encumbered with sand, mounds of rubbish, and the houses
of the modern village.* The obelisk in front of the pro-

pened, the Arabs were in such numbers, and in such a state of excitement, that a retreat was attended with some difficulty.

* It is surprising that the French did not clear away this and other
antient monuments, when they had possession of the country and the
command of the inhabitants, whose employment would have been desirable in every respect.

pylæa is considered the finest in Egypt, but is, in my opinion, inferior to that in the Temple of Karnac; possibly owing to its being seen to disadvantage, as the adjacent mounds hide nearly half of it, and as its companion has been sent to France.

30*th.* — The temples at Karnac have been repeatedly described, and much accurate information respecting them is contained in Mr. Wilkinson's book, to which I am enabled to add little from the short time I remained there; I shall therefore confine myself to such general observations as occurred on the spot. Having obtained horses from the Catchief of Karnac, I set out for that place along the causeway, or avenue of sphinxes, by which the Great Temple was formerly connected with Luxor, and afterwards passed through several magnificent propylæa covered with innumerable hieroglyphics. To the eastward was another avenue of sphinxes, and near it a large reservoir of water surrounded by antient foundations, and by a variety of mutilated statues chiefly of basalt. Besides the propylæa, which on every side surround the Great Temple, many stupendous ruins constructed of enormous blocks present themselves in all directions, each of which in any other situation would merit particular attention. But the principal approach to the Great Temple is from the westward, the side towards the river; and here the grandeur of the propylæa, forming probably the most magnificent entrance ever constructed by human science, must be seen to be comprehended. The stones, that compose its exterior, are laid in horizontal courses, and like the casing-stones of the Pyramids at Gizeh, have been cut according to the required obliquity of the surface, and afterwards smoothed down from the top. It may give some idea of the vastness of these buildings to observe that great spaces, particularly in the inner face, have not yet been finished. The doors, of proportionate size, appear to have been suspended in the same manner as at Edfou, and in other temples.[5] Immense figures of granite guard each side of this entrance, which opens into a spacious court surrounded by buildings of proportionate grandeur, and on the eastern side by the entrance to the Great Temple.

This gigantic portal was decorated with the finest sculpture, and hieroglyphics, and likewise with two enormous Colossi; and, although surrounded by ruin and desolation, stands without a rival in the world. What edifice, antient, or modern, can vie with this structure, in grandeur and simplicity? and what, in comparison, is the boast of Michael Angelo, that he would raise in the air a dome similar to that of the Pantheon? The multitude of columns, the massive architraves, suspended above 100 feet high in the air, the vast scale of the component parts, rendered beautifully attractive by the exquisite finish and variety of the painted sculptures, are of a magnitude and perfection not to be described; and the whole effect is far superior to that of any building of uncoloured stone, and of smaller proportions. The cella once had an upper range of columns, like that of the Temple of Neptune at Pæstum; although few of them

---

[5] This mode of construction seems to have been universally applied in very antient times to all doors of whatever dimensions, but at some few places — at Patara, for instance, in Asia Minor — the stone doors of antient tombs slide in grooves.

now remain.  It is also filled up to a considerable height
by enormous masses of broken columns and of ruined
architraves, some of which appear to have been destroyed
by fire, notwithstanding the great height to which they
have been raised; and the surface of some of the columns
towards the eastern end of the hall have not been faced
down, but merely roughly chiselled into the proper
shape and dimensions.[6]  What it must have been when
fresh and uninjured, and filled with multitudes of priests
and worshippers, in all the pomp and splendour of
Egyptian idolatry, can scarcely be imagined; but I consider that the spectacle it affords, even in its present
dilapidated condition, an ample compensation for the
time consumed, and the trifling inconveniences necessarily incurred in a voyage from England.  Beyond this
temple other sacred buildings extend in a right line,
the works of successive monarchs from the earliest times;
and an open space near the centre had been adorned with

[6] Having been informed that the blocks were kept together by
wooden fastenings, I examined several; but instead of wood, I found in
the joints of one, which had partly been thrown over, cuttings about
an inch deep in the shape of wedges, with the smaller ends meeting at
the centre of the column, full of an exceedingly fine white cement of
the consistence of pounce, which, notwithstanding an exposure of probably many centuries to the intense heat of the climate, still retained
a degree of moisture.  I brought away some of it with the intention
of having it analysed.  In the corresponding stone, that had been placed
upon it, were similar cuttings filled up in like manner.  The slabs
forming the roof of another part of the Temple had been cut in a somewhat similar manner; but I did not find any thing in them, nor discover
by what substance they had been fastened.  The extreme tenacity of
the cement used in antient buildings was afterwards evident, when the
casing-stones of the Great Pyramid of Gizeh were discovered.

four obelisks: one at present remains, a monument of surpassing beauty, and appears to great advantage, shooting up, as it does, into the azure vault of an almost cloudless sky. It is composed of the finest rose-coloured granite, and has been grooved down the edges, and worked with the utmost exactness. The few hieroglyphics inscribed upon it are also of the finest workmanship. Many of these buildings were no doubt hypæthral, and the effects of light and shade seem to have been well understood by those who planned and executed them. Mr. Wilkinson remarks, that the central temple is more than 100 years older than any other building at Thebes, and that the cartouche of Osirtesen is inscribed in it: the cartouche however of Thothmes the Third is also to be found towards the bottom of a doorway.[7] The ceiling had been formed of large slabs of granite, ornamented with gilt stars upon a blue ground. The figures upon the walls were sculptured, and painted upon the stone in some places with different and appropriate colours, and in others with a greenish gray, which formed a pleasing contrast with the warm tints of the polished granite. The cartouche of Osirtesen was also inscribed upon some ruined columns in an adjoining building, which are called polygonal, but which are essentially Doric, excepting that the echinus, annuli, and hypotrachelion are wanting. Mr. Wilkinson has justly observed, that they prove the pure taste of the

---

[7] The doorway is much decayed, having been composed of basalt, which seems ill adapted to withstand the corroding effects of the desert sands; but the whole apartment has been materially injured by antiquarian researches, carried on, as it is said, under the direction of Mr. Dronetti.

most antient Egyptian architecture, and were the pro-
totype of the Greek Doric; nor can any one, I think,
see these pillars, and those at Benihassen, without being
of the same opinion, and without being convinced that
the Greeks took with them from Egypt amongst other
sciences, those of architecture and of sculpture, and, as
has been already stated, the art also of colouring the
interior of their temples upon stucco. It should likewise
be remembered that the Doric was the oldest order in
both Egypt, and in Greece. Some of the blocks composing these columns are three feet seven inches in
diameter, and have been fitted together by pommels and
corresponding cavities,⁸ their flutings are nine inches
wide. In an adjoining temple, the capitals of the columns have the appearance of being inverted; and at
right angles to this, another building contains many of
the Doric columns nearly in a perfect state. Beyond
these temples are magnificent propylæa,⁹ through which
the distant mountains and bright blue sky are seen
with great effect; and on all sides vast mounds of ruined
materials, enormous masses of solid masonry, fragments
of columns and of architraves, attest the former splendour of this extraordinary place, and at the same time
the wonderful efforts that have been made to destroy
it. On the exterior of the northern wall of the Great
Temple are the famous battle scenes, which are also

⁸ The same fastenings are to be observed in some of the architraves
at Stonehenge.

⁹ It is extremely probable, as Mr. Wilkinson observes, that Homer's
εκατομπυλαι may allude to these portals; and, also, that from them tri-
umphal arches were derived.

partially recorded at Abou-Simbel, and at other places, and which are supposed to relate to the times of Sesostris. Was the knowledge of hieroglyphics as perfect as in some publications it is supposed to be, the doubts that exist respecting the subjects of these sculptures would be soon removed, as tablets of hieroglyphics are inserted over the prisoners, the representations of cities, and in other parts which evidently relate to the subjects described, and would probably throw much light upon antient history and chronology, and possibly upon Homer's poems. For instance, the hieroglyphics in the margin are placed over a town near a river, supposed, from the insertion of crocodiles, to be the Nile. There are several figures on horseback introduced, the horses are in general executed with so much spirit, and thrown into attitudes so true to nature, that such imitations could only have been the result of a very accurate observation of the most beautiful originals. They were sometimes out of proportion, and of ideal forms; but in spirit and in general effect, reminded me of Vernet's drawings. Many of the figures were well imagined, particularly a chief killed by the gigantic hero. The cars, particularly the wheels, appear to have been made of metal; and the reins were fastened round the body of the driver, as they are represented in Roman sculpture. I did not perceive any cars drawn

RUINS AT CARNAC.

*Lithographed by James Fraser, Edgeware Row.*

Fig. 1.

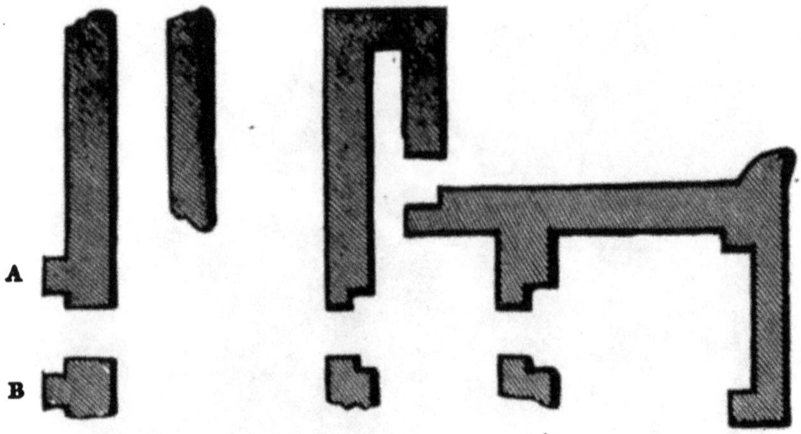

Fig. 2.

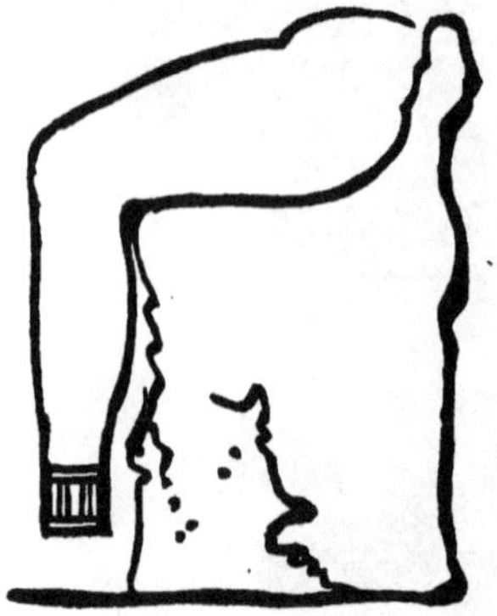

Fig. 3.

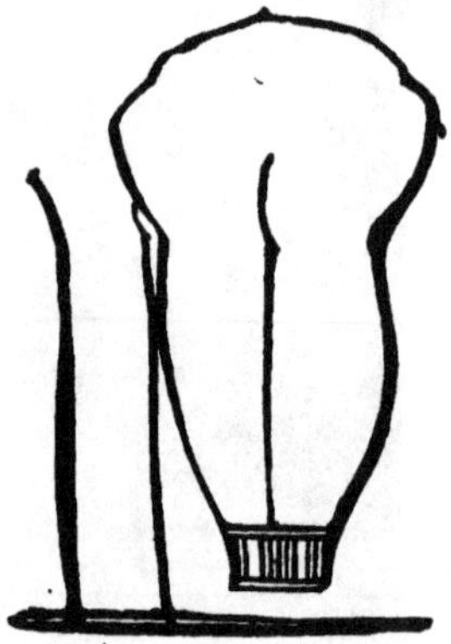

Fig. 4.

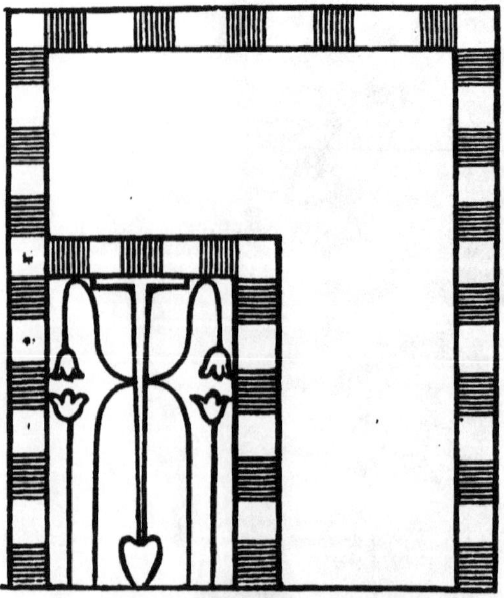

Fig. 5.

Fig. 6.

Fig. 1.—Plan of the Ruin.

2. } Views of the Pedestals, each Side of the Entrance, at A and B.
3. }

4.—Ornaments upon the Pedestals.

5. } Inscriptions.
6. }

by more than two horses. Great attention seems to have been paid in these designs to national costume and physiognomy; and in some of them human sacrifices are certainly represented, notwithstanding the supposition that the figures are allegorical. The sculpture, that records the wars of Shishak in Palestine, is remarkably well executed, particularly a recumbent figure on the lower part of the wall.

I went back by a ruined tank towards the reservoir of water, already mentioned, and observed, to the eastward of an avenue of sphinxes, the foundation of a building, which had been adorned with small Doric columns. The blocks had fifteen flutings of seven inches and a quarter each, and had been fastened together in the usual manner by wedge-shaped grooves crossing each other at right angles at the centre. On each side of the entrance were the pedestals, and lower parts of two basaltic statues,[1] in the same position as the Colossi in

[1] The sculptures on the sides of the pedestal are the common ornamental border and the peculiar representation which may be called an anaglyph; it represents a terebra or bore placed between two groups of the flowers of papyrus and lotus, the stem or cord of each central flower rises to the height of the stick of the bore, passes to the top of the picture, and droops pendent over the exterior flower. This anaglyph has not been explained. The central symbol (the bore) is used in the texts for the letter *c* (*s*) as the initial of a group reading *c ee r* " to accuse, reprobate, command;" and the lotus and papyrus respectively represent " the upper and lower hemisphere," the "north and south." The whole apparently indicates " commanding the upper and the lower world." The inscriptions, placed parallel to the legs of the statue, contain the names and titles of Amenoph the Third, or Memnon. To the left is the gracious God, Lord of dilating the heart (the Sun, Lord of Truth), beloved of Pasht, Neith the giver of life eternal." To the right is " the son of the Sun of his race loving him" . . . . . beloved of Pasht, Neith.—Mr. BIRCH.

the plain of Thebes. The torso of one of them was near these pedestals, and by the cartouche on the girdle, proved to be that of Oisirtesen the First. I obtained leave to take it to England, and it is now in the British Museum. I found Mr. Wilkinson's book particularly useful at Karnac.

In returning to the boat, I was sorry to observe a number of people employed in constructing magazines of gunpowder within a mile of the antient buildings. The approach to Luxor must have been extremely magnificent, but is, as I have mentioned, much disfigured by the accumulations of sand and rubbish, and also by the loss of the obelisk taken to Paris, which has destroyed the effect of the one remaining. There are ruins of other temples in a distant part of the plain near the mountains; but I had not an opportunity of seeing them; nor, by the accounts that are given of them, do they appear to be of much importance.

The plains of Thebes are very extensive on both sides of the Nile, and well calculated for the site of a powerful city; for, as water can probably be found in most places at the level of the river, they are capable of great fertility. At present however, owing to a scanty population, and to other causes, they are very imperfectly cultivated. The inhabitants of Luxor, and of Karnac scarcely amount to 2000, and the conscription is likely to reduce even that number. The summer is very hot, and lasts ten months; and during the extreme heats the people of Karnac take refuge amongst the ruins. Bathing is dangerous, owing to the number of crocodiles, which are said to destroy animals, and even women who approach the river; and to strike down their prey

with their tails into the water before they devour it.
The Catchief sent me a present, and came himself in
the evening, when I procured the use of his horses for
the examination of the plain on the other side of the
river. [Thermometer at night, 57°.]

31st. — Thermometer 78°. I again went to Karnac,
and examined the ruins where the torso was found; and
afterwards the Great Temple: the more I saw of it, the
greater were my admiration and delight. In the evening
the boat was removed to Gournon.

*January 1st*, 1837. — I set out early in the morning
for Biban El Moluc. Beyond a strip of cultivated land
near the river, and the ruins of a temple, apparently
of great antiquity, and supposed to have been built
by Osirei, father of Sesostris,[2] the plain is covered
with barren sands, which towards the mountains form
mounds, and hillocks, some of which seem to have
been tumuli, and others the effects of repeated excavations amongst the shafts, and mummy pits. Vast
quantities of blanched bones, black rags, broken mummy
boards, gums, and resinous substances present a scene
of extensive and of wanton spoliation, altogether peculiar to this extraordinary place.[3] The mountains
likewise abound with ruined tombs, whence thousands

[2] It is called El Ebek by Mr. Hamilton.

[3] It may with great probability be inferred, from the authority of
Homer, and from many of the fables and traditions of antient mythology,
that, together with longevity, mankind were originally endowed with
superior intellectual and bodily faculties. It would also appear that
castes were established, that brass and iron manufactured (without which

of bodies have been dug out, despoiled, and broken up, and afterwards scattered on all sides in surprising numbers.

neither wood nor stone could have been worked), and that the arts had arrived at great perfection before the deluge; and it may reasonably be inferred that many of them survived that great event. The power and skill displayed in the different magnificent sepulchres, in the pyramids, and in many other stupendous remains of remote antiquity, appear, therefore, less surprising than the powerful motive that caused their construction, and the vain contrivances, by embalment and other precautions, to preserve inviolate the body after death.

This motive seems to have acted with equal force upon all classes of the Egyptians, the most learned people of antiquity, and also upon the shepherd kings, of a totally different religion and nation; and could only have arisen from a profound conviction of the resurrection of the body, and of a future existence, connected with the doctrine of expiation, and of sacrifice.

It is evident that natural religion could never have arrived at this great and important truth, but that it must have been originally imparted by direct revelation, although afterwards obscured, and in the end entirely lost sight of from the corrupt and base superstitions notoriously prevalent among this wonderful people, from whom the same errors, together with civilisation and learning, were diffused throughout the rest of the world. And it is also probable that this doctrine was but slightly alluded to by Moses, and that his tomb was expressly concealed to avoid the superstitious veneration that has, in many instances, even under a more perfect dispensation, been paid to the dead; and which has so greatly conduced to idolatrous and sensual practices, and to such absurd notions, that without the most positive testimony could not have been supposed to have existed even amongst the most ignorant people.

Many arguments might here be adduced of the inefficacy of mere human acquirements with respect to an after existence, which the authority of Cicero himself might be brought to support, who confessed the doubt and gloom in which it was involved. And it is also to be observed, that the antients seem to have been deeply impressed

The people of Gournon live in huts, or in sepulchres on the sides of the mountains, and make use of the fragments of mummies and of their cases for fuel, and for other purposes. Mr. Hay had formerly a house near the village; and Signore Werdie, a Greek, has resided there for the last ten years.

The approach to Biban El Moluc is by a natural valley, through which however it may be concluded that a sufficient road formerly existed for the processions which, according to the evidence of antient sculpture, attended funeral ceremonies. Were it not for these representations, it might be supposed that interments were performed with secrecy, and that concealment of the tombs was the main object, as the entrances are in obscure and hidden situations, and as the surface of the mountains has been left entirely in a natural state. These lonely glens are however highly picturesque, and form a strong contrast to the elaborate decoration of the interior of those sepulchres. The mountains are of an imposing grandeur, but in many places of a loose friable texture. Shortly after you enter the valley it becomes narrower, and winds round towards the southeast, where it is connected by a steep path with the plain of Thebes.

The tombs that are accessible have been numbered, so that reference can easily be made to Mr. Wilkinson's book.[4] The first I visited was No. 17, discovered by

with the idea of a superintending Providence; as scarcely a heroic achievement is recorded by the antient poets without an invocation for supernatural assistance, or a hero represented in Egyptian sculpture without a tutelary deity.

[4] This book, to which I have so often referred, is equally useful on the eastern side of the mountain; but it is to be lamented, that

Signore Belzoni. It fully equalled my expectations; but I was sorry to observe how wantonly it had been disfigured, it was said, but I trust without foundation, by M. Champollion. One square pillar had been entirely destroyed, and several of the apartments were strewn with large fragments, which had been cut from the painted walls, and columns. The sepulchre, however, had been violated before Belzoni's discovery, who found the sarcophagus removed from its original position, and a descending passage of considerable length opened beneath it, which could not have been effected when the sarcophagus was in its place. In most of these tombs, as also in the Pyramids of Gizeh, the sarcophagi have been removed, and excavations made beneath, and around them, in search either of treasure, or of secret communication; but this is, I believe, the only passage that

many of the interesting objects described have been since destroyed. As the tombs, however, which contained them are pointed out, much needless inquiry is saved. According to all accounts, Mr. Hay has with laudable industry caused casts and copies to be taken of these, and of other antiquities in Upper and in Lower Egypt, which will probably in a few years be entirely destroyed. Government should publish collections of this sort, and save from oblivion records that can never be replaced. They would do well to emulate the wise and liberal manner in which M. Champollion's and Signore Rosellini's works have been published. The fine obelisk at Thebes and the colossal statue at Metrahery are at our disposal; but it appears that this country is now too much impoverished to remove any of those masses which antient Egypt had both the power and the skill in numberless instances to fashion and to erect, and which, it may be remembered, the Romans found it easy to convey not only to Italy, but also across the deserts to Palmyra. It is to be regretted that the obelisk from Thebes has not been erected in this country as a monument to Lord Nelson: it would have been a more appropriate and glorious record of his fame than any sculpture which modern times can produce.

has yet been found under a sarcophagus, nor is any vacancy or hollow to be observed in any of the pyramids, where treasure could have been lodged. I then entered several other tombs well worthy of examination, although greatly injured, as might be expected, from the length of time they have remained open. The entrances are not in general so much inclined as those in the pyramids, nor do they appear to have been filled up with solid masonry, but are generally covered with inscriptions. In the entrance of No. 15 there were two large medallions executed in white stucco, that have precisely the appearance of ivory, and may have been intended to represent that substance, in which, and in gold Phidias, and Praxiteles are said to have chiefly carved; and as the Hebrews, as well as the Greeks, may be imagined to have carried arts, and sciences with them from this wonderful country, these sculptures may serve to explain, not only the works of the above-mentioned artists, but also the ivory palaces mentioned in Scripture. Processions of prisoners, or of victims, are frequently represented, with their arms fastened behind them, and with a rope round their necks, possibly to denote, in the Grecian manner, slavery, or Helotism. Some of these appear to be Jews; others have scarfs over their shoulders, and their hair, which is extremely bushy, cut square before, and behind, with a perpendicular bald stripe behind their ears, and a large tress hanging down each side of their faces. Negroes, and different nations, are also portrayed, some of whom are dressed in flowered garments. In other places are figures without their heads, which are separately represented with a sacrificial knife; also decapitated persons in a kneeling position, with their arms tied behind them to a stake surmounted by a jackall's head. In one instance I observed a row of kneeling figures, each of whom was held down by a priestess, whilst the blood spouted out, like a fountain, from the top of his head into a cup or basin placed before him. One of these victims appeared to be struggling with two priestesses, and endeavouring to escape. There is, therefore, little doubt that human sacrifices are represented by these designs, and that they formed part of the sepulchral rites of persons of consequence; a conclusion to which Mr. Hamilton also appears to have arrived. The several divinities, it may be added, are represented in the usual forms, but generally with more decorous emblems than in the temples, and other buildings. A child in the character of Harpocrates seated on a winged globe, is supposed by Mr. Wilkinson to typify regeneration after death, and another figure seems to be rising out of a tomb at the command of a divinity; I shall not however attempt even a general description of these interesting paintings, as it would not only require considerable detail, but much more observation than I had time to bestow upon them.

2d. — Sig. Werdie was so good as to shew me his collection, which contained a number of interesting antiquities, amongst which were some very handsome mummies, and several buff embroidered scarfs which were considered extremely antient, but which appeared

BRICK ARCH NEAR THE MEMNONIUM.

Published by James Fraser Regent Street

as fresh as when first out of the loom. This gentle-man's house was well arranged, considering its extra-ordinary situation. I then proceeded to the Memno-nium, where the famous Colossus excites almost as much astonishment by the manner in which it has been destroyed, as by the skill, and labour, which must have been employed in its erection, for it is impossible to con-ceive by what engine so vast a mass of solid granite could have been suddenly broken without some marks being left of the manner, in which the force was applied. The form of the arches near the Memnonium, and the lining of bricks placed edge-ways to retain cement, or mortar, would lead to the supposition that they were Roman; but had they been constructed by that people with materials taken from Egyptian buildings, several different cartouches would probably have been found amongst them, particularly as a considerable ruin, composed entirely of the bricks of Thothmes the Third (or Mœris),[5] was close at hand.[6]

[5] See Rosellini, Tav. 2. tom. 1.

[6] It is also to be observed, that these bricks are of the same size as those of Remeses the Great, one foot four inches long, seven inches broad, and five inches deep. They are composed of mud and cut straw, and between the courses layers of straw, which were wonderfully fresh, are inserted with the slime, that serves for mortar. In some instances

This, however, is not the case; the only cartouche discovered at these arches is that of Amunmai Remeses
(called in Mr. Wilkinson's list Remeses the Great,) by
which it would appear that they were built in the reign

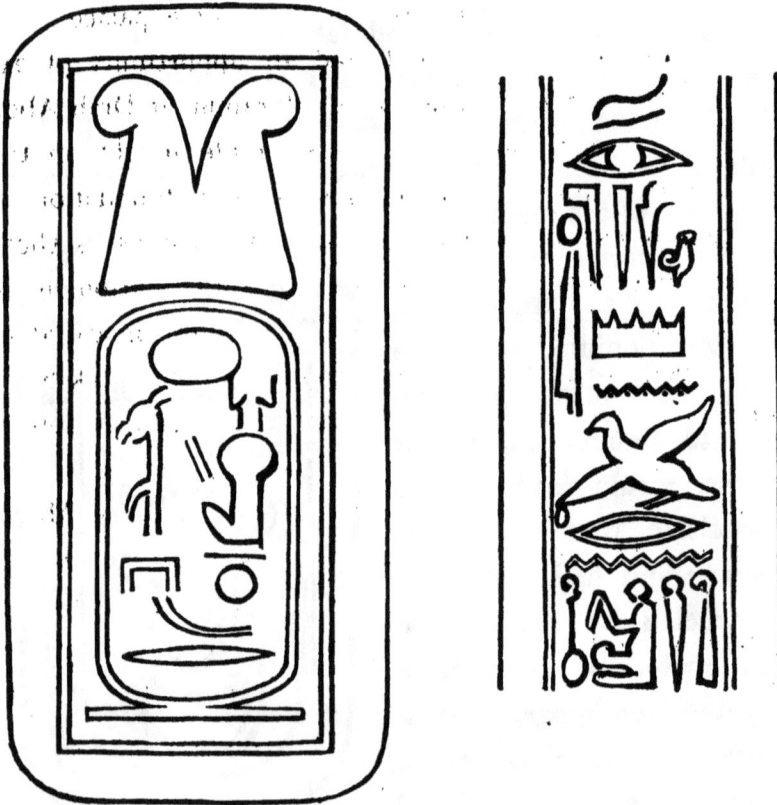

the bricks are laid in alternate courses, endways, and lengthways.
The cartouche of the king is not impressed upon all of them, but the
marks of a man's hand having been drawn over were visible on the
reverse sides.

7 This inscription, which consists of a single line of large hieroglyphics, contains the names and titles of the person, for whose tomb the
bricks were made. " The Osirian (deceased), divine father, chief prophet, priest of Amon, Piran-nofre, the true." It bears the name of
Piran-nofre, a deceased chief-prophet of the god Amon, the eponymous

of that monarch. They seem to have been a sub-structure of some other edifice: bodies have been taken out from beneath them. I did not hear whether they were those of Egyptians; but if they were, and coeval with the Memnonium, it would go far to prove that that building was a tomb, or a temple, and not a palace.

On the following day I had an opportunity of examining the arches in the ruined Pyramid at Drah Abou Negger. It is situated at a considerable height on the side of the mountain, and consists of a foundation of unburnt bricks of nearly the same dimensions as those already described, and impressed with the cartouche in the preceding page. A few squared stones appeared to have been used in the superstructure; the brick-work contained an apartment, which had been regularly domed over on the principle of an arch, and had been lined with bricks placed edgeways, like the arches near the Memnonium. Opposite to the entrance a large niche had been worked in the same manner; and on the left-hand a smaller one had been constructed by horizontal courses gradually approaching each other from the bottom. This building had every appearance of antiquity, and as the arches were in the foundation, they proved, in my opinion, that the Egyptians were acquainted with that mode of construction; indeed, if a large space was to be built over by brickwork, it could scarcely be effected in any other manner. In the caverns and sepulchral ex-

---

deity of Thebes: this evidently refers to the person, for whom the edifice was erected, and not to any mark for a collection of revenue from bricks, the term Osiris, or Osirian, which is placed before the name, always indicating a deceased person.—Mr. BIRCH.

The other cartouche belongs to Amunmai Remeses.

cavations, which occupy the space between Medinet Abou
and the mountains, brick arches are every where visible.
And an arch has also been constructed with bricks, bear-
ing the cartouche of Thothmes the First, to support the
roof of a cavern in the adjacent hills, where the rock
happens to be of a very loose texture. Mr. Wilkinson
may have alluded to this tomb when he observed, that
arches were known in Egypt 1540 years before Christ;
and it must have been of importance, as the French are
said to have taken away a very fine sarcophagus from the
bottom of a deep shaft, which has been sunk in it.

I did not, however, observe any remains of arches
built with stone. The portal, mentioned by Sig. Belzoni,
behind Drah Abou Negger, is composed of stones laid
in horizontal courses, and cut into a coved shape like
the roof of the temple at Abydos, and those of the
Mamertine prisons at Rome.

The sculpture at the Memnonium seems to relate
to the same great event, that is recorded at Karnac,
Abou Simbel, and at other places, and is equally worthy
of admiration; indeed in some respects more so, being
executed with greater care, and more highly finished.
The horses in particular must have been designed from
very beautiful originals, although greatly differing from
those represented in Grecian sculpture; and many of
them are described in spirited, and natural attitudes,
such as I never observed in any other place. The
whole is in nearly the same style, and has the same
merits and defects, as those at Karnac. The adjacent
ground abounds with gigantic fragments of fine workmanship, and no doubt many still lie concealed below
the surface.

*3d.* — In continuing my examination of this interesting place, I proceeded to the two famous statues, one of which is said to be that of Memnon. They have evidently been placed, together with other Colossi, as ornaments upon a causeway, that formed the approach to a considerable building, the site of which may yet be made out, and which is said by Mr. Wilkinson to be of the time of Amenoph the Third. No apparent superiority distinguishes one of these images from the other; but the most northern, from the inscriptions, with which it is covered, and also from tradition, is supposed to have emitted the musical sound, and to be the monument of the mighty hero. Mr. Wilkinson appears to consider that the sound was produced by artificial means, and that a sonorous block, which he found in the lap of the figure, was struck for that purpose. It would seem however more probable, that it was occasioned by the vibration of the stone, of which the figure is composed, under the powerful action of the morning sun; a phenomenon not entirely without precedent.

Medinet Abou is situated on a knoll, and is surrounded by Arab huts. This building is evidently composed of two distinct parts: the smaller and more antient, said to have been built in the time of Thothmes the Third, contains Doric, or polygonal columns, like those at Karnac. The larger has been a most stupendous edifice; although not equal to the temples at Karnac in extent, or in grandeur, it certainly exceeds them in excellence and variety of decoration. These, besides describing with considerable detail the usual battle-scenes, processions, triumphs, &c., are rendered peculiarly interesting by the introduction of ships and of the sea-shore, and give

an extensive idea of the conquests and dominion of antient Egypt.[8]   In one of these curious representations
I fancied that I observed a hostile chief making a yet-
tatura, with an extended hand, and arm, to avert the
evil eye of the conqueror, who, it may be remarked, is
always represented in the flower of youth.   The similarity of some of the costumes with those discovered
in America, and many other interesting particulars, have

[8] An explanation of the sculpture so frequently found in tombs
and in other places, is extremely desirable; and particularly of these
writings, which are of the greatest possible interest as far as profane
history is concerned, but they have not yet been deciphered, even with
the help of the figures.   Whatever progress has been made in hieroglyphics seems to have been effected by a careful examination of the
triple inscription on the Rosetta stone, which was brought to England
in 1801.   Yet in 1835, Mr. Wilkinson, the highest authority in these
matters, thus expressed himself: " No one is yet sufficiently advanced
in the language of antient Egypt to enable him literally to translate an
inscription of any length, or moderately complicated, though a general
meaning may frequently be obtained."   This assertion is unfortunately found to be true, notwithstanding the pretensions set up to the
contrary.   Nor does it appear that even Mr. Wilkinson has been able
to establish any undoubted chronology, or succession of the antient
kings, even with the aid of the stone found at Abydos, and of the Greek
historians, or to reconcile in any way the differences which exist between
the accounts of Manetho, and those of Herodotus.   The earliest periods
are still involved in complete mystery, and the most important events
remain as yet unexplained, although described both in sculpture, and in
written characters.   Some great mistake must indeed exist in those
antient accounts, which carry back the dynasties to a period before the
creation, and record four, in which twenty-seven kings reigned one hundred and forty-six years; sixteen, forty-three; sixty, one hundred and
eighty-four; and seventy other monarchs seventy days; whilst at the
same time to Cheops is attributed a reign of fifty; and to his successor,
Chephren, fifty-six years.

been adverted to by Mr. Wilkinson, and by other travellers.   The interior of this building is on a noble
scale, and has a most splendid appearance, notwithstanding the remains of the church, with which it is
encumbered; and its walls contain representations of
processions, and other remarkable ceremonies, which give
it in some degree the appearance of a palace, although
its situation in the midst of tombs seems to constitute
it a temple.   It is impossible however to distinguish
with much accuracy the respective destinations of
Egyptian buildings; as the appearance of the several
ruins fully warrants the observation made on Petræ,
that the early inhabitants connected almost all their
works of art with the idea of mortality, and of a state
after death.

Not far distant is a small temple of no great antiquity,
but of considerable interest from the sculptures it contains, which are said to elucidate the succession of the
Ptolemies.   It has been surrounded by a peribolus of
unburnt brick, nd is remarkable on account of the
manner, in which the stones have been fastened by pieces
of wood inserted between the different courses.   The
ground between these buildings, and the mountains has, as
I have before mentioned, been entirely occupied by subterraneous tombs constructed with brickwork, and the
whole range of mountains is covered with the fragments
of embalmed bodies and the spoils of innumerable sepulchres, which attest by their numbers the immense population, and by the excellence of their sculptures, the
wealth and prosperity of the antient city.   In one of
the interior valleys the violated tombs of the queens,
and likewise of the Pallades, probably the first mon-

astic order of either sex, that ever existed, exhibit on their painted walls several curious memorials of antient worship.

Still further in the mountains are the remains of a large convent, built upon a terrace, in a most romantic situation; and behind it are the portals of an Egyptian temple, excavated in the side of a lofty cliff, over which there is the path to the valley of Biban El Moluc. In these lonely recesses ruined tombs abound in every direction, together with mounds of broken pottery and of sepulchral remains. And it is to be observed with regret that the work of destruction is still going on, for in one of the most beautifully excavated tombs at Assasseuf I saw ox-wains busily employed in carrying away large masses of stone, torn forcibly from highly sculptured walls, for common purposes, and which could have been obtained with equal facility from the natural rock. In a very extensive tomb at the same place, which had a long inclined entrance, there were fluted pilasters of smaller proportions, but of the same kind of architecture as those at Medinet Abou, and at Karnac. Innumerable objects of great interest might be alluded to, but I must refer to Mr. Wilkinson's work for a more detailed account of the unrivalled remains of antiquity, which yet distinguish this remarkable scene of ruin, and of desolation.

In the evening I returned to Luxor, where Mr. Lakin, Mr. Rutherford, and Dr. Wilson had arrived. They were on their way to Nubia.

4th. — Thermometer 65°. I spent the day at Karnac, and took an opportunity of recommending the Catchief to exert his authority in preventing the further destruction of the ruins and tombs. He promised to do so; but of course I did not much rely upon the professions of an Arab. A fine young crocodile, about fourteen inches long, was offered for sale, which had been caught when asleep upon a sand-bank; but as there was little chance of its living, I did not buy it.

*5th.* — Thermometer 65°. I again went to the temples of Luxor, and of Karnac, and returning to Gournou in the afternoon, I rode to the Memnonium. In the evening I called upon Lord Lindsay, and Mr. Ramsay, who had arrived from Cairo, and we agreed to visit the ruins on the following day. A letter from that place informed me that M. Caviglia had at last received a firmaun, but that on account of some informality it had been returned, and that another was expected.

*6th.* — Thermometer 53°. I set out by myself early in the morning, and afterwards examined the sculptures at Medinet-Abou, Deir Abou Negger, Biban-El-Moluc, and various other tombs, &c. with Lord Lindsay and Mr. Ramsay. I sailed in the evening, with much regret that I had not leisure to see more of this wonderful place.

The weather was at times comparatively cold, as may be seen by the variations of the thermometer.

*8th.* — I did not land at Cous (Apollinopolis Parva), nor at Coft (Coptos), four miles distant from the river on the eastern shore, as scarcely any remains now exist at either of these places; but proceeded to Kenneh, and visited the well-known temples of Tentyra (Dendera).

I was sorry to observe again at this place, that, in proportion as what is called the civilisation of the country extends, these noble edifices become more and more dilapidated, and that neither perfection of art, nor antiquity are any protection, when materials are wanted either for public buildings, or for private palaces.   In short, the difficulty of removing the enormous masses, of which they are composed, forms their only defence.   The Great Temple even has been assailed, notwithstanding the quantity of loose materials, with which it is surrounded.   The Arab village has been removed towards the river.

*9th.* — I landed near Quasr-e-Syad, and the site of Chenoboscion, in search of the tombs mentioned by Mr. Wilkinson.   Having crossed a plain slightly cultivated to the desert mountains at about two miles' distance from the river, I found a rough cavern, containing a Greek inscription, but without any vestiges of painting, or of sculpture, or of a regular doorway ; neither did it appear to have been used as a tomb.   The floor had not even been levelled.   These mountains are composed of white stone interspersed with small black pebbles.  Beyond this grotto were two others near a canal, in which doorways, and a raised bench often seen in sepulchral excavations had been roughly hewn.   The villages in this neighbourhood were nearly deserted, as the inhabitants had fled to the mountains, and wandered from place to place to avoid conscription, and compulsory labour in the manufactories.

How (Diospolis Parva) is a straggling village built on mounds of rubbish, and of broken pottery.  It contains manufactories of sugar, and of indigo, and is situated in a rich, and fertile plain abounding with crops of every description. The cotton appeared to be very luxuriant, as well as the sugar canes, which were to be cut in March. There were the remains of a large reservoir, but the temple no longer existed. In my way to the tomb of Dionysius I passed two handsome mosques, that had been built, by the Mamelucs, opposite to each other, and consequently the niche in one of them, which should have indicated the position of Mecca, pointed in a contrary direction. The tomb, supposed to have been built in the time of the Ptolemies, was nearly covered with stones, and sand, so that the lower apartment was inaccessible. Amongst the sculptures which were visible, the protecting genius was represented in the form of a female as at Philæ. The Mahometan burial-grounds on the adjacent plain were said to have been the scene of a great battle; and a considerable number of mummies have been from time to time dug out of the distant mountains — the necropolis of the antient city.

Farshiout, about six miles inland from Girjeh, is the modern capital of the province, and Arabet-El-Matfoun is not very distant from the latter place.

10th. — I set out from Girjeh with some officers, who were returning to England from India, for Arabet (the antient Abydos). We could not at first procure a sufficient number of horses, but, upon meeting the Sheik on the outside of the town, he readily supplied the whole party. Our road lay over cultivated plains, and in about an hour and a half we arrived at Arabet, near a large pond, the banks of which were encrusted with natron. The village is built (apparently

upon the mounds of the antient town), at the verge of
the cultivated ground, which seems formerly to have extended to the mountains, but the space is now covered by
the sands, which have overwhelmed the ruins at this place,
and also those further to the southward, where the plain
is of greater extent.  It cannot be supposed that these
magnificent structures were erected in a desert, and as
the sands from the neighbouring mountains were probably always encroaching, industry must have been as
necessary in this country, as in others less productive,
not only to increase fertility, but to arrest the progress
of the desert by canals, and by other means of irrigation.
Besides the testimony of antient history, fragments of
obelisks, pieces of alabaster, and other costly materials
evince the former splendour of the two buildings, which
alone are at present visible, and even they are so deeply
buried, that they scarcely merit the attention of a cursory traveller.  The masonry is good, and the ceilings
of the chambers in the larger one are composed of stones
cut into a coved shape, like those in the gateway at
Thebes.  They are adorned with the finest sculpture,
and are surrounded with sepulchral shafts, and the remains of tombs that have been despoiled of their contents; but as the famous tablet was found here by Mr.
Bankes, further excavations near the buildings might
possibly lead to interesting discoveries.  On returning
to Girjeh I again met the Sheik, with whom I took
coffee, and in the evening sailed for Eckmim.  The
officers proceeded to Cairo.

El Birbe, near Girjeh, is supposed to occupy the site
of the antient town (This).

SHEIK'S TOMB AT ECKMIM.

Printed by C. Hullmandel.

Published by James Fraser, Regent Street.

*11th.* — Eckmim, the antient Chemmis (Panopolis), is a considerable town, well situated on an eminence, in a fertile plain bounded by desert mountains, in which was the necropolis. A Sheik's tomb, held in high veneration, has been built upon the site, and partly with the materials of the antient Temple of Pan, and contains a large stone, that, from a cavity, and groovings cut in it, seems to have been antiently used in sacrificial ceremonies. The Arab women, who are childless, and desirous of having a family, are in the habit of sitting upon this stone, and of performing ablutions with water drawn from an adjacent well, over which, to make the charm efficacious, they must have previously stepped. It seems, therefore, that in former times the Mahometans allowed their converts to retain local superstitions, provided the name of the tutelary influence was changed, under which the practices were observed ; as the Catholics have done in Italy, where most of the local traditions, that now prevail, may be traced to a Pagan origin. Many squared stones, inscribed with hieroglyphics, are scattered about, and in a hollow at a little distance is an architrave with a Greek inscription, which has been copied by Dr. Pococke, Mr. Hamilton, and other travellers. Several remains, such as fragments of columns, &c. may likewise be seen in the town.

On the opposite bank is Souhaaj, where the Mameluc chief—Morad Bey was buried; it is built on the mounds of an antient town, by some considered to have been Crocodilopolis. I then passed Sheik Hereedee, and the supposed site of Passalon, and proceeded to Shendowee. on the western shore. The surrounding plain extends about four miles to the desert mountains, and is irrigated by a canal, that probably joins the Bahr Yousef near Benisouef.[9]  Having applied to the Nazir of Shendowee for horses, and guides to the Red, and White Convents, (the latter of which is also called Amba Shnoodeh), he sent his nephew, some armed attendants, and a Coptic secretary, with whom I immediately proceeded.  Such was the fertility of the plain over which we passed, that the crops were reaped in four months after sowing.  They were extremely luxuriant, and quantities of cattle, camels, sheep, and goats tethered in rows to long ropes, were depastured on all sides.  The sheep, as in other parts of the country, were badly shaped, and marked with brown, and white; but the cattle, and particularly the oxen, were very handsome, and fine in the horn.  The best were of a dark brown, or of a cream colour.

We crossed the canal at a ford, and arrived in about two hours at the White Convent, which is a lofty quadrangular building situated in the sands, at the termination of the cultivated ground, and not far from the mountains, where several antient tombs have been found. The walls are of stone, and have a projecting cornice. The door is very strong, and opens into a square, cloistered court.  The church is in the form of a Greek cross, and contains four arched recesses, surmounted in the middle by a cupola.  The arches are rounded.  The altar is of common stone, but appears to have been plated. The coved roof above it had been originally adorned with mosaics, and a wooden screen before it had been painted with figures of the Holy Virgin, of St. George and the Dragon, and of other saints.  The whole is in

[9] An oasis is distant four days' journey from this place.

a most dilapidated, and dirty state, as sheep and cattle are brought into the cloister every night for security. It did not appear that much service was performed, although three Coptic priests constantly resided there. They invited me to take coffee, and complained that the grounds belonging to the convent had been seized upon by the government, and that they were much impoverished; but, as they had sheep, and cattle, they must have had land for their support. They are however in a great measure maintained by the Copts, who live in considerable numbers together with the Arabs in the neighbouring villages, and who visit the convents on holydays. This building, as well as that, which I afterwards visited, was well adapted for defence, and also protected by an Arab guard, said to be necessary on account of the bad disposition of the population, the Coptic part of which, it is to be observed, was exempted from conscription. Several large mounds, broken pottery, and a few squared stones indicate the site of antient buildings. On some of the blocks I observed hieroglyphics, and on one the remains of a tryglyph.

The Red Convent was similarly situated, and built on the same plan, but had been constructed with burnt bricks, and appeared of a more recent date. The columns in the church were rather larger, and had something like Corinthian capitals, and in several of the architectural ornaments, particularly under the cupola, shells were introduced. The communion-table was composed of granite. The church was locked up and neglected, and the whole building in a worse condition than the other, and merely inhabited by a few Coptic peasants, with their cattle. Some mounds in the cultivated ground at a short distance from these convents, and at present occupied by an Arab village are the only remains of Itfou (Aphroditopolis.) The ruins of Athribis are said to be at some little distance to the southward, but I did not visit them. I came back to Shendowee by a circuitous road, in order to pass the canal at an easier ford, so that it was night before I arrived at the Nazir's house; whence I returned to the boat, and immediately sailed. During this excursion, I witnessed a ceremony which was new to me; one of the attendants happening to meet an acquaintance knelt down on the ground, and made several prostrations, as if at prayer. His friend did the same; after which they got up, and embraced with the usual salutations.

12th. — The temple at Gow-El-Kebeer (Antæopolis) has been entirely removed, for the sake of the materials. It was situated in a fertile plain, at present interspersed with a few scattered hamlets, and supposed to have been the scene of the fabled contest of Isis with Typhon, after the death of Osiris. The connexion of this story with the name of Antæus is remarkable. The desert mountains which encircle the place to the eastward, approach the river at the southern extremity, and also at the northern, where several grottoes and antient tombs have been excavated, which, having procured guides, I proceeded to examine. The fastenings of stone doors, and the remains of painted stucco were in many places visible; and also a brick wall, which had the appearance of great antiquity. There was likewise an inclined passage, which was said to lead to other apartments; and further on an Egyptian figure in a sitting position had been sculptured near a grotto, which seemed to have been a temple, as it contained a stone altar. At some

little distance, in front of a large excavation, a considerable space had been levelled, whence a staircase ascended
to a chamber at right angles to the excavation, which
had a window opening into the court: grapes, and other
devices, apparently Roman, had been painted on the
walls of these apartments. The inhabitants of the place,
with what justice I cannot say, had a bad character, and,
indeed, during the time I was examining these grottoes,
a number of people, many of them armed with guns,
assembled, and seemed inclined to be troublesome; and
I have no doubt that a Frank, unacquainted with their
language, and unattended by a janissary, would have
met with inconvenience. There were extensive quarries
higher up the mountains to the eastward, which contained Egyptian figures, hieroglyphics, and also inscriptions of a later period, and small pieces of alabaster
were scattered about. It was difficult to imagine how
the large blocks could be safely conveyed from these
lofty situations, as the mountains were precipitous, and
full of ravines. I saw in the plain below, the ruins of
a church built with arches, and likewise those of another
building upon an adjoining eminence.

. I did not again disembark till I arrived at E-Siout.

On the eastern bank, a little above that town, a Sheik's
tomb had been built upon a mound close to the river,
under which a great treasure was said to be concealed.
The mound seemed to have been a tumulus, and, by
excavation, some antient memorial might possibly be discovered.

13*th*.—E-Siout is a place of importance, and is situated
on the site of Lycopolis, but does not present any object
of antiquity, excepting some excavations in a high range

of hills near it. One of them, called Stahl-Antar, is very extensive, and contains many apartments, which seem to have been chiselled out of natural caverns, and to have been decorated with painted hieroglyphics, the figures of divinities, processions, &c. The ceiling of the principal chamber has been coved; a descending passage, which probably conducts to other apartments, was closed up with rubbish, and fragments of human, and of other mummies were scattered about in considerable quantities. I did not visit the alabaster quarries, nor the convent at Dronka, where a good many Copts are said to reside.

The gardens, with which the town is surrounded, and the principal roads, are upon raised banks, as the adjacent plain is annually inundated; and in consequence extremely productive. Indeed, the whole place was better built, and more flourishing than the generality of Arab towns, and contained several hareems, and whitewashed houses. A battalion of infantry was encamped near it, and appeared to be in good order; the arms were remarkably clean. In my way to Stahl-Antar, I met a concourse of people bringing from a neighbouring village, for the governor's inspection, the body of a man who had been murdered. The delinquent had fled, but, from the nature of the country, escape is very difficult. Before I returned to the boat I called upon the Governor, Mohat Bey, to express my thanks for his civility; he had been in command in Nubia, and was a very agreeable person. In going thither a circumstance occurred, which shews the foolish mistakes that may arise in this country between persons, who cannot understand each other. As I passed through the bazar with the governor's janissary, and attendants, I met near a gateway an Arab officer, who called out with much earnestness, and made violent gestures for me to stop, and to get out of the way. His horse was rather troublesome, and, as the one I rode was the same, I concluded that he was afraid of their coming into collision. I knew perfectly well, however, that I could easily prevent any accident, and accordingly passed through the gate, keeping on the left hand, and making signs to him to keep on the other side, at the same time giving him the usual salutation; when, to my surprise, he became more excited, and talked louder than ever. I was afterwards informed that what I intended as a civility he took as an affront, and that he had been insisting that I should wait, in order that he, being a Mahometan, might go first through the gate. My attendants appeared much offended, and wished me to represent his conduct to the governor, which of course I would not do.

I wrote to Colonel Campbell from this town, desiring to hear, by a letter directed to Benisouef, whether any discovery of importance had taken place at Gizeh, as, in that case, I intended to return immediately to Cairo, instead of visiting the Faioum.

In proceeding down the stream I was informed that a boat, which was moored to the eastern shore, belonged to an Arab, and had no European aboard, although it carried an English flag. I therefore went over with the intention of taking it away, when a Maltese appeared, and claimed it. Of course I declined any further interference, but noted down the particulars, and transmitted them to Colonel Campbell, who took measures to prevent the repetition of a similar abuse. European flags are often obtained in this manner for trading speculations in native boats, that could not otherwise be carried on.   A practice, which, besides giving just cause of complaint to the government, exposes the flag to disgrace, from the misconduct of the Arabs who sail under it.

14*th*. — Thermometer early in the morning 49°, afterwards 56°.  I arrived at Manfaloot, situated on a high bank on the western shore, which is gradually undermined, and carried away by the stream.   The changes that take place in the channel of the river, together with the progress of the desert sands, increase greatly the difficulties, that on other accounts exist in ascertaining the position of antient cities.   As I could not obtain horses to examine the bank opposite to the town, I proceeded to El Karib, the supposed site of Hieracôn, situated at the back of the cliffs of Djebel Abou Faydee. The ruins, consisting of walls and of foundations built of small unburnt bricks, are on one side of a valley; and on the other several caverns have been excavated, in which mummies of dogs, and cats are said to have been found.   They were, however, completely closed up with sand.   I found in the adjoining quarries a tablet of hieroglyphics, some Egyptian sculpture, and a Greek inscription, but they were much effaced; and also some curious diagrams drawn in red lines, and apparently intended as marks for hewing the stone.   I observed likewise some antient remains near

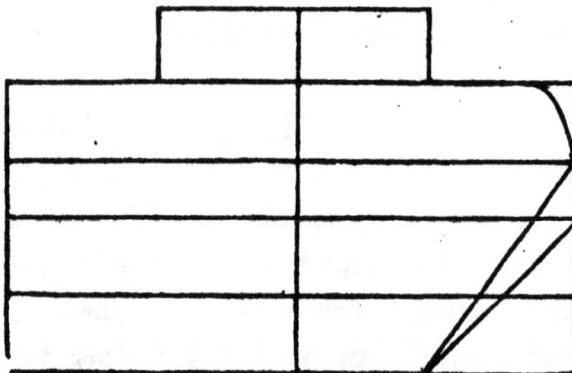

a small Arab village at some little distance. The convent at Deir-El-Cosseir (on the site of Pesla) had been destroyed, and no signs of sculpture remained in the grottoes. I did not visit Djebel Toona on the western bank, as it was at a considerable distance from the river, and as the only remains consisted of tombs similar to those at Tel-El-Amarna, and accordingly arrived in the evening at Hadji Kandeish near Coseah, the antient Cusæ.

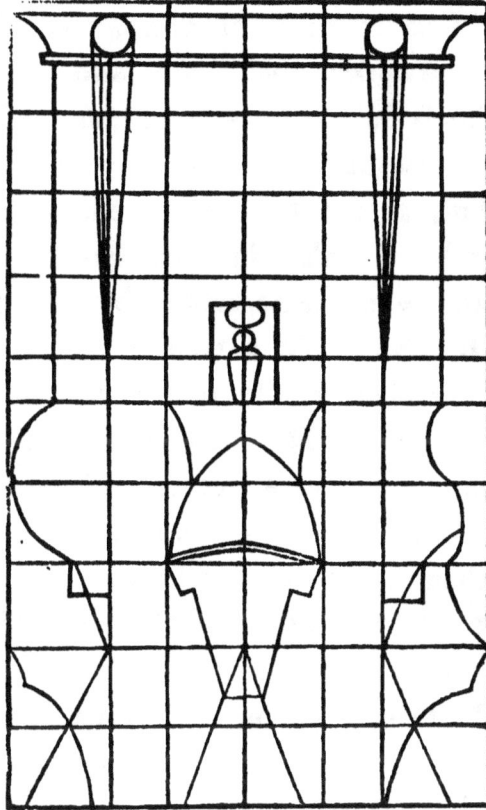

15*th.* — The ruins at Tel-El-Amarna (formerly Alabastron) are situated in a plain of considerable extent, and surrounded by a semicircular chain of desert hills, that come down to the river at its northern and southern extremities. The promontory to the northward is called Sheik-Said. A large island is opposite to the plain, and a strip of cultivated ground in an open grove of palmtrees extends along the bank of the river, near which the villages are situated. The rest of the plain is neglected and covered with sand; but the ground under tillage is very productive, and sugar-canes, cotton, and other crops, are raised in great abundance. The remains of the

antient town consist of mounds of rubbish, of the foundations of small buildings, and of two large masses of
brickwork ; there are also vestiges of walls under
Sheik-Said. In several parts of these mountains the
surface has been roughly chiselled, and grottoes formed,
but, as far as I observed, without sculpture, or regular portals; in one, however, there was an altar,
and some remarkable channels had been cut before
it. No doubt a considerable necropolis exists, as the
hills abound with natural caverns. Most of the tombs
opened by Mr. Hay had been closed up with sand,
but some were accessible, and were interesting from
the representations on their walls; and near one of
them a winding staircase of some length descended
to an excavation, which had been lined with painted
stucco.

Over the door of this tomb, a solar disc was inscribed,
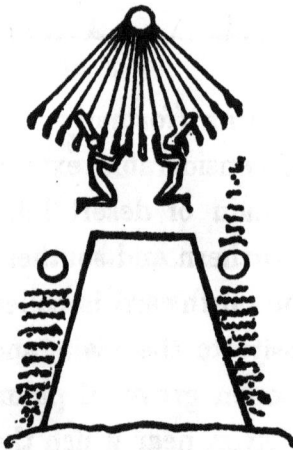
from which rays with hands at
their extremities extended as from
a common centre; two figures,
one of them apparently that of a
king, were represented as worshippers in a kneeling position;
and on each side hieroglyphics,
and circles, or discs were introduced. The interior consisted of
three small apartments, and appeared to have been covered with
paintings, which were almost entirely defaced. Processions of prisoners of a red complexion, but with the
features of Negroes, were amongst the figures, that could
be made out; also a solar disc with rays, like that

over the entrance, and beneath it the figures of a king, and of a queen dressed in high caps; the whole being surrounded with various hieroglyphical inscriptions. The principal cartouches had been entirely destroyed in every part of the tomb, and, as the form of the caps appeared to be Persian, they might have belonged to the era when that people possessed the country. The following cartouches

were inscribed on the walls, and the same are also said to exist at Djebel Toona.[1]

[1] The hieroglyphical cartouches at Tel-El-Amarna contain the honorific titles of the sun, in reference to the solar disc, whose rays of light terminate in human hands: the Deities, on account of their mythic reign over Egypt, had all cartouches in which their names were inscribed. The cartouche A, which may be considered as the prenomen,

In another excavation sacrifices, and chariot races had been described, but the principal cartouches were in that also obliterated. There had been two rows of columns, the outer had disappeared; but of the inner, six, and two pilasters connected by a low wall, yet remained.* On each side of the portico, or entrance, were recesses, with the remains of figures seated in the usual, formal position. Many smaller apartments branched off in different directions; and, opposite the doorway, a narrow chamber of some depth contained at the furthest end a mutilated image, to which the floor ascended by steps to within four feet and a half of the ceiling. The paintings in these excavations had been well executed, but were much effaced. I did not visit the quarry of alabaster. I was informed that the ruins of Sbayda were six miles above Hadj Kand.

15th. — The French superintendent conducted me with much civility over the works at Reramoun, where a considerable quantity of fine sugar is produced, chiefly for the use of the Pacha's hareem. He complained of the great difficulties he met with in obtaining the necessary supplies, and likewise in effecting the improvements which, at his suggestion, had been sanctioned by the Pacha, in consequence of the idleness of the Arabs, and of the jealousy of those under him, who thwarted him in every possible way. This is universally the case when Franks are employed as overseers, and the Pacha,

reads: " The living Har (Horus), rejoicing in his solar abode." The cartouche B, reads: " Who superintends the splendour of his disc." Similar cartouches appear in M. Rosellini, tom. i. — Mr. BIRCH.

* For the capitals of three columns, see preceding page.

naturally becomes dissatisfied, and is easily induced, by the artful representations of those about him, to direct that instead of Europeans, natives should be employed, who are incapable of conducting a large establishment even in the customary manner, much less of adopting such improvements as from time to time might be made in the different operations.

The ruins at Medinet Antholee are on an elevated plain, and are separated by the Wady Garoos from Sheik Abadeh (the site of Antinoopolis).[3]   The latter town must have been also finely situated, and very extensive, but most of the materials have been taken away by the Defterdar Bey; and a few columns, a mass of brick building, which seemed to have been a bath, and some broken materials, and mounds of rubbish are all that remain of this celebrated place.   The streets appear to have been spacious, and adorned with rows of columns in the same manner as those at Djerash, the foundations of which in many places remain.   I did not visit the catacombs at Sheik Timay, where the lofty cliffs come down to the brink of the river, which soon afterwards expands into a noble sheet of water, and appeared, when I saw it, to great advantage—glowing with the peculiar beauty imparted by a setting sun in this fine climate. [Thermometer 75°.]

16th. — The tombs at Beni Hassan are on the eastern

[3] The Arab, whom we procured as a guide at this place, was accompanied by his son, about seven or eight years old.   I happened to take notice of the child, and to give him a piastre, when his father immediately took him away, exclaiming that I wanted to murder him, in order to find hidden treasures by means of his blood.

shore, and at a considerable height above the level of the river; they are excavated in a range of low cliffs on the side of a sloping bank, and are connected by a kind of terrace or path. The most northern has been either entirely ruined, or never finished. Before the portal of the next are handsome columns of the same kind as those already described at Karnac, and which are perfectly Doric, excepting that, as in other instances, the echinus, annuli, and hypotrachelion are wanting. The interior of this excavation is singularly beautiful; it is divided into three compartments by two rows of columns, painted of the colour of porphyry;[*] and, according to Mr. Wilkinson, of the following dimensions: Sixteen feet eight inches and a half in height, of five diameters, slightly diminishing towards the top, and of sixteen flutings of eight inches in breadth, and of half an inch in depth. The inner face of each column has been left flat for the inscription of hieroglyphics. The whole of the interior of the chamber is painted upon stucco. The ceilings of the three divisions are coved, and are separated by bands, or flat spaces of the same width as the abaci, and painted in alternate squares of gold, with red; and of white, with light blue ornaments; a broad band also runs down the middle of each ceiling. The whole is remarkably elegant, both in proportions and also in decorations, excepting a painted cornice, which has not a pleasing effect. The walls are covered with various figures employed in leaping, wrestling, &c., many of which are in excellent drawing. Gymnastic exercises, the breeding, and rearing of cattle, and different

[*] The same colour is to be seen on several blocks of the Temple at Ægina.

rural occupations, are also described, and explained by appropriate hieroglyphics. The third tomb from the north has similar columns and decorations; and in one of them a group of strangers is portrayed, amongst whom are women, and children carried in panniers on asses, and an ibis, and ostriches are presented to a king.[5] This drawing has been supposed, (but it appears without much probability,) to represent the arrival of the Israelites in the time of Osirtesen I.; whose cartouche is inscribed in various parts of the hieroglyphics, together, however, with several others, which belonged to later monarchs. The same columns appear in the two adjoining excavations, which have not been finished; and it is remarkable, that although they are also to be seen in the most southern, that, in the intermediate tombs, the pillars peculiarly called Egyptian, with capitals composed of the flowers of the lotus, (and in this instance of extremely bad proportions,) have been introduced. Many of the excavations communicate with each other, and in most of them are shafts, and niches for the reception of mummies, but, in general, they do not appear to have been completed: some of them have been furnished with stone doors. The view from the terrace in front of these sepulchres is very extensive, and comprehends the river studded with fertile islands, a plain to the southward interspersed with the ruins of several Arab villages,[6] and also a chain of hills,

[5] Some of the strangers are clothed in party-coloured garments, that bring to recollection Joseph's coat of many colours.

[6] These villages had been plundered by the Mamelucs, and also by the French, &c., in 1800; and several had been abandoned on account

intersected by deep gullies, and ravines,—the effects, apparently, of torrents.

In exploring the valleys in search of the *Speos Artemidos*, several portals, and sepulchral excavations were discovered; but I was obliged to get a guide from the villages to find out the place in question, which was called Stahl-Antar, and proved to be on the southern side of a valley, or glen, that extended eastwards for a considerable distance. The entrance was by a portico, composed of a double row, each of four columns, which may possibly have been hewn into the shape of colossal figures: the inner row was destroyed, and of the outer only three remained, and they were entirely defaced. In the centre of this portico, or colonnade, a square chamber of no great size had been excavated, which opposite to the doorway contained a niche about seven feet from the floor. The remains of an image might be distinguished; and hieroglyphics had been inscribed on the columns, and also upon the walls near the door-

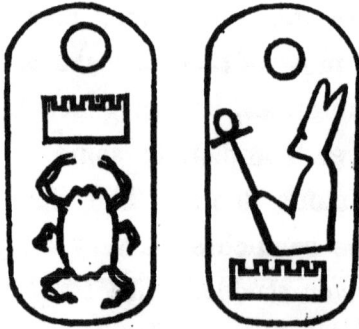

way, and near the niche, where the cartouches of Thothmes III. and of Osiri-Menephthah I. had been inscribed; but the whole was exceedingly rough, and the marks of a chisel were every where visible.[7] The rocks

of the plague, which was very destructive in 1836: the inhabitants are at present few in number, and in bad repute.

[7] These cartouches are the prenomens of Thothmes the Third (or Mœris), and of Menephthah the First, both monarchs of the 18th dynasty.—Mr. BIRCH.

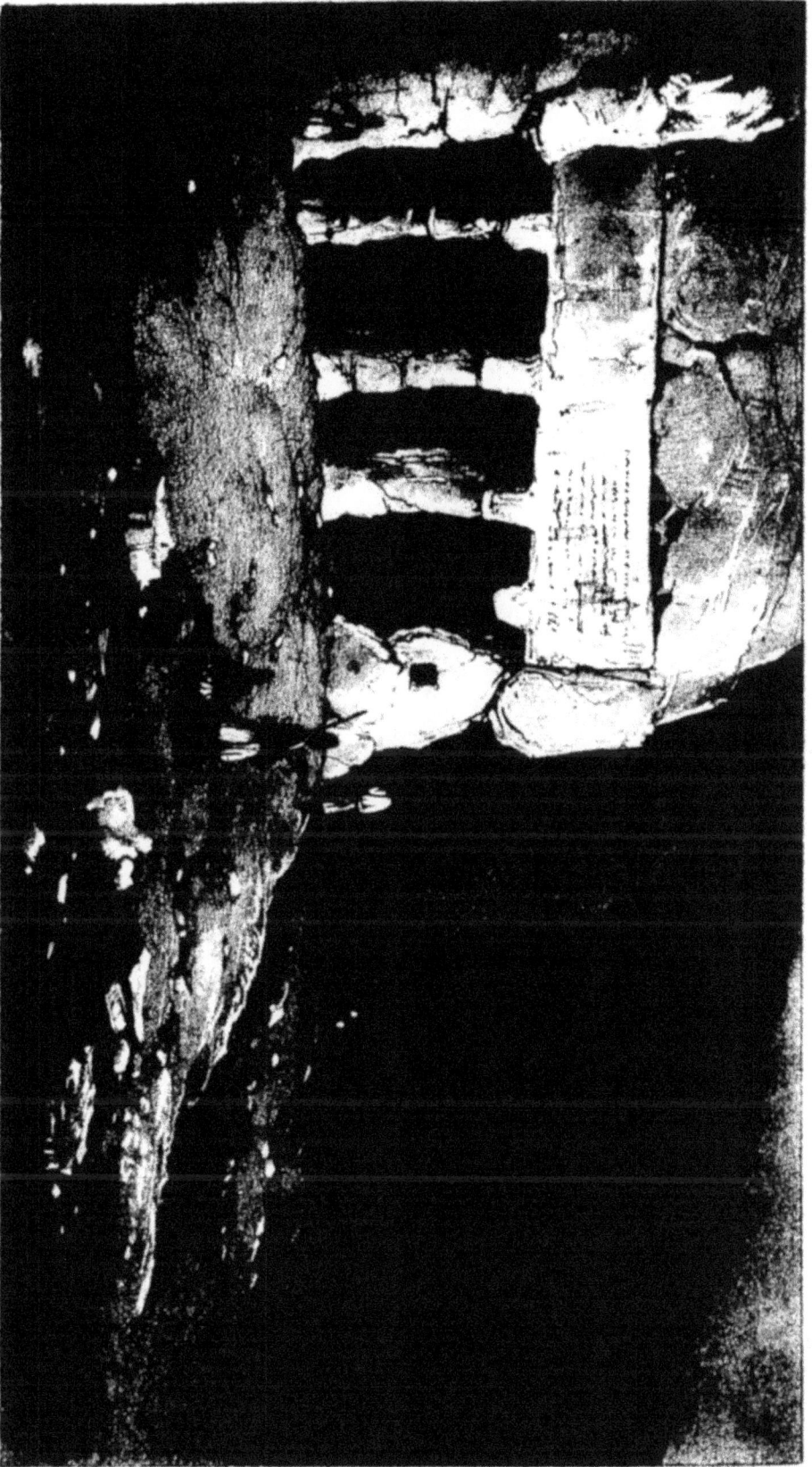

SPEOS ARTEMIDOS.

over the entrance had been faced down, and towards the right, or western side, rows of hieroglyphics had been cut, but seemed to be illegible. One or two small chambers, and the remains of steps leading to them, had been also hewn out on the sides of the colonnade.

There did not appear to be any excavations in the higher part of the valley, but there were several, on both sides, which contained deep shafts,⁸ between the Speos, and the plain. One of them was of a consider-

A               B

---

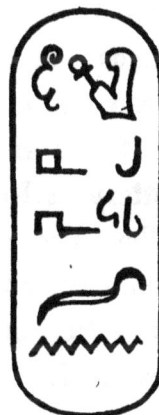

⁸ The cartouches at this place, which are numbered from the left, are apparently the prenomen, and name of Alexander, the son of Alexander the Great. The prenomen repeated in B, 2, 4, 7, 9, reads Pe ⲉⲁⲁ ⲟ̅ⲏⲧ, ⲥⲱⲧⲡ ⲛ̅ⲁⲙⲏⲛ "The sun rejoicing the heart approved of Amon." The name occurring alternately in A, 1, 3, 5, 6, 8, 10, ⲟⲗⲕⲥⲁⲛⲧⲣⲥ, ALEXANDER. The first symbol, a bird or eagle, is a phonetic variety of the common form. See Rosellini, tom. ii. tav. xvii. b. 1, b. 2. The reason given by M. Rosellini for this name not appertaining to Alexander the Great is, that Alexander particularly assumed the title of the "son of Amon," which would have appeared in the composition of his name,—a reason hardly adequate, as the title of the "son of Amon," similar to the "Epiphanes and Theos Philadelphos," &c., in the Ptolemies, would probably have been added to the name out of the cartouche, and consequently, the name may as well be

able size, and consisted of several chambers roughly
chiselled;[9] and over the entrance a figure was inscribed
in the act of worshipping, and five cartouches on either
side facing inwards, of which 1, 3, 5, 6, 8, 10, were like
A, and 2, 4, 7, 9, like B.[1] The interior of another tomb
had been painted with the white flowers and stalks of
the lotus, in compartments upon a dark blue ground;
and in another place a design had been sketched out,
but not executed. Mummies of cats are said to have
been found near the Speos. The channel between the
islands and the plain near the Speos is only navigable
during the inundation.

There are large mounds and a quantity of broken
pottery at Kom Achmar,[2] and a quarry in an adjoining
valley, also several tombs excavated on the side of the
mountain, and decorated with painted figures, processions, &c., in which the drapery is remarkably well represented. The river takes a fine bend under these
rocky mountains, and afterwards stretches away with
great effect towards Minyeh. The village of Souadee,

that of Alexander the Great. The prenomen is assumed from the
name of the monarch Hophra, or Apries, of the 26th Saite dynasty,
with the addition of "The approved of Amon."—Mr. BIRCH.

[9] Notwithstanding the great care with which the interiors of some
of the tombs have been finished, in many others no attempt at decoration is visible, either from the premature death of the persons for whom
they were intended, or from other causes at present inexplicable. In
Campbell's tomb at Gizeh, for instance, sarcophagi of the most exquisite workmanship have been placed in rough grottoes cut in the rock,
without the least attention to symmetry, or to any regular shape.

[1] See preceding page.

[2] Several places are called by this name, which signifies a red
mound.

where a number of boats were being built, amongst open
groves of beautiful palm-trees, luxuriant plantations of
sugar-cane, and abundant crops watered by a succession
of sakias, was highly picturesque. Some antient tombs,
built of calcareous stone, have here been destroyed, in
order to make lime for the Pacha's service. It is much
to be regretted that they were not composed of the sand-
stone from the neighbouring mountains.

Minyeh appears at a distance to be a considerable
place, as many of the houses are whitewashed. I arrived
there about four o'clock, when a number of Bedouins
were crossing the stream in small boats; the women
wore the usual blue dress, but the coverings of their
faces were red. I went on shore to see a cotton manufactory, and was invited by the commandant, Hassan Bey, to
his barge, which was moored beneath the bank. I found
him surrounded by his attendants, and received great
civility from him, and also from the governor, Churchid
Effendi, who soon afterwards arrived. I understood that
these dignitaries usually spent the mornings in their barge,
on account of the heat. The cabin was very narrow,
extremely low, and so much encumbered with cushions,
that, when I took my leave, I thought that I should have
been obliged to request both their excellencies to move
before I could extricate myself from my embarrassment,
which was not a little increased by a low awning before
the cabin, under which a secretary was seated, surrounded
with a quantity of papers. During the course of this visit,
I expressed strongly my regret at the devastations, to
which the antient monuments were constantly subject,
and explained how much it was the Pacha's interest to
prevent future spoliation, particularly where sculpture and

hieroglyphics were in question. They both promised to give orders accordingly, but most probably with as little intention of keeping their word as the Catchief of Karnac.

The Governor sent a janissary with me to the factory, which was a large establishment. Some of the rooms contained two hundred looms, but many of them were not at work. The labour was as usual forced; and a man was confined in irons in the court-yard for having attempted to escape. I passed through the bazars, which were very crowded, and also well supplied, to a school, that contained about one hundred boys; they looked healthy, and comparatively clean; and were seated on the ground in circles of ten or twelve together round small tables preparatory to supper, which consisted of abundance of good Arab bread, and of soup. The children are taken by force to this school, (possibly the only method by which education can be at present carried on), and are not allowed to go out excepting on Fridays, when they walk through the town. They are taught to read, and to write, and are ultimately sent to the academies at Tourah, or at Boulac. The plague raged violently at Minyeh in 1837.

17th.—I went on shore at Dewadee, a village on the eastern bank, and walked across the cultivated ground to a number of brick walls, and foundations at the foot of the hills, which might have been supposed to have been those of houses, had they not contained sepulchral shafts, and an immense quantity of bones, which are continually dug up by the Arabs, whenever they take away the earth as dressing for the cultivated land. A boundary wall had enclosed these remains, and at the entrance of

a narrow pass, more ruins and foundations were to be
perceived of the same kind, and further up in the mountains parts of the Gisr El Agoos, (the wall, that is said
to have extended from the sea to Es Souan) still exist.
This wady, or pass, soon after turns to the right, and
continues its course through the mountains till it reaches
the Nile near Kom Achmar. To the northward, near
Djebel Sheik Embarek, a grotto, which contained in a
niche opposite the entrance the remains of two figures,
and a sepulchral shaft, had been excavated in the rocks;
and near it was a descent, that probably led to other
tombs. These excavations, and several others of the same
kind were full of loose stones, and rubbish. Whilst I was
examining these grottoes, several Arab girls arrived from
a small encampment of Bedouins, who had come down
the wady from the desert; they possessed a few sheep,
and goats, but were extremely poor. The weather was
fine, and, together with the fertility of the crops, and
the singing of the birds, reminded me of an English
spring.

Mounds of rubbish, broken pottery, fragments of architraves, of cornices, and of squared stones, and masses
of brick work apparently Roman mark the site of Acoris,
near the Arab village of Tehneh, which is situated at the
eastern extremity of a fertile, but neglected plain, about
two miles from the river. These ruins are at the entrance of a valley, which extends still further to the eastward in several directions, and also to the south behind
a range of cliffy mountains, which in every part contain
excavations, and tombs, and are ascended by means of
terraces carried along from one grotto to another. The
river, and the adjacent country are seen to great advan-

tage through a natural arch in a cavern near the summit, whence there is a mountain path down a wild, and barren valley to the eastward. Several quarries, and also sepulchral excavations are to be seen on the adjacent hills, but the latter have been opened, and despoiled of their contents. I did not observe any hieroglyphics, nor did I find the Roman figures, Greek inscriptions, and reservoir mentioned by Mr. Wilkinson. Amongst the ruins, I noticed some stones that had been cut in a remarkable manner, and had apparently formed part of an altar; and before an altar placed in the entrance of the adytum in one of the excavations, a deep pit, sufficiently large to receive a sarcophagus, and several holes connected by groovings, which might possibly have been intended to convey the blood of sacrifices into it. Between Tehneh, and the convent, Deir El Adra, the Gisr El Agoos is to be traced in many places.

As soon as the boat appeared in sight of the convent, two of the monks came down, at first by a ravine, and afterwards by a subterraneous passage to the river, and plunging into the stream swam off to it. They were very stout men, and I can well imagine, if an opportunity occurred, would be again as troublesome to passengers, as they are reputed to have formerly been. They are chiefly maintained by the inhabitants of the adjacent Coptic villages. The place is difficult of access from the river, on account of the rapidity, and depth of the stream, so that with Arab boatmen a large vessel cannot safely approach it. The cliffs, however, terminate about two miles to the northward, whence it can be easily visited by land. The lofty minaret of Samaloud is seen on the opposite shore.

18*th*. — There seems to have been an antient town near Sheroneah, where there are extensive Mahometan burial-grounds, and a canal, that proceeds from the river near Darhabeah, and conveys the water of the inundation across the adjacent plain. The dog mummy-pits mentioned by Mr. Wilkinson are probably in the neighbouring mountains.

Mr. Waghorn, who was employed under Colonel Campbell to convey the East India Company's despatches to Bombay, overtook me near this place on his return from Cosseir, and soon afterwards proceeded to Cairo.[3] I received a letter by this gentleman from M. Caviglia, dated December 22d, 1836, which had been accidentally detained at Kenneh. I was informed by it that he was still of opinion that the southern air-channel in the Great Pyramid at Gizeh, after having ascended vertically fourteen feet, changed its direction towards the centre of the pyramid, above Davison's chamber; that he had not hitherto been able to intercept it, but was continuing his labours for that purpose; that the firmaun had not arrived; that he was preparing to measure the pyramid; that he had received several strangers, &c. &c.

Not far from the mounds of Kom Achmar, which I intended to visit, the people of the neighbouring village of Habyeah had assembled on a rising ground with flags, and with Arab music, which the women loudly accompanied with their voices, to celebrate the arrival of two

---

[3] The mails of 1836 for India left Falmouth May 3d, and arrived at Bombay July 5th; left Falmouth June 3d, arrived at Suez 28th, and at Bombay July 17th; left Falmouth July 4th, arrived at Mocha August 23d, and at Bombay September 3d.

priests. I therefore landed with the janissary, and, join-
ing the crowd, I observed three or four men entirely
naked, excepting a cloth round their waists, dancing upon
some mats, and amongst them a man, with a white cotton
cap, and a short apron, exerting himself in the most
furious manner, foaming at the mouth, and brandishing
a scourge of small cords in his right hand, and another
instrument in his left with the most violent gesticulations, whilst a person stood behind to assist in case he
should fall from excitement, or from exhaustion. This
man, I found to my surprise, was one of the priests, and
that the ceremony, which I then witnessed, lasted three
or four days, and nights. A respectable looking man was
seated upon the ground on the opposite side of the mats,
dressed in a green robe, and turban, whom, I concluded,
from the colour of his dress, and appearance, to have
been the other functionary. I was told, however, that he
was only an attendant, and that the priest was a naked
wretch with a cloth round his waist, who knelt before him
in a state of the greatest possible exhaustion, and excitement, and who made the most horrible contortions, and
noises, whilst the man in green in vain attempted to
pacify, and to sooth him. Upon our approach, the priest
jumped up, and came towards us with a large palm branch
in a threatening manner. I do not suppose that he would
have struck me; but Selim, the janissary, probably in
order to enhance his own consequence, said, that he certainly would, and that the rest of the people would have
joined him, unless he had interposed. As soon as he had
done so, the priest dropped the stick, and, standing
upright, raised his head, and muttered a prayer; after
which he embraced, and kissed Selim the janissary, and

then favoured me with the same benediction, no doubt in full expectation of receiving a backshish. With such instructors, can the savage state of the population be any longer a subject of surprise? I was informed that the priests received no regular pay, but that their privileges consisted in being exempt from conscription, and in being provided with a house, fuel, and a servant.

I found at Kom Achmar mounds of rubbish, and foundations composed of burnt, and of unburnt bricks, amongst which the walls of the town could be made out, and a gateway, or entrance opposite to a ravine in a chain of hills, where there had been quarries. The place must have been of importance, but the materials had been taken away to Benisouef. I examined a subterraneous passage of considerable length, but did not find any thing worthy of notice. Several of the unburnt bricks had been stamped with hieroglyphics, some of them in double columns; but the characters were so much effaced, and the surface of the bricks so rough, that I could but imperfectly make out those in the margin.*

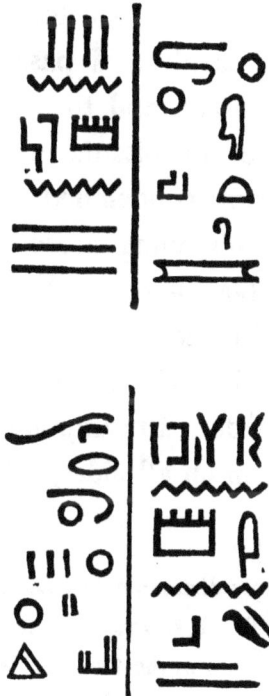

* The hieroglyphics given in the first section are exceedingly difficult to recognise, and it is still more so to offer any connected interpretation of their meaning. The line on the left seems to coincide with the line on the right hand side of the second, of which, although rather

*19th.*—As I did not find on my arrival at Benisouef any answer to the letter which I had sent to Colonel Campbell, and as the one I received by Mr. Waghorn did not induce me to suppose that any discoveries of consequence had been made at Gizeh, I determined to take a cursory view of the Faioum, and, accordingly, having procured horses from Phil El Effendi, the governor, I left Benisouef at ten o'clock.

The plain was covered with abundant crops of cotton, of beans, and of other produce, amongst which were herds of cattle of all descriptions, and the horses of a regiment of cavalry. I passed, soon after, two villages, the one entirely, and the other nearly deserted, from the dread the inhabitants entertained of the conscription, or of being condemned to compulsory labour without a hope of obtaining more than a scanty subsistence for themselves, and for their families. I met afterwards several of these unfortunate people brought back as prisoners with their cattle, and, like them, fastened together with cords. Encampments of Bedouins were likewise to be seen on all sides, whose cattle were turned into the crops

more distinct, only a conjectural restoration can be offered. "Prophet, Priest of the abode of Amon, Lord of the thrones of the two worlds ;" but this explanation is given with considerable diffidence. It is possible, especially in the upper copy, that there may be the poniard, which in the texts replaces the human head, as determinative of head, chief, or, and in that case it would be the " Chief Prophet, Priest," that is, the high-priest. Should this conjecture be well founded, the illegible characters in the second line are the name, and the whole indicates that the bricks were destined for the hypogea of a deceased sacerdotal functionary.—Mr. BIRCH.

belonging to the inhabitants. Beyond El Hadjar, (one of the depopulated places already mentioned,) a ridge of barren land on a higher level intersects the cultivated plain, which continues to the two villages of Illahoon, where the pyramid, which forms a prominent object from Benisouef, has been constructed on the verge of the desert. At this place a dam, connected with a bridge, regulates the water of the Bahr Yousef: it is well built; and had been, I heard, lately repaired; and was, no doubt, erected on antient foundations, as many are to be seen near it, together with shafts and ruined tombs. A palace belonging to the Pacha is pleasantly situated in a grove of palm-trees, on the grassy banks of a large pool, and the scene is not only enlivened by the picturesque figures, that repair to it for the water, and by the persons belonging to a magazine, where a number of carts are employed, but also by occasional travellers, as a considerable traffic is yet kept up from Medinet El Faioum, (the present capital of this once fertile province,) with Cairo, and with the other towns to the northward of Benisouef.[5] The common route to the greater oasis likewise passes through it.

From Illahoon, the road to Medinet passes over a tract of ill-cultivated ground at the verge of the desert, leaving the pyramid to the northwards; and, on the distant barren hills to the southward, the remains of

[5] There is, however, a much shorter communication through the desert, from the northern part of the Faioum by Dashoor to Gizeh, which requires about twenty-four hours, and the journey thence to Alexandria occupies about six days. It is remarkable that the two other tracts reach the banks of the Nile near pyramids, one at that of Lysht, and the other at the false pyramid.

some Coptic monasteries.  Not far off a large canal is crossed by a dyke supported on arches, (which appear to have been originally of Roman construction), and afterwards the beds of several water-courses that have been cut round the brow of the desert plain, upon which the pyramid of Howara is built.[6]  The village itself is inconsiderable, and stands on a bank between the road, and the water.  About seven miles further the road turns to the right, on the western bank of the Bahr Yousef, and, having passed a magazine, and an unfinished palace belonging to the Pacha, enters Medinet El Faioum by a bridge built over clear and sparkling streams, that no doubt flow from the above-mentioned canal.  The journey from Benisouef occupied about seven hours.  The ruins of Antinoe, the antient capital, are situated on a high range of hills, at some distance to the north of Medinet, which, in consequence of an abundant supply of water, is surrounded by luxuriant vegetation, and lofty trees.  It is also adorned with handsome minarets, contains several good houses, and a well-supplied bazar, and is better built than the generality of Arab towns.  On approaching it over the bridge, it brought to my recollection Windsor, and Eton, without possessing any exact resemblance to either of these places.  After passing through a number of winding streets, I arrived at the residence of Ali Dud, the Madyr. He was not in his house, but in a small square apartment on a level with, and on the opposite side of the street. The room, which appeared to be his hall of audience, was crowded with Coptic secretaries, Turks, and Arabs of

---

[6] The pyramids of Howara and of Illahoon have been already described.  See pages 8 and 9.

every description.  He gave me a very civil reception,
and, after the usual ceremony of coffee, and pipes, I produced my firmaun, and requested his assistance in visiting
the interesting province over which, he presided.  This
he readily promised; but how the important affair was
to be performed gave rise to a discussion of nearly two
hours, in which every person present participated.  At
length, however, an arrangement was made, and I accompanied the Madyr to his own residence.  We passed
through a court, in which there were several horses,
and then through long passages and a dirty staircase to
a spacious, but cold apartment, as the large windows of
lattice-work were but partially covered with oiled paper.
A well-grated window, over a door into the hareem,
afforded to its inhabitants an opportunity of observing
what took place.  The floor was paved with red tiles,
but a carpet was laid before a low sofa covered with
cushions, and extending round two thirds of the room.
These, together with a small mirror, and a basin and ewer,
constituted the furniture ; and the whitewashed walls
were adorned with a solitary group of three small prints
of Britannia, cut out of an English shop-bill.  The room
was not particularly clean, although probably the best in
the whole province.  After pipes, and coffee had been
introduced, a plentiful supper was served in the usual
manner; and as the Madyr, myself, and the janissary,
who served as interpreter, sat together on the floor,
round a circular tray in front of the latticed window of
the hareem, we must have presented an amusing spectacle
to those within, whose lights from time to time appeared,
although their persons could not be distinguished.  The
Madyr was an old man, and had been a considerable

merchant, and, probably on account of his wealth, had
been obliged by the Pacha to accept the government of
the province.   He appeared extremely credulous, but was
very civil, and obliging, and contributed all he could to
my convenience.   He remained for a considerable time
after supper, and a long conversation was carried on by
means of the janissary Selim.   I then retired to the sofa,
but not to sleep, owing to the quantity of gnats, and of
vermin, with which the place abounded.

20th.—I left the town early in the morning with
the Sheik of Shadowee, by the way I had arrived, and
leaving at some distance to the left the mounds which
occupy the site of Antinoe, we proceeded through cultivated plains, and groves of olive, and of fig-trees, to
some ruins, which are supposed to have belonged to an
antient pyramid.   The inhabitants of the different villages were employed in threshing out their corn, under
the superintendence of the Sheiks, and of the Pacha's
officers, who take away two-thirds for their master, which
sufficiently accounts for the reluctance, with which the
fellahs work, particularly as they are at the same time
subject to the oppression of the Sheiks, and to the devastations of the Bedouins, twenty thousand of whom were
said at that time to have taken up their quarters in the
province.   The ruins in question may have formed part
of one, or of two monuments, as they consist of two
large masses perfectly unconnected, and at some distance
from each other, but neither the form, nor foundations
can be ascertained.   The stones are large, well squared,
and firmly set in mortar, and the masonry much resembles that of the pyramids at Gizeh.   After having ex-

amined these remains, we passed through an undulating country, where my companion got several fair shots at cranes, but without success, although he dismounted, and knelt down to take deliberate aim. This instance, and what I had previously seen in the desert, near Palmyra, gave me a bad idea of the prowess of the Arabs. In a few miles we came to the village of Shadowee, situated on lofty mounds near a deep glen, through which a large stream flows towards the Lake Mœris.[7]

[7] I was informed, that the population of this place only amounted to four, or five hundred, although it formerly exceeded six thousand, and that many of the Sheiks had been killed, or forced to run away to the desert. The Faioum presents a striking contrast to the alluvial plains of the rest of Egypt, as it consists of high undulating ground, and of picturesque valleys well watered by streams, which flow from the Bahr Yousef, and from the other canals. A variety of timber and of fruit-trees, gardens of roses, and vineyards, amidst groves of olive, and of mulberry-trees, vary its appearance. The Lake Mœris presents a fine expanse of water to the westward, and beyond it is the interminable desert. The antient canals, and watercourses seem to have been constructed with great skill, and it is to be regretted that no regular survey of them exists, as it would probably shew the former level of the Nile, and afford information respecting the Bahr Bela Mar, and might also lead to the discovery of the famous labyrinth, and of other celebrated remains. Yet, notwithstanding its fertility, in no part of the country is distress more apparent, or cultivation less attended to: indeed, a considerable part of the land is entirely neglected; for, besides the oppression which affects the whole country, the Bedouins, as I have mentioned, are allowed to encamp in great numbers, and their cattle are turned out amongst the crops in perfect security; whilst those of the inhabitants are obliged to be driven home every evening to the villages; and the report of fire-arms, shouting of men, and the continual barking of dogs during the night, shew that, even there, they are not in safety. The Sheiks of the villages connive at depredation, and keep on good terms with these savage intruders, that,

Upon our arrival the Sheik conducted me to his divan, a dirty upper room with mud walls, that had probably once been whitewashed; and some loose bricks having been removed from a small aperture, which served for a window, sufficient light was admitted to shew that no rest was to be expected either on the dirty cushions laid against the walls, or upon the stained carpets spread over the mats on the earthen floor, which, to judge by the state of several small recesses, or cupboards in the walls, had never been cleaned since it was built, and must therefore swarm with vermin of all descriptions. In due time dinner was brought in, at which the Sheik's brother, and eight or ten persons assisted, and amongst them one of the Bedouin Sheiks, a stout, handsome man, dressed in a clean Arab blanket, and red tarboose, and much superior in appearance to the Arabs of the villages. He seemed to be an intelligent person, made many inquiries respecting my journey, and readily answered any

in case of necessity, they may find a secure retreat amongst them. They themselves oppress, and plunder the people to the last degree, not only to meet the demands of the Pacha, and to preserve an interest by bribing his officers, but also to amass treasure for their own purposes, which they keep in a portable and available shape, and ready for immediate flight whenever caprice, or other circumstances may make it expedient. The dilapidated state of the villages may, therefore, be easily imagined, but the habits of rapacity thus produced can be scarcely conceived. I saw an astonishing instance of this in crossing the Lake Mœris on the following morning. The boatmen, who rented the fishery from the Sheik, brought two large fish for sale, and also a jar of fresh water for our accommodation. The Sheik immediately seized upon the fish, and the jar, and, unless my janissary had interfered, a scuffle would have ensued, as the poor people, to whom these objects were of value, although not intrinsically worth a piastre, were determined to defend their property.

questions about the oasis, and the ruins in the neighbourhood of the lake, without being able, however, to afford any particular information.

Owing, to the distance of the village from the lake, and to the difficulty of procuring a boat, I could not cross the water till the following day. In the evening supper was brought in, and afterwards coffee, and pipes, when the fishermen, who owned the boat upon the lake, and many other persons, came up, and a conversation lasted for some hours.

21*st.*—I set out with the Sheik, and a number of attendants, at six in the morning for the lake. We passed a fine plain, abounding with crops of clover, beans, and different sorts of grain, and affording pasture to herds of goats, camels, and other cattle, which were guarded by armed Bedouins, much stouter, and better clothed than those in Syria. They wore white blankets, red tarbooses, and sandals, and many of them were armed with pistols, suspended under the left arm by a broad Moorish belt, that passed over the right shoulder. They appeared in perfect security, and were strolling about in various directions on foot, and also on horseback, but none of them were well mounted. Their black tents were pitched on the grounds, that had been eaten down by the cattle, and, in many instances, were surrounded by yards enclosed with reeds.[a] Beyond the cultivated

[a] The Faioum, from the abundance of pasture, is better adapted to the feeding of cattle than any other part of Egypt, and, from its isolated position, is peculiarly fit for the reception of strangers. In these respects it would answer the description of the land of Goshen; and if the canal,

land, a barren plain covered with stunted bushes, and which appears to have been formerly under water, extends for about two miles to the lake, where some people were employed in building a boat. The water was so shallow that we were carried to the vessel which was to convey us to the other side. The lake abounds with fish[9] and with various kinds of waterfowl, and great quantities are taken by hooks attached to long lines, that are stretched at intervals over the surface. I saw a large black fowl with a sharp serrated bill caught in this manner; and two fish called Shillbee Beeri, with flat heads, and beards, or whiskers six or seven inches long, which were said to be very fine, and were nearly a yard in length.

We arrived on the western shore in about an hour, and landed in the same way, in which we embarked. Having passed a narrow strip of bushes, where the slots of leopards, and of antelopes were visible, we ascended a steep ridge, on which there had been evidently vineyards, as the remains were to be perceived struggling through the sand, that now covers the extensive ranges of desert mountains to such a depth, that their rocky summits are the only objects perceptible in the undulating waste. As the sand is deep and drifted, it is impossible,

Bahr Yousef, could be supposed to have been the work of the great patriarch, it might be an additional argument.

9 Certain varieties of fish are said to be peculiar to the Nile, and to the Caspian Sea. I do not believe that the assertion extends to those in the Lake Mœris; but, considering the antient traditions respecting this lake, it would be interesting to discover any fish in it, which are peculiar to the Caspian Sea, and still more so if they were not found in the Nile.

without very extensive excavations, to determine what was the former surface of the country, but it is evident that the part next the water had been cultivated, and that the antient town, we came to visit, had been placed to great advantage; and that before the plains and mountains, between it and the lake had been overwhelmed with the vast body of sand, that it commanded a magnificent prospect of the lake, from which it is not three miles distant, and of the fertile province on the eastern shore.

The ruins, (said by Mr. Wilkinson to be those of Dimay, or Nerba,) are situated on an eminence, and are approached from the eastward by a causeway, composed of black stone, which may be traced to some distance amidst brick foundations, mounds of broken pottery, fragments of talc, and of squared stones, as may be also the walls of the town, built of unburnt bricks, which in many places are nearly white. Layers of reeds had been inserted between the courses; and to the right hand of the entrance, and about two feet above the ground, a remarkable cavity, one foot in height, and in width, and nine feet in length, had been worked from the outside into the wall, and contained three pieces of flat, and as many of round wood, placed across the bottom, at equal distances. I could not discover a cartouche, or any inscriptions upon the bricks. I fancied with the assistance of a glass that I could discover stone quarries, and the remains of a necropolis in some cliffs about two miles to the westward. There were likewise square masses of ruins on a mountain between the town, and the lake.

I had intended, in my return to Medinet, to have examined the obelisk at Biggig; but after a long detour,

I found, that, on account of the number of water-courses, there was not any direct road from Shadowee to that place, and that it would be necessary to return to within a mile of Medinet, and then to go a considerable distance in order to arrive there. It was night, and as the obelisk was broken, and thrown down, and the inscription well known, I did not think that the mere inspection of it was worth the journey. I was sorry that I could not remain longer in this beautiful province, where I had received so much hospitality, and where so many interesting antiquities may yet be concealed, but my anxiety to return to Gizeh induced me to set out on the following morning.

22*d.*—I took leave of the Madyr, and proceeded at eight o'clock, with the Sheik of Illahoon as a guide, to the pyramids at that place, and at Howara; but he soon lost his way among the ravines, and watercourses, that intersect the country in every direction, and I was obliged to procure other assistance. We met a considerable number of Bedouins, and of country people on their way to Medinet, and passed over a tract of land evidently capable of great fertility. We then crossed a stream in a part of the large ravine, which I had observed at Howara, and which, at this place, appears to have been formed in a natural gulley. And having left on the opposite bank, a considerable Arab village, we turned to the right, and pursued our way over a desert plain to the pyramids, and afterwards proceeded to Benisouef. I received on the road to that place a letter from M. Caviglia, enclosed by M. Piozan. It was an answer to that which I had sent to Colonel Campbell from E-Siout, and was dated

January 17th, 1837. It informed me, that the works in the Great Pyramid were much advanced; that in the Second[1] he had discovered a passage, communicating by a pit with the lower descending passage; and that he had proceeded with the excavation on the northern front in search of a lower entrance, which he hoped to find in a few days. That at the Third Pyramid he was already within sixty feet of the centre. And that he had been also employed on some mummy-pits. He likewise added, that his discovery in the Second Pyramid had excited the envy of the French to such a degree, that Colonel Campbell had been obliged to exert himself with the government to secure the exclusive privileges granted by the firmaun.[2]

On approaching the town, I met a number of mounted Bedouins, their horses, and several that I saw in the town were very bad, and many of them only two years old. Colts of the same age are used in Syria, which might be adduced as an instance in favour of early training; indeed, in that country, old horses do not appear to stand fatigue.

23d.—Having expressed my acknowledgments to the governor for the assistance I had received from him, I left Benisouef at six o'clock, and arrived at Gizeh on the following evening, when I went to Cairo, and returned

---

[1] See vertical section of Second Pyramid.

[2] It will subsequently be seen what progress M. Caviglia had made in the three pyramids, particularly in the third, where, by Mr. Perring's admeasurement, his excavation had only arrived at the length of six feet on the 13th of February.

at night to the boat, which was moored under the western bank.[3]

24*th.* — Being extremely anxious to see what progress had been made, I set out early in the morning, and went immediately to the Great, and to the Second Pyramids, where I expected to find M. Caviglia, and his men, but I did not meet with a single person, and I afterwards discovered the people at work on three mummy-pits between the Sphinx, and the Second Pyramid. M. Caviglia, however, informed me that parties had been employed by night, and by day at the southern side of Davison's chamber, in search of the southern air-channel; and in continuing the excavation, near the entrance to the king's chamber, along the course of the northern air-channel in the Great Pyramid; and also at the excavation in the Third. He then shewed me his discovery in the Second Pyramid. It appeared that, in clearing the horizontal passage, he found that a part of the floor was composed of masonry, near the chasm formed in that communication by the descending passage, which returns beneath it to the northward; and that, when this masonry was removed, he discovered another descending passage, above, and parallel to the lower one, which terminated at a short distance in

[3] On arriving near Tourah, one of the boatmen was dressed in a white robe, a high fur cap, and a white beard, and came round the boat for a backshish, on account of our having returned from Upper Egypt. This custom is something like that observed in crossing the Line.

The boat belonged to the company established on the Nile, and was of about fifty or sixty tons; it was therefore very roomy, and, as it was newly painted, perfectly clean. The figures in the annexed sketch are given to shew the costume, and appearance of the people.

A NUBIAN BOATMAN, MAJOUB THE SON OF THE REIZ & ABDULLAH A SLAVE.

Published by James Fraser, Regent Street

the rock, and was connected by an hole with the other passage.[4]   It might therefore be supposed that it had been made for the sake of ventilation in forming the subterraneous passages before the pyramid was built, or that an alteration had, for some reason or other, taken place in the original construction of the pyramid.

A narrow excavation had also been carried by M. Caviglia, through the mound of rubbish in the centre of the northern front of this pyramid, to within about thirty-eight feet of the base, whereby the rock, and a pavement in the form of a step had been uncovered, which he imagined had been painted of a red colour upon stucco. I was myself at first of the same opinion, till further observation proved that it was merely a partial discoloration, produced from the particles of red cement.[5]   This work had been commenced on too small a scale, and only at the bottom; and the materials had not been removed to a sufficient distance; consequently, as the mound was composed of very large blocks, and upwards of forty feet high, the removal of it was attended with great difficulty on approaching the building, and was not completely effected.   It should have been carried on at the top, and on both sides, as well as at the bottom. M. Caviglia then shewed me the three pits, upon which the people were employed.   The two, nearest the Second Pyramid, were large quadrangular shafts of considerable

[4] The reader is in this and similar instances referred to the plans in this book, and also to the large plates of the " Pyramids of Gizeh," published in numbers by Mr. Fraser of Regent Street.

[5] Upon what foundation the other opinions respecting this pyramid, published, (apparently by M. Caviglia), in the " Malta Gazette" of March 22d, 1837, were founded, it is impossible to say.   See Appendix.

depth; but the third, near the Sphinx, (afterwards called Campbell's tomb,) was evidently of a very curious construction, although the sand had only been partially removed from the north-western corner of the fosse, and from the shaft near the south-western angle, as it was proposed to clear out the fosse first, and then to fill it up again with the sand from the interior excavation in order to save expense.[6] A cawass, (or janissary,) from government, and the Sheiks of the neighbouring villages were in attendance.

In conversation with M. Caviglia, I expressed my disappointment that greater progress had not been made, particularly at the Great Pyramid; when he informed me, that more men could not be obtained; and that, as the French had a party amongst the Arabs, it was necessary to occupy the ground, to prevent any interruption on their part. With respect to these statements, it is only necessary to observe, that a greater number of people subsequently attended, and that during the period I remained at the pyramids, I never experienced the slightest interference. It was, at this time, settled, that whatever communications might subsequently become necessary, in consequence of important discoveries, they should be made from time, to time to Mr. Hamilton; to which arrangement Colonel Campbell afterwards readily assented.

Mr. Hill came in the afternoon, with Sir Edward

---

[6] The portions of rock left as buttresses across the fosse were extremely curious; and it was supposed that water would be found at the bottom. Plans, and sections of this monument are expected from Egypt, and will probably be published.

Pearson, and Captain Smith; and, in the evening, I went with them to Cairo; at which place a number of persons had arrived from India, and, amongst them, Mr. Turton, to whom I subsequently gave a letter of introduction to M. Caviglia, in order that he might examine the pyramids.

26*th.* — I sent my baggage from the boat to the pyramids, and, returning there in the evening, I found Mr. Maltas, and several other persons; as also Mr. Turton, and his family, who soon afterwards set out for Cairo.

27*th.* — I began, with M. Caviglia's assistance, to measure the interior of the Great Pyramid; and, in the course of the day I copied the hieroglyphics inscribed on the rocks to the northward of the Second;[7] where M. Caviglia pointed out a cutting, (apparently the beginning of a doorway), but which he considered an Hebrew character, and informed me that there was a shaft beneath it, supposed to be connected by an underground passage with the building itself. The works were continued at the three pits, as also in the interior of the Great, and in the chasm at the northern front of the Third Pyramid. I had a long conversation in the evening with M. Caviglia, in which he observed that I hurt his feelings by continually urging him to turn his attention towards the pyramids, instead of employing the people at the mummy-pits. I assured him that I had no such intention, but that as I had undertaken the opera-

_____

[7] Which are afterwards inserted, see February 17th.

tions solely with a view to these magnificient structures, particularly the great one, I naturally wished to make some discoveries before I returned to England. I remarked, that the pits had been most probably already opened; that, if not, mummies were of little, or no value; and that, as the pyramids were the great object for which the firmaun had been obtained, I confessed myself surprised, and disappointed that greater efforts had not been made to discover their interior construction. He repeated what he before said respecting French interference, and intrigue, and the difficulty of procuring more men; expressed his opinion that the mummy-pits might produce several objects interesting to the scientific world, and, in short, that having begun the excavations, it was necessary to finish them.

28th. — I continued the admeasurements. Affairs went on as usual. Several bones were found in some grottoes in the sides of the shaft nearest the Second Pyramid. Mr. Hill came.

29th. — I proceeded with my examination of the Great Pyramid; and in the course of the day went to Cairo with Mr. Hill to get sieves to sift the sand taken out of the mummy-pits, in which small particles of leaf-gold, and other trifles are often found, and also for a windlass to assist in raising the sand, that these operations might be finished as soon as possible. I likewise determined to procure some boring rods, which I imagined would have been more useful, than they afterwards proved. Mr. Hill had assisted me in measuring the Great Pyramid, and also engaged to do the same in mapping the ground,

but he observed that a Civil Engineer had arrived with
Mr. Galloway, who was furnished with the proper instruments, and who, he had no doubt, would undertake the survey in the best manner. In consequence
of what he said, I took an opportunity of mentioning
the subject to Mr. Galloway, who in the handsomest
manner immediately acceded to my request, and promised Mr. Perring's able assistance, which that gentleman afterwards most kindly, and disinterestedly continued, with what effect the masterly plans, and drawings,
together with the map formed by himself, and Mr. Mash,
will best testify.[8]  I again beg leave to acknowledge the
great assistance which I received from those gentlemen,
and to express my satisfaction, that accurate elevations,
and plans of these most antient, and noble monuments
will at last be published, which, besides other excellences,
will possess that paramount, and most unusual quality,
truth.

30*th.*—I dined with Mr. Galloway, and Mr. Perring,
and had a good deal of conversation with them respecting
the measuring of the pyramids, and the mapping of the
ground.

31*st.* — I went to Mabietta with Mr. Hill, where we
succeeded in procuring some boring rods, and in the
evening I again met Mr. Galloway, and Mr. Perring.[9]

---

[8] See No. I. of the " Pyramids of Gizeh," published by Mr. Fraser.

[9] An incident occurred at Mabietta, that shews the incapacity, and
ignorance of the Pacha's superintendents.  The one in question was
a Levantine, and, I was told, a very respectable person, and had the

*February 1st.*—I returned to the pyramids, and found matters going on as usual. A sarcophagus was discovered in a rough grotto on the southern side of the central mummy-pit. It had been opened, and, as I was informed, only contained the following articles; some pieces of bone, and of linen; a few small green ornaments, (apparently of a necklace); a green idol; a brown scarabæus without any inscription; a piece of red cornelian; some narrow strips of leaf-gold; thirty-two gilt balls about the size of a pea; a lump of resinous substance with more of these balls adhering to it; a blue scarabæus without any inscription; a bull with his legs tied together for sacrifice, composed of stone, (about an inch long;) and two pieces of polished stone, about half an inch long, and a quarter broad, stuck together with gum. The grotto was about eighteen feet long, and thirteen broad. Sixty-three green idols were found amongst the sand in, and about it. I was also told that some pieces of bone had been brought out of the shaft at the south-western corner of Campbell's Tomb.[1]

charge of several extensive establishments. As he had promised Mr. Hill to furnish me with the boring-rods at a fair price, provided he could part with them consistently with the Pacha's interest, I thought it proper to express my acknowledgments; when, to my surprise, he asked, what sort of a machine the instrument in question was, and whether it was as large as the great steam-engine belonging to the copper mill in the citadel? and seemed much astonished when I told him that, although of considerable length, it was about the size of the nabout, which I held in my hand. With such superintendence it is not wonderful that the establishments fail.

[1] Every thing discovered under the firmaun was to belong to the Pacha. The articles found before the 13th of February, were in the charge of M. Caviglia.

*2d.*—I examined the above-mentioned antiquities. It is remarkable that all these idols,[*] and many more subsequently found, differed from each other, either in physiognomy, or in inscription.  Some of them appeared to have been portraits, those made of *terra cotta* seemed to have been cast, and afterwards inscribed.  Selim arrived with the boring-rods, several of which were missing, and were never afterwards recovered.  I concluded that they were taken out of the box at the factory; as I had no reason to suspect the janissary of dishonesty, or of carelessness.  He returned in the evening to Cairo, with my English servant, who had been suddenly attacked by fever.

M. Caviglia informed me that Colonel Campbell had authorised M. Piozan to advance for him another subscription during his intended absence in Upper Egypt.

A party was sent to remove the rubbish from the northern front of the Second Pyramid.

At night there was a heavy storm of wind and rain.

*3d.*—Instead of the party at the Second Pyramid, thirteen women and children were employed there.

A few additional men came from an adjacent village; but the people worked very badly, and nearly one half of them sat still, under pretence of relieving the rest.  They

---

[*] They represent a human mummy holding a hoe and pickaxe, with a basket slung over the left shoulder, and are supposed by M. Champollion, and by other authors, to personify the deceased, equipped for the mystic cultivation of Hades.  These in question bear the name of Psametik, whose surname is Aahmôs, or Amasis, born of Pasht Ertais. He appears to have been some functionary of state—attached to the care of the pure abode.—Mr. BIRCH.

also came late in the morning, and were not fairly at work before seven, or eight o'clock. They were allowed an hour at twelve o'clock for dinner, and were dismissed before sunset. A Reis received two piastres per day; the men, and larger boys one piastre; and the women, and children twenty, or thirty paras, according to their size.[3] The men employed in the interior of the pyramids, and those subsequently procured from Cairo, and from the quarries at the Mokattam, had of course higher wages; and after the 13th of February, every person received double pay when any discovery of consequence occurred. This, however, instead of being an additional stimulus to exertion, proved a mere waste of money. The people at first assembled every morning and evening, to be counted off, on the terrace, where the tents were pitched; but, by a more convenient arrangement, they afterwards collected, according to their villages, upon the plain beneath.

In the course of the day a large stone, which seemed to cover the aperture of a pit, was found near the grotto where a sarcophagus had been discovered in the middle shaft. It was broken with some difficulty, but nothing, excepting sand, was beneath it. A rough wall had been built from east to west across the lower part of this shaft, apparently to divide it for separate interments. More bones were taken out of the grottoes, which seemed to have been enlarged from natural fissures.

*4th.*—I completed my copy of the hieroglyphics on

---

[3] For the value of money see Appendix. Forty paras make a piastre, and five piastres are worth a shilling.

the rock near the north-western angle of the Second Pyramid; and afterwards examined the Third, the three smaller, and the periboli, and boundaries near them. In the afternoon Mr. Hill came with Paulo, a Maltese, who was engaged to superintend the boring; they immediately went with M. Caviglia into the Great Pyramid, and re- solved to commence operations in the centre of the king's chamber. But it was found impossible to bore through the blocks of granite, or to remove them on account of the closeness of the joints, I therefore directed Paulo on the following morning to clear out an old excavation at the north-western corner, and to begin boring at the depth of six feet four inches below the surface of the granite blocks, and at the distance of three feet from the northern, and ten feet nine inches from the western side of the chamber. A party was employed at the Second Pyramid. Mr. Hill set up several triangles, to raise the sand from the fosse at Campbell's tomb, which would scarcely ever have been got out without the assist- ance of machinery.

In returning to the tents in the afternoon, I asked M. Caviglia when he would probably have finished his excavations at the mummy-pits, and be able to take the bulk of the people to the pyramids. He said in about a fortnight, but that he then intended to begin upon another.* I remarked, that in that case it was useless for me to remain any longer, as no discovery could be made before I should be obliged to return to England.

* This pit was on the hills beyond the southern dyke, and M. Ca- viglia informed me that the French had failed in attempting to open it. It is described 26th March.

He observed that the ground would be surveyed, and that I could take the map with me; and asked what I would advise him to do with the pits that were already begun. I recommended him to give up the two higher shafts, which had evidently been opened, and to employ the people at the pyramids; but to continue the excavation at Campbell's tomb, on account of the peculiarity of its construction, although it had been, no doubt, already plundered, as the superstructure was destroyed. To this he agreed, and, on going to Cairo in the evening, I informed Colonel Campbell accordingly. Indeed I had often expressed to him my regret, that so much time and money had been wasted upon these works; but he seemed to have a great opinion of M. Caviglia's experience and skill; and a disinclination to interfere with his projects.

5th. — I remained at Cairo.

6th. — M. Caviglia came early in the morning, and informed me that he had received Colonel Campbell's directions to proceed with the mummy-pits as usual. As soon, therefore, as I was dressed, I went in search of the colonel. I found him at the house of M. de Laurin, the Austrian consul-general, and explained to him how un-satisfactorily the works had been carried on at Gizeh; when he promised to send orders to M. Caviglia to employ the people without delay at the pyramids. He introduced me in the course of the day to Mr. Lakin, Mr. Rutherford, and Dr. Wilson, who were proceeding to Upper Egypt.

7th. — I went to Gizeh in the afternoon with Mr. Galloway, and Mr. Perring; and we began to measure the interior of the Great Pyramid.

*8th.*—We continued the admeasurements. In the evening, Mr. Perring and Mr. Galloway returned to Cairo with Mr. Hill, who had arrived in the morning.

*9th.*—The work was resumed at the Second Pyramid, probably in consequence of Colonel Campbell's letter. Two German and two English travellers paid us a visit. Several bones were found in the fosse of Campbell's Tomb.

*10th.*—M. Caviglia went to Cairo to make arrangements respecting the Arabs, who, the Sheiks had informed him, would be required to work at a canal.

A quantity of bones were found upon one of the buttresses, and in other parts of the fosse at Campbell's tomb. Whilst I was employed in the Great Pyramid, I was informed that a sarcophagus had been discovered in a grotto proceeding from the shaft, near the south-western corner of the tomb.[5] I immediately went to the spot, and finding that M. Caviglia's servant (Giachino) had entered it, I ordered him out, and forbade any person to go down before M. Caviglia's return. The sarcophagus was empty.

The Sheiks came to me in the course of the morning, and offered to furnish two or three hundred additional men, if I could obtain a protection for them from being sent to the canal. I immediately accepted them, and

---

[5] A plan of the tomb will be given.

promised to consult with M. Caviglia respecting the protection. I paid the people in the evening,[6] and, upon his return, gave an account of them to M. Caviglia, and informed him of the discovery of the sarcophagus, and of the additional men offered by the Sheiks. He observed, that he did not like to employ more men, as the weekly bills were already very high. I told him that I thought he was right about the weekly bills,[7] but that, as time was every thing to me, I would pay the rest of the people, whom he did not want, and employ them in distinct operations. He then alleged, that he had not leisure to attend to any additional works. I stated that I would undertake both their payment, and superintendence, and avoid all interference with his excavations. In the evening Mr. Hill and Mr. Perring arrived. A smith's forge was established in an adjoining tomb. At dinner, M. Caviglia produced a programme of his intended operations. I informed him, that I had no objection to it; and, as I had before stated, that I should employ the rest of the people according to my own judgment, and at my own expense.

11*th.*—Mr. Hill went away early in the morning.

[6] Their numbers were—men, sixty-eight; women and children, fifty-three; with Paulo, in the Great Pyramid, four; at the excavation in the Great Pyramid, six; at the excavation in the third pyramid, two.

[7] I had repeatedly stated my apprehensions, that Colonel Campbell would give up the affair on account of the increasing expense; and, as that might materially embarrass our operations, that I was ready to advance any reasonable sum, besides our regular contributions; and, in fact, M. Caviglia had been furnished with provisions, and stores of every description by Mr. Hill on my account.

Soon afterwards I found it necessary to recall Paulo, and the party, who were boring in the Great Pyramid, and to withdraw the rods, owing to circumstances, which it is unnecessary to detail, but which subsequently induced Colonel Campbell to give up his share in the undertaking, and to dismiss M. Caviglia from the pyramids.[8] I wrote to Colonel Campbell, and went with Mr. Perring to the Great Pyramid, where we took the angles, examined the excavations, and likewise the stone at the northern end of the great passage, which appeared to Mr. Wilkinson to have been granite. We also directed our attention to a considerable settling on the western side of this passage, occasioned, probably, either by the excavation made by the Caliphs, or by the chasm connected with the grotto in the well. Dr. Wilson, Mr. Rutherford, and Mr. Lakin arrived; with whom, and with Mr. Perring, I went in the evening to Cairo; where I saw Colonel Campbell, and explained to him my reasons for declining all further co-operation with M. Caviglia.

12th.—I returned with Mr. Galloway and Mr. Perring to the pyramids, where the Arab Sheiks had been some time in attendance. I desired them to send, on the following morning, the additional men, whom they had promised; but this they now refused to do. Mr. Galloway, Mr. Perring, and myself, measured the exterior of the Great Pyramid; and Mr. Perring, in passing over the centre of the northern front for that purpose, discovered the mouth of the northern air-channel.[9] On return-

[8] See Appendix.

[9] As there had been an excavation to the length of thirty-seven feet along the upper end of the channel, and a great many stones removed

ing to the tents from these operations, I received a letter from Colonel Campbell, informing me, that he gave up the works carried on under the firmaun, and inclosing a copy of one, which he had sent to M. Caviglia, to recall him from the pyramids. Mr. Galloway returned to Cairo. Mr. Perring and myself passed most part of the night in examining the interior of the Great Pyramid; particularly Davison's chamber, the passage leading to it, and the excavation made by M. Caviglia on its southern side.

### *February 13th.*

Reis, 7.       Men, 78.       Children, 57.

Great Pyramid.—Davison's Chamber.
———       Northern Air-Channel.
———       Passage to Queen's Chamber.
———       King's Chamber.
Third Pyramid.—Temple to the Eastward.
———       Excavation between the Temple and Pyramid.

The numbers of people employed are regularly stated, as they varied considerably from day to day; but, to avoid unnecessary repetition, the day's works are omitted, when they are the same as the preceding. With one or two exceptions, no work was done on Sundays. The people employed at piece-work, and the quarry-men from Cairo, are not included in these accounts.

M. Caviglia having sent me word, (in consequence, no doubt, of the letter which he had received from Colonel Campbell,) that he did not intend to employ the people, I counted them off, and sent them to the

from the face of the pyramid near it, it is surprising that it had not been sooner discovered; particularly as, according to M. Caviglia, sulphur, rope-ends, and pitch had been burnt in the lower part of it, and " des hommes experimentés" sent in various directions over the exterior, in order to detect its direction by the smell, or by the smoke.

works above mentioned.[1] The excavation, begun by
M. Caviglia behind the blocks of granite, which form the
southern wall of Davison's chamber, with a view of in-
tersecting the southern air-channel, was continued; and
another party was also employed at the same place, to
carry up the excavation above the roof of the chamber,
where, as I before mentioned, I expected to find a sepulchral apartment, to which, I thought it probable, that that
chamber was an entresol, and the top of the great passage
an entrance. Some men were employed in clearing out
the mouth of the northern air-channel, which had been
discovered by Mr. Perring on the exterior of the pyramid;
but the excavation along the course of this channel near
the king's chamber was discontinued from the great difficulty attending it. The candles would scarcely burn;
not more than six inches were cut out in twenty-four
hours; and I knew, from examination, that at least thirty-
five feet remained without any opening, or apartment.
The connexion between the upper and lower parts of this
channel was not then ascertained; but, even if it had,
a communication from it to other chambers, was highly
probable. The men sent into the passage leading to the
queen's chamber were ordered to clear out the rubbish
from the bottom of the step, as far as the apartment. In
the king's chamber, the boring rods, withdrawn on the
11th instant, were replaced; and Paulo resumed his
former operations.

The greatest part of the people were sent with the

---

[1] In order to understand the details contained in this journal, a refer-
ence is recommended not only to the accompanying plates, but also to
Mr. Perring's plans and sections, published by Mr. Fraser, 215 Regent
Street.

two janissaries to clear the space between the eastern front of the Third Pyramid and the ruins of the temple; and likewise to excavate the adytum of the latter building, in the hope of finding an entrance into the pyramid.

Giachino, whom M. Caviglia had discharged, entered my service, and had the general direction, and superintendence of these works. Having made these arrangements, I assisted Mr. Perring in taking the level of the entrance from the base of the Great Pyramid.

In the evening, that gentleman returned to Cairo; and a number of Arab Sheiks and Turkish officers paid me a visit.

When the people were paid off, a guard was placed upon Campbell's tomb, which was continued till M. Caviglia's departure for Alexandria, when I took away the windlass, ropes, &c., and the machinery that had been erected.

An old basket having been dug up in the passage leading to the queen's chamber, I concluded that it had been already examined, and ordered the rubbish to be replaced, and the operation to be given up.

### February 14th.

Reis, 7.      Men, 95.      Children, 73.

Great Pyramid.—Davison's Chamber.
—— King's Chamber.
—— Northern Air-channel.
—— Subterranean Passage and Chamber.
Third Pyramid.—Temple to the Eastward.
—— Excavation between the Temple and Pyramid.
—— Interior.

Mr. Perring had informed me on the preceding evening, that having again examined the works near Davison's

VIEW OF THE THIRD PYRAMID.

Published by J. Fraser, 215 Regent St.

chamber, he had directed Paulo, to take away the men
employed over the granite blocks on the southern side,
and to set them to work in the end of the passage at the
north-eastern corner of that apartment, where we had,
on the evening of the 12th instant, observed a small
crevice in a joint, by the side of the corner-block of
granite, which allowed of the insertion of a reed for about
two feet in an upward direction; and which the men were
to follow up.   I expressed my thanks to Mr. Perring, and
gave directions accordingly.   The place was rather less
confined, and more convenient for the object which I
had so anxiously in view, namely, to penetrate over the
chamber, yet it was still a most difficult operation, as the
passage was not much more than three feet in height,
the stones extremely large, and hard, and the whole
overhand work.   The Arabs can stand heat, but are
feeble workmen, and have neither proper tools, nor skill
for such undertakings.   We' had parties employed by
night and day for many weeks, which required constant superintendence.   I tried piece-work, without success; and but little progress was made, until quarry-
men arrived from the Mokattam, who understood their
business, and could use gunpowder; yet even then the
joints were obliged to be cut to get room for the blasting;
and the great fragments, immediately above the workmen, were afterwards drawn out with much difficulty,
and in many instances with considerable danger.   The
other party, employed on the southern side of the chamber, was soon withdrawn.   Owing to the idleness of the
Arabs, the boring rods in the King's Chamber were not
constantly turned, and a notch was made at the bottom
of the hole, in which the chisel snapped off at the depth

of five feet,—it was reported, upon granite. Nothing, therefore, remained but to cut through the stones for the chisel. The subterraneous chamber, and the passage proceeding from it to the south, were strictly examined, but without any other result, than the conviction that they were unfinished excavations; nor could the purpose, for which the passage had been intended, be discovered.

Some bones, and a skeleton, probably of a common Arab, wrapped up in coarse linen, were found amongst the stones near the Third Pyramid; and people were employed in carrying on the gallery, which M. Caviglia had made to the length of six feet, from the chasm to the northern front. Several strangers visited the works. Mr. Hill arrived in the evening.

### February 15th.

Reis, 7.        Men, 96.        Children, 85.
The same works were repeated.

The excavation for the chisel was begun in the King's Chamber. About fifteen feet of the northern air-channel had been cleared.

Litter and decayed forage were taken out from the place where the bones were discovered, at the Third Pyramid. The Adytum of the temple was cleared to its rocky foundation; it was seventeen feet below the top of the present wall, and was stained in places with red cement in which a pavement had been laid: no pavement or lining, however, remained, nor were any inscriptions or sculpture visible upon the enormous blocks, with which it was built; but a shallow square had been cut in the centre of the western side, and slight indications of pedestals appeared on the floor.

I examined the several pyramids with Mr. Hill; and, on arriving at the portcullis of the Second, we imagined that, if it was entirely taken out, access might be obtained through the vacancy or groove, in which it moved up, to other passages, and chambers, that might possibly exist in the higher part of the building. Had we extended our researches a few paces further, the great excavation across the horizontal passage would have shewn our mistake, for it was from twelve to fifteen feet high at the distance of twenty-three feet eight inches from the portcullis, and must, therefore, have intersected any passage that ascended at the usual angle. Not being aware of this circumstance, however, we lowered the portcullis, in order to break it, and, in doing so, endeavoured to shut in two of the Arabs, that they might work the harder to effect their escape; but no persuasion could induce them to remain, although Mr. Hill offered to stay with them; and the granite, owing to the confined situation, resisted all our efforts from without. Some men were therefore employed to cut grooves across it.

I was informed that M. Caviglia had arrived with a janissary to remove his baggage, but I did not see him.

### February 16th.

Reis, 7.      Men, 90.      Children, 82.

Great Pyramid.—King's Chamber.
——————— Davison's Chamber.
——————— Northern Air Channel.
Second Pyramid.—Portcullis.
——————— Lower Entrance.
Third Pyramid.—Interior.
——————— Boring.
——————— Excavation between the Temple and Pyramid.

Mr. Hill went to Cairo. Having ordered that the tomb, which had been occupied by M. Caviglia, should be cleaned out, and made fit for use; I was told that he had left behind him a quantity of clothes, furniture, and various other articles. These were given in charge to Giachino, his former servant, who said, that he had received directions to keep them till M. Caviglia's return, which he expected would be in about two months.

A large party was employed in removing the mound from the northern front of the Second Pyramid, in search of a lower entrance.

The gallery in the northern front of the Third Pyramid, was extended an additional six feet, and a tent was put up in the chasm, that Giachino might superintend the work by night. As there were no accounts, antient or modern, respecting the entrance of this pyramid, or of its having ever been opened, notwithstanding the attempts that from time to time had been made,[2] it was an object of the greatest curiosity, and I fully expected to discover the interior chambers and passages, by carrying on the gallery to the centre, and by afterwards sinking a large shaft to the foundation. I also ordered Paulo to bore for a passage in the lower chasm, behind the granite blocks that form the base of this pyramid.

### February 17th.

Reis, 7.    Men, 85.    Children, 65.

Great Pyramid.—King's Chamber.
——          Davison's Chamber.
——          Northern Air Channel.

[2] I was not then aware of the extract translated by Burckhardt from Edrisi, which will be afterwards alluded to.

EXCAVATIONS &c. AT THE BASE OF THE THIRD PYRAMID.

Published by J. Fraser, Regent Street.

In the course of the morning, Giachino reported that the men, employed at the northern air-channel, had arrived at a portcullis; but when the sand had been completely cleared out, the supposed portcullis was found to be the termination of the forced passage, (three feet, by two feet nine), made to the extent of thirty-seven feet, upon the air-channel, which continued nine, by nine and a half inches, (at about an angle of twenty-six) in the solid masonry. It was full of sand and stones, which, owing to the smallness of the aperture, and its inclined position, were with difficulty taken out, though various instruments were contrived for that purpose. For many days scarcely a bushel of sand was drawn up; but, by Mr. Hill's, and afterwards by Mr. Raven's perseverance, and with the assistance of the boring rods, above ninety feet of this small channel were entirely cleared, and ventilation restored to the pyramid.

Another groove was cut in the portcullis in the Second Pyramid. The sand was removed, in search of a shaft, below the cutting mentioned by M. Caviglia on 27th of January.[3] No shaft was discovered, but the

---

[3] M. Caviglia appears to have always entertained an idea that Hebrew characters were connected with the pyramids; for, in a letter to Mr. Hamilton, dated Sept. 21, 1818, is the following passage:—" La forme du premier (pyramid) exprime ce pentagramme, הנימה, qui est, constaté par les cinq lignes perpendiculaires, qui sont au dessus de la chambre, où il y a le sarcophage."

bottom of the rock had been excavated to form the lower part of a doorway, and the cutting beneath the hiero-glyphics marked the outline of the top. Similar works had been begun at the bottom of the rock under the

On the northern side.

inscription on the western side, and Mr. Birch's explanation of the characters leaves no doubt that entrances were intended. Al-though the operation was a failure as far as the original object was concerned, yet it led to the discovery of lines of the quarrying, by which the rock must have been levelled when the pyramid was constructed. They formed squares of about nine feet, and had been preserved under a depth of sand; but in other parts, where they had been exposed to the air, they were almost entirely effaced, which proved their great antiquity.

On the western side.⁴

⁴ The line of hieroglyphics, sculptured above the quarries levelled for the Second Pyramid, contains the names and titles of a functionary of the age of one of the Remeses, (the second, or third,) or, of one of the nine-teenth dynasty; he is named Maei, and is stated to be superintendent of a certain office* under Remeses (beloved of Amun), "in the abode

* The "bearers" of the . . . peculiar office undiscovered. The heron, a sieve, occasionally preceded by the lituus, form the phonetic group oⲥⲃⲁⳓ, "clear," "splendid," and are accompanied in the Egyptian ritual by the determinative of a disc shedding light, and elsewhere by

At the Third Pyramid the boring had got down seven feet five inches, and the gallery in the chasm had advanced about two feet. I gave up the operation between this pyramid and the temple on account of the great difficulty and danger attending the removal of the granite blocks, and of the little probability that existed of finding an entrance, at all events from the temple. In the evening Mr. Hill arrived with the unwelcome intelli-

of Haröeri, son of the superintendent of the carriers Bokenamûn, justified in Egypt."* The inscription underneath contains the name of his son Pöeri, "vivifying his name."† The names and titles of the same Maei appear in the hieroglyphics on the western side, with the variation of Chief of the Bearers, or Builders, in the abode of the Sun. Although, from the position in which they were found, it might be supposed that these characters were of the era of the pyramid, the whole mass of hieroglyphic evidence is against it. Were it not almost certain that the stone was removed in preparing for the base of the pyramid, the name and titles of the functionary might justify the supposition that he superintended the quarryings at a later period for the construction of a temple in honour of the god Re or Haröeri in the time of the eighteenth or nineteenth dynasties, long after the erection of the pyramids; but this does not appear to have been the case, and, from the sepulchral tenor of the inscription, it must be concluded that the site was at that epoch considered desirable for the excavation of Hypoges, or tombs, and that the name inscribed indicated the locality marked out by the beginning of a doorway for the vault of Maei. It is impossible to connect the comparatively complex name of Remeses in the inscription with those of the early dynasty, under which the pyramids were built. —Mr. BIRCH.

---

a symbolic eye. In one text Horus is said to illuminate the world with ⲟⲩⲃⲁⲁⲩ, "the splendour of his eyes." (Vide Champollion, Mon. de l'Égypte.) It frequently formed a sacerdotal title.

* The pure Land of Truth.
† A common sepulchral appellation of the relations of the deceased.

gence that Mr. Galloway and himself were going to
Alexandria; and that Mr. Perring, owing to important
business, would not be able to attend for some days.
At night Mr. Hill went round, and examined the works.

### February 18th.

Reis, 7.        Men, 128.        Children, 56.

| | |
|---|---|
| Great Pyramid.— | King's Chamber. |
| —— | Davison's Chamber. |
| —— | Northern Air-channel. |
| Second Pyramid.— | Portcullis. |
| —— | Lower Entrance. |
| —— | Quarries. |
| Third Pyramid.— | Interior. |
| —— | Boring. |

The morning was so extremely foggy, that the pyramids were quite obscured.   My time was occupied as
usual.

19th.—I went to Cairo early in the morning; where
I saw Mr. Galloway, who was on the point of setting out
for Alexandria, and also Mr. Perring, who was engaged
in laying down a railroad at Tourah, and was obliged,
therefore, to suspend for the present the survey, which
we had undertaken.   He gave me several useful admeasurements of the Great Pyramid.   Mr. Hill having
mentioned that a person, who had arrived at his house
from India, desired to go with me to the pyramids, I took
an opportunity of calling upon him, and had the pleasure
of his company on my return in the evening.   This gentleman, I was afterwards informed, was a Mr. Ashburner
from Bombay.

*February 20th.*

Reis, 6.        Men, 63.        Children, 36.
The same works were repeated.

The gallery at the Third Pyramid had been carried on about three feet, the boring nearly twelve. A Russian colonel, and four other strangers, paid me a visit.

*February 21st.*

Reis, 6.        Men, 90.        Children, 59.
The same works were repeated.

The works did not go on to my satisfaction in the King's and Davison's Chambers, notwithstanding that Paulo remained during the night in the Great Pyramid. I therefore ordered an agreement to be made for piece-work at twenty-two piastres per foot. Seventeen feet of the northern air-channel had been cleared. The centre of the southern front of the Great Pyramid was marked on the same level with the doorway on the northern, that an entrance might be searched for as far to the westward of the centre on that side, as the present doorway is to the eastward of the centre on the other, for I conceived it possible that a communication might proceed from a southern entrance. I had not at that time any idea that the stupendous masses of the pyramids were composed of solid masonry, and that, (with the exception of the King's, and Queen's Chambers, and the adjoining passages and chambers of construction afterwards discovered in this pyramid,) the apartments were invariably excavations in the solid rock. Indeed, after having ascertained the fact almost beyond the possibility of a doubt, it was difficult to believe it, or to comprehend an adequate motive for the construction of these magnificent buildings merely as sepulchral monuments over a tomb, unless it was the all-powerful influence of superstitious feelings.

The rubbish had been nearly removed from the base of the Second Pyramid. The two grooves in the portcullis were finished, and another was begun across them.

I measured the chasms on the northern front of the Third Pyramid, and directed that the excavations should be carried on by piece-work; and that, instead of daily pay, the men should receive a thousand piastres on arriving at the centre of the pyramid. There was a difficulty, however, in making this arrangement, because the same people did not regularly attend, and because those, who were employed, from their extreme poverty, required money for their daily subsistence.[5] Mr. Ashburner returned to Cairo.

[5] Whatever may have been the result of these operations, the villages of Koum el Eswith and of Cafr el Batran have been greatly benefited, not only by the daily receipt of more money than they ever before obtained, but by their exemption from public labour at an adjacent canal. In the present state of the population all labour must be compulsory, but the mode in which it is exacted is often extremely cruel, and the cause of great distress. When a public work is to be carried on, the people, or a considerable portion of them, are demanded by the Madyr of the district from the Sheiks of the villages, who make a selection at their own discretion, and are also obliged to attend in person. A system of injustice, bribery, and extortion is the natural consequence: the Mamoor (the officer under the Madyr), oppressing the Sheiks; and the Sheiks, in their turn, the defenceless people, who are reduced to the lowest state of misery. In many instances a guard is stationed to prevent the return of the people to their homes before the completion of the work; and as no respect is paid to age, sex, sickness, or poverty, the consequences on the infirm, from age or

*February 22d.*

Reis, 7.        Men, 96.        Children, 43.

Great Pyramid.—Excavation in southern front.
———        King's Chamber.
———        Davison's Chamber.
———        Northern Air-channel.
Second Pyramid.—Portcullis.

infancy, and the effects upon a beautiful and intelligent race of children, particularly in wet and cold situations and seasons, can scarcely
be imagined.    Yet, with all the advantages of regular wages, and
exemption from severe labour whilst employed at the pyramids, of
attention to their comfort, and to any little accidents that might occur,
and of medical aid and of food to the sick, and likewise of a positive
prohibition of severe measures, and of corporal punishment, these unhappy
people were totally insensible to the kindness shewn to them.    Indeed,
on the contrary, they practised every possible imposture and deceit
to obtain money, food, medicine, &c. &c.: and, at last, their insolence
and idleness arrived at such a pitch, that the only alternative was to
give up the work, or to have recourse to the usual means of coercion.
What might be effected by a long and continued exercise of rewards
and punishments, with power, at the same time, to enforce obedience,
and habits of industry, I know not; but, I am certain, that in the present state of things, no business can be carried on without the dread of
corporal punishment.    The children work with the greatest alacrity, and
appear susceptible of great improvement; but, with a few exceptions,
the men, from some cause or other, appear incapable of exertion,
and incorrigibly idle.    In justice to the Pacha, it must be confessed,
that he has established schools in every large town, and appears to be
extremely anxious to civilise his people; but the education of the boys
can have but little effect, while the female part of the population are
plunged in the grossest ignorance.    It has been well observed, that the
antient system of Egyptian superstition survived the repeated conquests
to which the country was subject, and at last yielded only to the
Christian dispensation; and it may be doubted whether the present
degraded and miserable condition of these people can ever be effectually improved, except by the same beneficial influence.

The excavation for a southern entrance in the Great Pyramid was begun at the distance of twenty-four feet westwards from the centre, and carried on to the depth of thirty feet, which was a work of considerable difficulty and labour, and was not finished till the 29th of May.[6] The stones were very large, and the half of each of them was keyed in under the upper layer, besides which, many of them were in slanting directions, although in horizontal courses; it became therefore necessary to break almost every block before it could be removed.[7] The mortar was nearly as hard as the stone itself, so that with Arab workmen, and common tools, it was a most tedious operation.  To obviate some of these difficulties, I ordered the people to get up twenty or thirty feet, and to cut perpendicularly down behind the stones; but very little advantage was gained in proportion to the increased

[6] The principal part of the blocks composing the pyramids were quarried from the rock on which they stand, and abound with fossil remains; but, for the casing of the exterior, for the lining of the passages, and for many other particular parts, they were brought from the Mokattam, and consisted of a compact limestone which contains few fossils, and is termed by geologists swine-stone.

[7] Mr. Perring observed, that the mortar used for the casing and lining of the passages was of lime only; that in the body of the pyramid it was composed of red brick, gravel, Nile earth, crushed granite, and calcareous stone, and of lime; and that for fillings in desert sand was employed in a grout of liquid mortar.

BRIDGE IN SOUTHERN DYKE.

Published by James Fraser, Regent Street.

number, which required to be removed. Towards the end of this work gunpowder was used with great effect.

A number of heavy blocks were taken away from the rubbish at the Second Pyramid; and an excavation for the base, on the western side, and near the north-western angle of that building, was carried across to the opposite cliff, under the hieroglyphics already alluded to.[8] At the Third Pyramid, the boring was discontinued at the depth of twenty-eight feet, which was then supposed to be below the foundation, although it afterwards proved to be seven feet above it. At one time a vacancy of two or three feet was perceived, most probably occasioned by a joint in the masonry. The stones of this pyramid are of an enormous size, particularly near the foundation.

When I was paying the people in the evening, Prince Pückler Muskau arrived, and requested to encamp in my enclosure; to this I did not consent, but directed a person to conduct his highness to the Great Tomb in the plain generally occupied by travellers; where he encamped. Captain Rowland and Lieutenant Campbell, of the East India Company's ship, Hugh Lindsay, then at Suez, paid me a visit.

The sand was cleared away under the bridge in the southern dyke, in order that it might be surveyed. It is evidently of great antiquity; the stones are remarkably large, and without carving or inscription of any sort. Other bridges are also mentioned, and may have been constructed in that part of the dyke which formerly extended across the plain, but at present only one has been discovered. This dyke is not a direct continuation of

[8] See page 160.

that near the Third Pyramid, which at first sight it appears to be. The whole plain to the foot of the mountains, from Saccara to Abou Reche, seems to have been formerly under cultivation, but, either from neglect of the antient canals, or from other causes, it is now covered with about nine feet of sand. The whole desert has evidently encroached upon the valley of Egypt, particularly from the westward; and there was probably little or no sand on the mountains at Gizeh, nor upon the plain beneath, when the pyramids were erected. An abundant supply of water must have been required for their construction, and also for the use of the workmen employed upon them; and as it can now be found in many places within a few feet of the surface, the land might be reclaimed without any great difficulty.

### February 23d.

Reis, 8.　　　Men, 106.　　　Children, 71.

Great  Pyramid.—Excavation in southern front.

—　　　　　　King's Chamber.

—　　　　　　Davison's Chamber.

—　　　　　　Northern Air-channel.

Second Pyramid.—Portcullis.

—　　　　　　Lower Entrance.

—　　　　　　Quarries.

—　　　　　　Excavation for base at north-western angle.

Third  Pyramid.—Interior.

Bridge near southern dyke.

Sphinx.　　　　Boring.

In going round the works, I particularly examined the excavation over the passage in the Second Pyramid. It is connected with the opening in the centre of the northern front, by which it is supposed that the caliphs en-

Roy<sup>l</sup> Hughe Lith<sup>rs</sup> to the Queen                                    F. Arundale lith

SECOND PYRAMID — UPPER ENTRANCE.

Published by James Fraser, Regent St.

tered, and in which Signor Belzoni worked, until he was obliged to desist from the loose and irregular construction of the building. In many parts the stones have collapsed, and a good deal of rain-water and drifted sand have penetrated, from time to time, from the north-west, through the loose joints of the masonry. The excavation must have been made with great difficulty, and Signor Belzoni's statement was not exaggerated, for when I attempted, on the 10th of March, to work in this place, the men hesitated to proceed; and, as there was no great chance of success, I gave it up. It is probable that most, if not all of these magnificent tombs, have been violated soon after their erection; but it will be afterwards seen that the three larger pyramids, and many of the smaller, were subsequently opened by Mussulmen, and apparently about the same time. Signor Belzoni found the regular entrance, concealed under a mound, which is now higher than the top of it, and obstructed only by loose stones and sand,[9] and it is remarkable how well the forms of the pyramids are calculated for the concealment of an entrance near the centre of their fronts, as the loose stones and rubbish produced by decay, or by violence, chiefly accumulate over these parts. I also observed that the lower portcullis in this pyramid, which had been forced out of its socket, moved up into a solid groove; and, concluding that the portcullis in the upper passage was similarly constructed, I gave up the idea of its removal, and raised it to a sufficient height, so that a person could conveniently enter. Signor Belzoni had only lifted it eight inches, which I ordered to be marked.

[9] See Athanasi's statement in Appendix.

I began to bore through the shoulder of the Sphinx, in order to ascertain whether or not it was hollow. The head seems to have been painted red, and upon the top of it there was a cleft four or five feet deep.

I called on Prince Pückler Muskau, who was encamped in the plain, with a considerable suite of the Pacha's people, janissaries, camels, horses, &c. In the evening he sent a message by his physician that he would pay me a visit on the following day.

### February 24th.

Reis, 7.        Men, 99.        Children, 66.

Great Pyramid.—Excavation on southern front.
——          King's Chamber.
——          Davison's Chamber.
——          Northern Air-channel.
Second Pyramid.— Lower Entrance.
——          Excavation for base at north-western angle.
——          Quarries.
Third Pyramid.—Interior.
——          Excavation for base at north-eastern angle.
Bridge in the southern dyke.
Sphinx.          Boring.

I discharged Selim at his own request, and sent a letter by him to Colonel Campbell.

Some desert sand, probably fillings in, had been found in the excavation made for the chisel in the King's Chamber. The Northern Air-channel was given up, as the men were unable to break, or to draw out the stones; with which it was filled. The depth of the boring at the Sphinx was nine feet eight inches.

The prince paid me a long visit. Mr. Perring and Mr. Mash (another able engineer) arrived. I went round the works late at night, and met the prince and his retinue returning to his tents.[1] The excavation for the survey at the north-eastern angle of the Third Pyramid was commenced.

### February 25th.

Reis, 7.        Men, 107.        Children, 85.

Great Pyramid.—Excavation in southern front.

——        King's Chamber.

——        Davison's Chamber.

Second Pyramid.—Lower entrance.

——        Excavation for base at north-western angle.

Third Pyramid.—Interior.

——        Excavation for base at north-eastern angle.

Bridge in southern dyke.

Sphinx.        Boring.

I had made an arrangement with a Reis from Kerdassee to remove the stones and rubbish from the centre of the northern front of the Great Pyramid in fifteen or twenty-five days, as the work might turn out, for two thousand piastres, the Reis to find all the tools except-

---

[1] The echoes near the pyramids are very surprising. They may be attributed to the number of subterraneous passages, and to the magnitude, forms, and relative positions of the buildings themselves. The vultures, which harbour upon them at night, bark like watch-dogs. (*Latrator anubis.*) Neither the Maltese, Turks, nor the Arabs, would go out by themselves after dark, from a dread (according to their own account) of lions, and of other wild beasts, but, in fact, from superstitious apprehension; so that, when either of the Maltese went at night to the pyramids, it was necessary to send two Arabs, as one would not come back alone. The contrast was striking, when an Englishman, Jack, who afterwards entered my service, went by himself every evening, for five months together, with his stick and his bottle, to spend the night in the Third Pyramid.

ing crowbars; but I afterwards broke off this agreement, as I thought it would probably interfere with the
other works, and lead to quarrels and disputes between
the villages. I requested the Sheiks of Koum el Eswith
and of Cafr el Batram to undertake this operation; they
refused to do so, but offered to superintend the work at
my expense, which, of course I declined. I had great
hopes of success in the excavation above Davison's
Chamber, and, upon the whole, every thing went on
well. In going round to the several works, I met at the
Second Pyramid Prince Pückler Muskau, who called to
take leave before he set out for Upper Egypt. Whilst
he was there, I sent my Arab (Darè) into the pyramid,
to find out, if possible, the entrance by listening to the
blows struck with a large hammer upon different parts
of the pavement; but the solid masonry, with which the
upper part of the subterraneous passage was closed, prevented any favourable result. In a short time we arrived
at the granite blocks in the lower part of the pyramid;
and a vacancy between two of them appeared to be the
entrance closed up with calcareous masonry, particularly
as the adjoining stones to the eastward shewed exactly
like a break, and gave to the granite blocks the appearance of a portal. The rubbish covered the western block,
which, I imagined, broke back in the same manner. As
I concluded that I had at last discovered the entrance,
I sent after the prince, who had gone to his tents. Fortunately he had not leisure to return, for immediately
afterwards I perceived that the supposed entrance was
filled up with rock; and that the granite was the revetment mentioned by Herodotus. It has been already
observed that this work had not been properly set out

at the commencement. It had now become extremely encumbered, the removal of the large stones from the higher part of the mound was attended with some risk; and continual attention was necessary to prevent accidents. Indeed, after all, a considerable quantity of rubbish was left upon the face of the pyramid.

26*th.* —I went to Cairo in the morning, and returned with Lieutenant Campbell, of the Hugh Lindsay, to dinner.

### February 27th.

Reis, 7.       Men, 122.       Children, 81.

Great Pyramid. — Excavation in southern front.
——       King's Chamber.
——       Davison's Chamber.
Second Pyramid. — Lower entrance.
——       Excavation for base at north-western angle.
Third Pyramid. — Interior.
——       Excavation for base at north-eastern angle.
Bridge in the southern dyke.
Sphinx.       Boring near the shoulder, and near the tail.

Mr. Campbell informed me, that in the preceding spring he went to the top of the Second Pyramid in company with an English traveller, Mr. Faber; and that, as the Arabs would not shew him the way, (although they subsequently followed him,) he found the ascent very difficult, owing to a great quantity of loose rubbish, and also to the projection, and slippery surface of that part of the casing, which yet remained. The joints of the casing were horizontal; and the projecting angles of the stones, which were not of a very large size, had been

finished down from the top.[2]   The western side was
the highest; and a large stone on the apex had been
displaced, possibly by lightning, but more probably
by human violence: the platform was about nine feet
square.

The boring in the shoulder of the Sphinx had penetrated sixteen feet.  I gave up the excavation at the
bridge in the Southern Dyke, until Mr. Perring was ready
to survey it, on account of the great difficulty of keeping
out the loose sand.  It was composed of two horizontal
stones; the northern was found to be twenty-two feet in
length, and six feet six inches in depth.  The length
of the bridge was eight feet nine inches; its breadth,
twenty-seven feet eight inches.  Three tiers of very large
blocks had been uncovered.  At the bottom of the rubbish at the northern front of the Second Pyramid, a
stratum, chiefly consisting of desert sand, and about four
feet thick, appeared to mark the first attempt to open the
pyramid, and some black spots upon its surface seemed to
have been occasioned by fire.  No other distinct stratum
occurred; but the remainder was an accumulation of
large blocks of stone and of rubbish.  The lower tier,
revetted with granite, had been forced apparently in
search of an entrance; but the pavement, as far as I
could observe, had remained untouched.  Two masons
arrived from the citadel to cut through the blocks of
granite, but they entirely failed, and returned on the
following day to Cairo.

I sent a message to Colonel Campbell by the lieu-

---

[2] They have been worked in the same way in the propylæa of the
Great Temple of Karnac.

F. Arundale del.

VIEW OF COL. CAMPBELL'S TOMB.

Published by J. Fraser, Regent Street.

tenant of the Hugh Lindsay, to express my regret that the tomb near the Sphinx, in which he took a particular interest, had not been cleared out, and to offer to complete it. He gave his consent, and desired to share in the expense, which I declined, but requested him to inform M. Caviglia of the circumstance, as I did not choose to interfere, on my own account, with any of the excavations, which that gentleman had undertaken in his search for mummies.

### February 28th.

Reis, 7.      Men, 95.      Children, 51.

Great Pyramid.—Excavation on southern front.
——      Excavation on northern front.
——      King's Chamber.
——      Davison's Chamber.
Second Pyramid.—Lower Entrance.
——      Excavation for base at north-western angle.
Third Pyramid.—Interior.
——      Excavation for base at north-eastern angle.
Sphinx.      Boring near the shoulder, and near the tail.
Campbell's Tomb.

The morning was cold and foggy, and at first every object, even the gigantic pyramids, were totally obscured; but as the atmosphere cleared up, the scene from the Sphinx became singularly beautiful. The picturesque forms of the women and children carrying baskets of sand upon their heads on the undulating mounds near Campbell's Tomb, the finely broken foreground extending to the rocks at the Southern Dyke, and the enormous masses of the ruined temple on the rising ground before the Second Pyramid were in the finest breadth of light and shade. For a time the lofty apex of the Second Pyramid shone alone in the clear blue sky, (like the top-gallant sails of a ship of war,) far above the clouds that shrouded its mighty bulk, which by degrees slowly appeared in all its grandeur; and soon afterwards the southern front of the Great Pyramid, glittering with the morning sunbeams, was displayed in full majesty as the light vapours melted away from its enormous space.

Owing to the oblateness of their forms, the want of proper objects of comparison, the proportionate small-ness of the stones, with which they are built, and many other adventitious circumstances, the exaggerated and undefined expectations of travellers are often disappointed in the hasty survey generally taken of these monuments; and they are consequently considered rude and misshapen masses of coarse masonry, without symmetry or beauty, and alone worthy of notice from their extraordinary size. A more deliberate examination, however, never fails to alter and correct these opinions; and it was universally acknowledged by those who remained for any length of time at Gizeh, that the more carefully and frequently they were inspected, the more extraordinary their gran-deur appeared, and also the striking effects which under the varying influence of the atmosphere they continually presented. Pre-eminent in dimensions and antiquity over all other buildings in the world, they are alike admirable for the excellence of their masonry, the skill and science displayed in their construction, and the imposing majesty of their simple forms.

As the lower entrance into the Second Pyramid could not be discovered, fires were lighted in the reascending passage, but it was so effectually closed up, that we did not derive any advantage from the smoke.

Several Turkish and Egyptian officers came to the pyramids in the morning; and in the evening a number of Arab Sheiks and Wahabees also arrived. They remained some time at the tents, and in the course of conversation remarked, that I did not make the men work hard enough, and dismissed them too soon at night.

*March 1st.*

Reis, 7.        Men, 112.        Children, 89.

The same works were repeated.

Lord Lindsey and Mr. Ramsey paid me a visit, inspected the several works, and returned to Cairo in the evening.

Some stones were taken up from the pavement at the Second Pyramid, but without success. The base at the north-eastern angle of the Third was sufficiently cleared for the survey. The excavation at the northern front of the Great Pyramid proceeded rapidly, but, as the regular passage led to the subterraneous chamber, I did not expect to find a lower entrance, unless it conducted to the apartment mentioned by Herodotus. The ramp, or inclined end of the granite block at the corner of Davison's Chamber was discovered, which confirmed me in the idea that there was a large apartment over it, and that the height of, Davison's Chamber was regulated by the slope of the roof in the great gallery.

We were disturbed during the night by the firing of guns, music, &c., and various other riotous demonstrations of joy in the villages on the plain below our tents, in consequence of the celebration of a wedding.

### March 2d.

Reis, 7.        Men, 110.        Children, 94.

The same works were repeated.

I again carefully examined the excavation across the horizontal passage in the Second Pyramid, and also Belzoni's Chamber. In the latter, square holes like the beginning of air-channels had been cut on the northern and southern sides;[3] and others below them marked out with red lines. If a northern air-channel had likewise been begun on the exterior, it might have been a guide for the forced passage. As I conceived that it was possible to find out, by means of the boring-rods, the lower entrance of the Second Pyramid, the operations carried on at the Sphinx were suspended, and the hole made near the shoulder, about twenty-five feet and' a half in depth, was plugged up. The excavation for the base at the north-western angle of the Second Pyramid was finished. The chisel in the King's Chamber was found to have been broken upon a calcareous stone, and not upon granite; all hopes therefore of an apartment in that direction were at an end.

Dr. Cummins came to the pyramids. The Englishman mentioned in the note page 171, arrived: he was indefatigable in his exertions, directed most successfully several operations during the day, and passed every night for

---

[3] Mr. Perring imagined that they might have been used in the construction of the roof.

five months in superintending the Arabs in the Third
Pyramid.   A number of Bedouins came to the works in
the course of the day: this was often the case, as the
pyramids may be considered close to the high road
leading from the Faioum to the Delta, and to Alexandria.
There are shorter routes, but this track, by skirting the
cultivated ground, is more convenient for camels, flocks,
&c.   Nothing could exceed the surprise of these savages
at hearing the ticking of a watch, and particularly at
the lucifer matches.   After a time, however, the Arab
girls found out the use of the latter, and were very eager
to have them.

*March 3d.*

Reis, 7.        Men, 124.        Children, 106.

Great Pyramid.—Excavation of southern front.
——            Excavation of northern front.
——            Davison's Chamber.
——            Queen's Chamber.
——            Passage to Queen's Chamber.
Second Pyramid.—Boring for Lower Entrance.
——            Belzoni's Chamber.
——            Passage.
Third Pyramid.—Interior.
Campbell's Tomb.

The janissary Osman had a dreadful attack of ophthalmia, which obliged me to send him into Cairo the
next day.   Another operation was begun in the passage
leading to the Queen's Chamber.   The upper stone,
which formed the step, was let in on one side under the
superstructure; but the stones beneath it were only
keyed in so that a small reed could be inserted for
several feet along their sides, and they appeared, there-

fore, to conceal the entrance into another passage. We began to remove the great block under the recess in the Queen's Chamber, and the whole of that apartment was carefully examined. The people commenced boring for a lower entrance at the Second Pyramid, and a party under an intelligent reis, carefully sounded Belzoni's Chamber, and the passage leading to it. The various chasms and imperfections in the rock, through which this passage was cut, were made good with masonry, and the sides had been stuccoed, and painted. On the sides of the chamber (cut out of the solid rock) a sparry secretion appeared, similar to that on the walls of the Queen's Chamber; although, it is to be observed, that the latter are composed of masonry. About half the floor from the eastern end of Belzoni's Chamber was rock, the remainder was a pavement of two tiers of calcareous stone, excepting some blocks of granite at the western end, in which the sarcophagus had been sunk.

*March 4th.*

Reis, 7.    Men, 152.    Children, 114.

The same works were repeated.

A stone in the southern side, and exactly opposite the entrance of the Queen's Chamber, was broken into; the joints appeared to indicate a door, but nothing was discovered. The gallery had arrived within thirty-seven feet of the centre of the Third Pyramid, when strong blasts of air were distinctly felt in it from the south, although the excavation was on the northern front. This was invariably the case when a Kamseen (southerly wind) was prevalent. As the joints were too close, and the bulk of the masonry too great, for the wind to penetrate through the building, I can only account for these currents by supposing, that they arose from the lower excavations which were afterwards discovered in the interior of the pyramid, and which had' a communication with the regular entrance; but then these excavations were distant from the gallery, and the regular entrance was also on the northern side, and completely buried under blocks of granite, rubbish, and sand. Similar gusts of wind were afterwards very perceptible in the gallery made from the northern front to the centre of the Fourth Pyramid; but the joints of this building were more open, and its bulk much less. I again examined the hieroglyphics on the rocks near the Second Pyramid.

*March 5th.* — I went to Cairo and got another janissary in the room of Osman. I saw Mr. Perring and Mr. Mash, who agreed to return with me to the Pyramids on the following day; I also called upon Col. Campbell, and informed him how matters went on at the tomb.

### March 6th.

Reis, 7.        Men, 137.        Children, 112.

The same works were repeated.

I left Cairo in the afternoon with Mr. Perring and Mr. Mash, in a most violent kamseen wind, by which, in crossing the Nile, we were exposed to some danger. The sky was completely obscured with sand, and the sun appeared as if eclipsed; the blast was hot, and affected the eyes most painfully.   Upon our arrival we examined the works, which had gone on well.[*]

*March 7th.*

Reis, 7.        Men, 99.        Children, 88.

Great Pyramid.—Excavation on southern front.

———    Excavation on northern front.

———    Davison's Chamber.

———    Queen's Chamber.

———    Passage to Queen's Chamber.

Second Pyramid.—Boring for Lower Entrance.

———    Belzoni's Chamber.

———    Passage.

Third Pyramid.—Interior.

Campbell's Tomb.

Fourth Pyramid.—Preparing to bore.

It rained early in the morning.   The janissary Achmet arrived.   The Second Pyramid was surveyed; the Arabic inscription could not to be discovered in Belzoni's Chamber.   A party was employed in clearing out the lower passages.   The sarcophagus in Belzoni's Chamber was minutely examined; it was composed of granite, and of the finest workmanship; the lid was made to slide on into a dovetail, which it exactly fitted, and it had been fastened by two pins, which went up into holes

---

[*] As several of the Arabs were attacked with ophthalmia, I applied to Naylor Bey, who had arrived from England for the purpose of establishing an Ophthalmic Hospital: the Pacha immediately gave him the rank and decorations of a Bey, and a house called Ater El Nebbi, near Fostat, for an establishment; he also sent a ship of war to bring his family from Europe. From some cause or other, however, the establishment was broken up, and, I believe, that Mr. Naylor returned to Europe.

VIEW of the PYRAMIDS S. of the THIRD PYRAMID.

Published by J Fraser, 215, Regent St.

in the lid, and dropped into corresponding holes in the sarcophagus when the lid was in its place, so that with-out having been broken it could not have been removed. Some resinous substance, which I brought away, was found at the bottom of these holes.

The Fourth Pyramid [5] (the middle one of the three south of the third) was prepared for boring by removing the stones from the top of it, as I expected to find the sepulchral chamber by penetrating through it. It was much dilapidated on the northern front; but the masonry on the other sides was very fine, and the stones exceed-ingly large, and apparently of great antiquity. Like the sixth (the one to the westward), it had been built in regular stages. The other works, particularly those of the Great Pyramid, were also attended to; and a scaffolding was put up in the great passage, that the stone at the northern end might be examined. It proved to be calcareous, but from its size, and situation, was an object of interest.

### March 8th.

Reis, 7.      Men, 122.      Children, 88.

Great  Pyramid.—Excavation of southern front.
———      Excavation of northern front.
———      Davison's Chamber.
———      Queen's Chamber.

[5] The three large pyramids are sufficiently distinguished. The other pyramids mentioned in this book were numbered as follows: The Fourth, the central of the three southward of the Third; the Fifth, that to the eastward of the Fourth; the Sixth, that to the westward of the Fourth; the Seventh, the most northern of the three to the eastward of the Great Pyramid; the Eighth, that to the southward of the Seventh; the Ninth, that to the southward of the Eighth.

Great  Pyramid.—Passage to Queen's Chamber.
Second Pyramid.—Boring for Lower Entrance.
————            Passage.
Third  Pyramid.—Interior.
Campbell's Tomb.
Fourth Pyramid.—Preparing to bore.

After having gone, as usual, round the several works,
I assisted Mr. Perring and Mr. Mash in measuring the
Second Pyramid.

### *March 9th.*

Reis, 7.     Men, 140.     Children, 112.
Great  Pyramid.—Excavation in southern front.
————            Excavation in northern front.
————            Davison's Chamber.
————            Queen's Chamber.
————            Passage to Queen's Chamber.
————            Large Stone in Great Passage.
Second Pyramid.—Boring of Lower Entrance.
Third  Pyramid.—Interior.
Campbell's Tomb.
Fourth Pyramid.—Preparing to bore.

We again inspected the pyramids, and also the ruins
to the eastward of the great one, particularly two in-
tersecting passages, which were afterwards excavated.
Having entered the Great Pyramid, we directed our attention to the Queen's Chamber, and to the large stone in
the northern end of the great passage.  It had a sparry
secretion, like that on the walls of the Queen's, and on
the sides of Belzoni's Chamber, and was different from
those in the other parts of the passage.  Whilst proceeding to the King's Chamber, Mr. Perring and Mr. Mash
were sent for to attend a council in Cairo.  At the

HIEROGLYPHICS NEAR THE SECOND PYRAMID.

Published by James Fraser, Regent Street.

Second Pyramid, the operations in the horizontal passage were given up, and the lower entrance was found in the pavement about forty feet from the base of the pyramid. It was completely filled up with solid masonry, closely jointed and cemented: the first stone was ten feet long, and the others six, or seven. I ordered parts of them to be removed so as to admit of a passage; but, on account of their hardness, confined situation, the badness of the tools (merely picks), and the unskilfulness of the Arabs, very little was effected before the arrival of the men from the Mokattam quarries.

Colonel Rainsford paid me a visit.

I measured the excavation in the Third Pyramid, and ordered four remarkable stones to be removed from the higher part of the western front, as I thought that they might conceal an air-channel.

### March 10th.

Reis, 7.       Men, 136.       Children, 121.

Great Pyramid.—Excavation in southern front.
——            Excavation in northern front.
——            Davison's Chamber.
——            Queen's Chamber.
——            Passage to Queen's Chamber.
——            Large Stone in Great Passage.
Second Pyramid.—Lower Entrance.
——            Excavating in forced Passage.
Third Pyramid.—Interior.
Campbell's Tomb.
Fourth Pyramid.—Preparing to bore.

Several pieces of bone and of decayed mummy-board were found in the square of Campbell's Tomb, also some fragments of stone inscribed with hieroglyphics. The hieroglyphics were in several places covered with plaster; the stone, therefore, must have previously belonged to some other building before the fragments were employed as fillings in, in this. Some men were set to work in the excavation across the horizontal passage in the Second Pyramid; but the masonry was so insecure that they were afraid to proceed. In the evening I went round the works with Jack.

### *March* 11*th.*

Reis, 7.        Men, 152.        Children, 126.

Great Pyramid.—Excavation of southern front.
——            Excavation of northern front.
——            Davison's Chamber.
——            Queen's Chamber.
——            Passage to Queen's Chamber.
——            Large Stone in Great Passage.
Second Pyramid.—Lower Entrance.
Third Pyramid.—Interior.
Campbell's Tomb.
Fourth Pyramid.—Preparing to bore.

Bones, earthenware, and small pieces of leaf gold, were brought out of Campbell's Tomb. One of the fragments of earthenware was handed to a boy, who, instead of placing it with the other things that had been discovered, put it into his dress; I immediately took it from him, and directed it to be preserved. In the afternoon I went back to look for this fragment, when it was missing. The sherd was positively good for nothing, but I thought it my duty to insist on its being restored; I therefore sent off all the people, and, in about an hour, I ascertained that the boy, from whom it was taken, had destroyed it in revenge. I directed that he should be sent to the Sheik, and not be allowed to work again, and I dismissed the reis from the tomb, who ought to have protected my property, or rather that of the Pacha, as every thing found belonged to his highness. At this time the gallery went on but slowly in the Third Pyramid, on account of the extreme hardness and solidity of part of its construction. It is built apparently in stages, and with two different kinds of masonry, which are both excellent; but the better sort, composed of very finely jointed stones, has been covered over by work of a looser construction.

M. Fresnell, attended by M. Massara, the French dragoman, came and entered the Second Pyramid.

12*th*.—I again carried the level of the entrance on the northern front of the Great Pyramid round to the excavation on the southern side, and also marked out the exact centre to prevent any mistake in searching for a southern entrance.[6]

### *March* 13*th*.

Reis, 7.        Men, 154.        Children, 123.

The same works were repeated.

Osman the janissary returned to his duty, which I reported to the British consul, and expressed a desire

---

[6] I received a letter from Mr. Galloway, containing an application from M. Caviglia to be again employed, which I answered on the following morning, expressing my regret that I could not accede to his request. My letter was addressed by mistake to Mr. Sloane, as the one, which I received, was either endorsed by that gentleman, or forwarded by Mr. Piozan as coming from him.

to keep Achmet also, as I had so many operations in hand.

I measured the lower entrance of the Second Pyramid, and sent the details to Mr. Perring.

I was informed by Abd El Ardi (the most intelligent and active of the reis), that there was a shaft, containing several sarcophagi, about five yards from the northern side of Campbell's tomb, and that it had been recently opened by some men from Koum el Eswith. I determined, therefore, not to excavate this shaft, unless it communicated with the fosse surrounding the Tomb, which was afterwards found not to be the case. Abd El Ardi also told me, that he had himself pointed out to M. Caviglia Campbell's Tomb, having found it too large for excavation on his own account.

The Arabs had made so little progress in the lower entrance of the Second Pyramid, that I determined to await the arrival of the stone-masons. The boring had been begun at the Fourth Pyramid; and several stones were removed at the Sixth to prepare it also for the same operation. The whole of the top, and part of the northern front of this edifice, had been taken down by the Pacha, that the materials might be sent to Alexandria. Several stones from the Third Pyramid had been removed for the same purpose, but, owing to the want of machinery and of skill, and to the depth of the sand, the Pacha had been unable to take them away. Indeed, their removal is impossible, unless a regular road be made for the purpose.

*March 14th.*

Reis, 7.          Men, 134.          Children, 127.

Great Pyramid.—Excavation in southern front.
——          Excavation in northern front.
——          Davison's Chamber.
——          Queen's Chamber.
——          Passage to Queen's Chamber.
——          Large stone in Great Passage.
Third Pyramid.—Interior.
Campbell's Tomb.
Fourth Pyramid.—Boring.
Sixth Pyramid.—Preparing to bore.
Passages to the eastward of the Great Pyramid.

In the morning, several officers, who had come from India, and, soon afterwards, Mr. Perring, Mr. Hill, and Mr. Mash arrived.

We examined the works, particularly those in the Great Pyramid, where several admeasurements were taken. I began to clear out the passages to the east of the Great Pyramid, which were examined on the 9th instant. They were excavations in the rock almost due north and south, the southern entrance not being very far distant from an extensive pit, or quarry, of an oblong form, extending north-east and south-west. I could not perceive any foundations near them. These passages had the usual angle, and nearly the same dimensions, as those in the pyramids,[7] and were exceedingly well cut, with grooves and fittings for doorways. The one from the south extended about thirty-eight feet; that from the north passed under it to the extent of sixty-five feet.

---

[7] The details of these passages will be given in the Appendix.

The lower end of the latter passage had not been finished, but was roughly chiselled in the rock, in which it abruptly ended, without any shaft or exit. A shaft, however, descended from the surface of the ground to the inter-sections of the two passages. These excavations may have been intended for a tomb, and, if finished, would probably have been covered by a pyramid. The oblong pit or quarry may have been the cause of their having been abandoned. The passage, however, from the south is not easily accounted for.

In the evening, all the officers went away except Mr. Rogers, who remained for the night.

### *March 15th.*

Reis, 7.      Men, 126.      Children, 133.

Great  Pyramid.—Excavation in southern front.
——      Excavation in northern front.
——      Davison's Chamber.
——      Queen's Chamber.
——      Passage to Queen's Chamber.
——      Large Stone in Great Passage.
Third  Pyramid.—Interior.
——      Stones on the western front.
Campbell's Tomb.
Fourth Pyramid.—Boring.
Sixth   Pyramid.—Preparing to bore.
Passages eastward of Great Pyramid.

Mr. Perring and Mr. Mash measured the base of the Second Pyramid. Mr. Hill removed the stones on the western front of the Third; they were very large, and in all probability key-stones for the revetment of the upper part of the pyramid; but nothing was discovered.

The excavation for the lower entrance of the Second Pyramid was resumed.

Mr. Rogers, Mr. Perring, and Mr. Hill returned to Cairo.

It was this morning reported, that on the 11th instant (Saturday), ten men, who were employed on the southern front of the Great Pyramid, upon being called to their work at the customary hour in the afternoon, sat down, and refused to proceed, notwithstanding the authority of the reis, and of Jack, who superintended the work, and that six of the men had not returned since that day. I directed that these men should not be again employed, and accordingly read over their names to the people at pay-time, in the evening, and, having sent for the Sheik of their village (Koum El Eswith), I informed him of the circumstance. He engaged that the men should be punished. I then told him, that, notwithstanding the repeated representations of the janissaries, I had hitherto strictly forbidden any harsh measures; but, since the people were insensible to good treatment, the only alternative left was either to give up the undertaking, or to allow them to be dealt with in the usual manner. I added, that I was determined to carry on the work, and that the change of treatment was to be considered as the necessary consequence of the misconduct of the people, and directly contrary to my own wishes and inclination. After this I had no complaints, and the works went on better. Of course I took good care that no abuse was made of this most unpleasant expedient.

*March 16th.*

Reis, 7.  Men, 117.  Children, 111.

Great  Pyramid.—Excavation in Southern Front.

—— Excavation in Northern Front.

—— Davison's Chamber.

—— Queen's Chamber.

—— Passage to Queen's Chamber.

—— Two Borings in Passage to Queen's Chamber.

—— Large Stone in Great Passage.

Third  Pyramid.—Interior.

Campbell's Tomb.

Fourth Pyramid.—Boring.

Sixth  Pyramid.— Preparing to Bore.

Passages eastward of the Great Pyramid.

I assisted Mr. Mash in taking the dimensions of the Third Pyramid. The boring at the Fourth was given up at the depth of eight or ten feet, as the stones were so loose that they would not retain water, and as the work was attended with great difficulty. For these reasons the removal of the stones from the top of the Sixth Pyramid was relinquished. The excavation at the passages eastward of the Great Pyramid was finished.

*March 17th.*

Reis, 3.  Men, 41.  Children, 1.

Great  Pyramid.—Excavation in Southern Front.

—— Excavation in Northern Front.

—— Davison's Chamber.

—— Two Borings in Passage to Queen's Chamber.

Third  Pyramid.—Interior.

Fourth  Pyramid.—Interior.

This day being the commencement of Beiram, very few people came, although I offered double pay as an inducement; and several of the works were, in consequence, suspended.

As the boring had not succeeded, I directed Jack to carry a gallery to the centre of the Fourth Pyramid, commencing ten feet eastward from the middle of the northern front, and at about three feet above the base.

After examining the works, I set out with Mr. Mash for Abou Rëche. These ruins are mentioned by M. Caviglia, and also by Mr. Wilkinson, and are situated about six miles to the north of Gizeh, on a high range of desert mountains, rendered conspicuous by white cliffs. We passed between the hills and the cultivated ground upon a plain, which must have been formerly under tillage; for, notwithstanding the depth of barren sand, a scanty vegetation might be here and there observed, particularly near a mound called Kom Achmar, the site of an antient town or village.

From the range, upon which the ruins of Abou Rëche are situated, a rocky promontory extends almost across the plain to a grove of palm-trees on the verge of the cultivated ground, and is covered towards the north with a large mass of brickwork; whilst the western and southern sides continue in a natural state, and do not exhibit the smallest vestige of any building, or foundation. The remains of inclined passages, which probably led to sepulchral excavations, are visible; but the whole is much dilapidated. A considerable part of the materials have been taken away for modern purposes, and the remainder will, no doubt, by degrees share the same fate. The bricks are unburnt, and of large dimensions like those at Illahoon, and at Howara, and are well made, but do not contain any straw: they should be

examined, as some of them may have been impressed
with a cartouche.

On a sandy plain to the northward of the promontory,
a small village, called Abou El Wali (Father of Bricks),
is surrounded with mounds of broken pottery and rubbish,
which mark the situation of a more considerable place.
After crossing this plain, we ascended by a winding path
amongst rocky hills, where antient tombs had been excavated, and proceeded to the objects of our research, along
a broad causeway, which extended in a south-westerly
direction.

The principal ruin consists of a few courses of masonry, forming a square of three hundred and forty-four
feet.  An entrance on the northern side, has the appearance of a road into a quarry, and descends to a large
quadrangular space, extending east and west, which, as
well as the passage, is at present entirely uncovered.
This excavation appears to have been made on a larger
scale than was afterwards found requisite, and to have
been built up with very large blocks.  They appear to be
very antient, and to have been quarried upon the spot:
many of them are scattered about; and others remain
suspended as it were against the sides, particularly towards
the eastern and western ends at a considerable height,
which shews that the apartment must have been lofty.
Two or three smaller square foundations of granite, and
those of a larger building upon an eminence are also to
be observed; and the ground is every where covered with
rubbish, broken pottery, and with the chippings of granite
blocks, that have been cut up for the purposes of removal.
From the decomposition of the latter material it has been
supposed that these buildings are of greater antiquity

than those at Gizeh; but I consider that the comparative smallness of the pieces, and their peculiarly exposed situation to the corroding air of the desert, will sufficiently account for their decay: besides, it is to be observed, that at this place the large masses of granite appear sound and entire, although the surface may have scaled off; and, also, that small fragments may be found near the Third Pyramid at Gizeh completely perished. Granite is known to be of different qualities, and one species is termed disintegrating, from its fragile texture. The stone, however, in both these instances, appears to be of the same quality; but it is evident that neither granite nor basalt can resist the action of the desert sand.

The valley to the eastward, and immediately below the cliffy side of the mountain, seems to contain antient remains, which I had not an opportunity of examining; but I hope to receive a detailed account from Mr. Perring, who has undertaken to survey them, in time for insertion in the Appendix. I have already mentioned that we ascended by a causeway from the north-east; we returned by another on the contrary side of the mountain, which had at first a south-westerly direction, and then turned to the south-east. We arrived at Gizeh in a heavy shower of rain. In going round the works we were informed by the Arabs that there were other ruins still further to the northward, but we could not obtain any positive information about them.

### *March* 18*th.*

Reis, 7.    Men, 109.    Children, 98.

Great Pyramid.—Excavation of southern front.

—— Excavation of northern front.

Great   Pyramid.—Davison's Chamber.
———               Queen's Chamber.
———               Passage to Queen's Chamber.
———               Two borings in passage to Queen's Chamber.
———               Large stone in Great Passage.
Second Pyramid.—Floor in Belzoni's Chamber.
Third   Pyramid.—Interior.
Campbell's Tomb.
Fourth Pyramid.—Interior.

The floor in Belzoni's Chamber was examined, and as the eastern part consisted of rock, and the remainder of a pavement of two courses of squared stone, it was supposed that the sarcophagus might conceal a secret passage to the principal tomb, as Herodotus states was sometimes the case; and a few blocks were taken up; but nothing was found out either at this time or in August, when the whole of the pavement was removed by Mr. Perring, in consequence of the discovery of the large apartment in the Third Pyramid.

We returned to Cairo during a strong Kamseen wind.

19*th.*—I gave to Mr. Brettel a letter of admission to the tents, as he set out in the evening with a party to visit the pyramids.

### *March 20th.*

Reis, 6.        Men, 118.        Children, 108.

Great   Pyramid.—Excavation in southern front.
———               Excavation in northern front.
———               Davison's Chamber.
———               Queen's Chamber.
———               Passage to Queen's Chamber.
———               Two borings in passage to Queen's Chamber.
———               Large stone in Great Passage.

Third Pyramid.—Interior.
Campbell's Tomb.
Fourth Pyramid.—Interior.

I was detained till late by business in Cairo, as Mr. Piozan (the consul, and also Messrs. Briggs and Thurburn's agent) had gone to Alexandria. On arriving at the pyramids with Mr. Mash, I found Mr. Brettel and three other gentlemen just setting out on their return to Cairo.

Two parties had, on the 16th instant, begun to bore in the passage leading to the Queen's Chamber, in order to ascertain whether the communication existed, which appeared to be concealed by the stones let in under the step, where we had been so long employed. The borings were made near a round hole in the pavement, about six inches deep. Similar holes had been found in the Queen's Chamber, at the exterior of the north-western angle of the Second Pyramid, and in other places.[8]

### March 21st.

Reis, 6.  Men, 99.  Children, 130.
The same works were repeated.

Fragments of earthenware were found in Campbell's Tomb. The gallery had arrived within fifteen feet of the centre of the Third Pyramid, and was continued for a short distance at an angle of forty-five degrees, when

[8] Mr. Perring says, that these holes may be observed wherever the upper part of the courses of stone are exposed, and that they were intended to support the wooden machines mentioned by Herodotus for raising the stones, which he thinks were like the polyspaston of Vitruvius, but this machine is supposed to have consisted of an apparatus of blocks, and pullies, which were probably then unknown.

a perpendicular shaft, about five feet in diameter, was begun. This was carried to the base, and the operation was attended with some trouble, as the workmen were obliged to come up from the bottom, every time the blasting took place, by means of a rope ladder; for those made of wood were destroyed by the pieces of stone, and the effects of the powder. Part of the gallery was also inconveniently narrow, and the stone was obliged to be broken up before it could be removed.

Mr. Harris (of Alexandria) and Dr. Walne, who was afterwards consul, encamped near the palm-trees on the plain.

In the course of the morning I assisted Mr. Mash in taking several admeasurements.

### March 22d.

Reis, 6.        Men, 104.        Children, 78.

| | |
|---|---|
| Great Pyramid.— | Excavation in southern front. |
| —— | Excavation in northern front. |
| —— | Davison's Chamber. |
| —— | Queen's Chamber. |
| —— | Passage to Queen's Chamber. |
| —— | Two borings in passage to Queen's Chamber. |
| —— | Large stone in Great Passage. |
| Second Pyramid.— | Lower Entrance. |
| Third Pyramid.— | Interior. |
| Campbell's Tomb. | |
| Fourth Pyramid.— | Interior. |

We examined the air-channels in the King's Chamber, and put up rods in the northern to the length of one hundred and nineteen feet; in the southern, of fifty-nine feet. In the course of this operation we were surprised to find that the latter was not in the vertical direction described

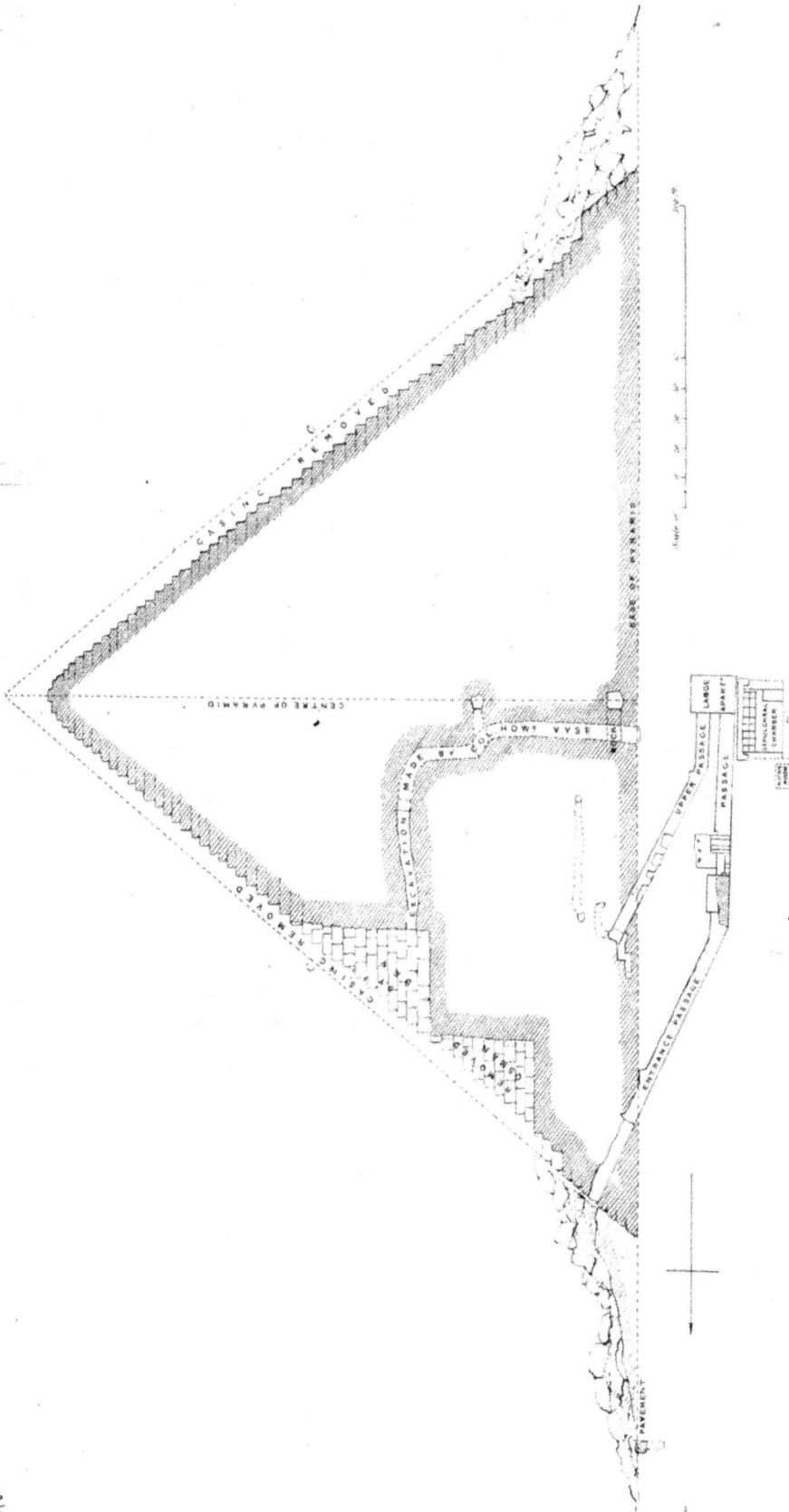

SECTION THROUGH CENTRE OF THIRD PYRAMID.

CASING REMOVED

CASING REMOVED

CENTRE OF PYRAMID

BASE OF PYRAMID

EXCAVATION MADE BY COL. HOWARD VYSE

ENTRANCE PASSAGE

UPPER PASSAGE

PASSAGE

LARGE APARTMENT

SEPULCHRAL CHAMBER

PAVEMENT

by M. Caviglia. A few more green idols were found in Campbell's tomb. Two quarrymen were employed in blasting the stones in the lower entrance of the Second Pyramid.[9]

### March 23d.

Reis, 7.          Men, 108.          Children, 115.

Great  Pyramid.—Excavation in southern front.
———          Excavation in northern front.
———          Davison's Chamber.
———          Queen's Chamber.
———          Passage to Queen's Chamber.
———          Northern Air-channel.
———          Large Stone in Great Passage.
Second Pyramid.—Lower Entrance.
Third  Pyramid.—Interior.
Campbell's Tomb.
Fourth Pyramid.—Interior.

As a cavity had not been discovered in the passage at the depth of ten feet, the boring rods were taken up to force the northern air-channel, which we were induced to attempt, from having found so great a length of the

---

[9] One of these Arabs, Daoud, remained with me during the whole time I was at Gizeh, and was employed after I left Egypt in sinking the shaft in the subterraneous chamber in the Great Pyramid; he was an excellent workman, extremely zealous and active, and possessed of great strength, although he was said to live entirely on spirits, and Hhasheésh (an intoxicating preparation of hemp). He had once a narrow escape when blasting for the lower entrance at the Second Pyramid. He had set fire to two shots, and only one of them going off, he returned to relight the other, which exploded whilst he was in the narrow passage; luckily no large fragments came out, and he escaped with a few trifling bruises about the arms. The previous explosion had thrown out many fragments of considerable weight to a great distance.

lower part of it entirely empty.   In consequence of a letter from Mr. Piozan's dragoman, I went in the evening to Cairo, accompanied by Mr. Hill and Mr. Mash.

### *March 24th.*

Reis, 6.      Men, 108.      Children, 108.
The same works were repeated.

I found the consul's office closed, as it was Good Friday, of which I was not aware.   I therefore returned without delay to the pyramids.   The Kamseen wind was extremely violent; and the sand got even into my watch and stopped it, which was a great inconvenience, as it could not be repaired, and as it had enabled me to regulate the people's work.   By means of the boring rods we cleared five feet of the northern air-channel.   The large stone in the Great Passage was cut through.   It proved to be a lining over a shallow cavity, about five inches square, which was formed in the eastern corner by the inclined position of the roof.   In order to complete the inquiry, the other side of the stone was begun upon. Daoud was sent to blast in Davison's Chamber; and small charges of gunpowder were used in the other works wherever they could be applied.   The shaft had been sunk about three feet in the Third Pyramid.

### *March 25th.*

Reis, 6.      Men, 119.      Children, 119.
The same works were repeated.

A quantity of black dust, apparently decayed stone, was discovered under the first stone that was removed in the lower entrance of the Second Pyramid.

The sand had now been cleared out in Campbell's Tomb to a level with the grotto communicating with the shaft at the south-western corner, in which a sarcophagus was found on the 11th of February. This was now well examined; it was composed of red granite, and inscribed with rows of hieroglyphics. It lay east and west on the southern side of the grotto, and the lid, which was also covered with hieroglyphics, had been removed, and placed near the wall. The grotto itself was roughly chiselled, without plaster or decoration; and a sort of groove ran round the walls close to the floor, in which small pieces of rough stone were placed at nearly equal distances. There were niches in the wall at the head and foot of the sarcophagus, and two apertures had been roughly cut through the sides of the grotto, one into the central part of the tomb, and the other into the shaft, which went down to a considerable depth. The sarcophagus was empty, but sixty-five green idols, in a perfect state, and several broken pieces were taken out from the sand, with which the grotto was filled.

26th.—I examined the southern dyke, and the tombs on the hills near it, which appear to extend to Abouseir and Saccara. The shafts were in general extremely deep. They had been, no doubt, pillaged by the antients, and many of them had been recently opened by Mr. Massara, and by other persons. One of the most considerable was that alluded to by M. Caviglia on the 4th of February. It was a large rectangular pit, forty-three feet in depth to the sand at the bottom. The edges were marked with hollows, that had the appearance of gutters, and a square passage like the inclined entrances in the pyramids had been cut through the rock on the southern side, and opened into the excavation, at about fifteen feet from the top, without any apparent means of descent, or any communication with the bottom: it is probable, therefore, that some building formerly existed in the centre, (like that afterwards discovered in Campbell's Tomb,) with which the passage communicated. The lower part of the perpendicular sides were hollow, and several large grottoes seemed to extend to a considerable distance, particularly towards the south-west. The bottom was covered by a pavement, which was said to have resisted every attempt to remove it. With gunpowder, however, this might be easily accomplished. The desert mountains abound with tombs in every direction. I examined three, which contained regular arches with key-stones, and vestibules with domed roofs. They were near each other, and there were probably many more constructed in the same manner. They had been closed with stone doors fixed on pivots. I did not consider them of very remote antiquity; and it is to be observed that, in the adjacent plain, there are heaps of burnt bricks, apparently Roman. Large tumuli, surrounded with masonry, and ruined sepulchres covered with sand, occupy the highest part of the hills; and the traces of a wall extend from east to west, upon the summit. I afterwards examined the periboli near the Third Pyramid, the excavations in it, and the other works.

*March 27th.*

Reis, 5.      Men, 101.      Children, 109.

The same works were repeated.

As more people were absolutely necessary, I sent to the Shieks of Koum el Eswith, and Cafr el Batran. The former came, attended with ten additional men; the latter, however, did not make his appearance at all, notwithstanding I sent by the janissaries in the evening, and again on the following morning. I accordingly reported him to the British consul. Mr. Perring informed me by Mr. Hill that neither Mr. Mash nor himself could attend for some days. I discharged Paulo. Hyænas and other wild animals came frequently round the tents during the night; but the dogs alarmed them, and prevented our getting a shot at them.

### March 28th.

Reis, 6.      Men, 140.      Children, 120.
The same works were repeated.

The work went on very slowly at the northern air-channel, and scarcely a bushel of sand was taken out during the day. In fact, this operation wanted more looking after than its situation (three hundred and thirty-one feet above the base of the pyramid) rendered at that time practicable. I inserted a candle at the end of a rod, through a small hole, that had been made in the chamber above Davison's (subsequently called Wellington's), and I had the mortification of finding that it was a chamber of construction, like that below it. More green idols were found in Campbell's Tomb.

### March 29th.

Reis, 7.      Men, 95.      Children, 101.
Great Pyramid.—Excavation in southern front.
——          Excavation in northern front.

In examining the ground to the northward of the Great Pyramid, I observed a line of rock projecting above the sand, which appeared to have been scalped down, and might, therefore, I considered, have contained an entrance to the subterraneous passage mentioned by Herodotus. It was parallel to the building, and about a hundred yards from it. But, upon removing the sand to the depth of six or seven feet, it was found to be in its natural state, and the work was given up.[1] I at first entertained an idea that a grand ascent might have been formed from the plain below to the brow of the mountain upon which the Great Pyramid is placed; but the side of the rock is covered with vast heaps of rubbish, fragments of stone, great quantities of coarse gravel, which have been brought from distant parts of the desert (probably from Dashoor), and with other materials, that have been used for fillings in, and for rubble work in the interior of the edifice. Two or three large holes of an angular shape have been cut in the platform before the

[1] A trench near this place, which does not exist, is inserted in the French map, probably through a mistake for the two pits further to the eastward.

pyramid, and a number of round ones about twelve inches in diameter, and eight or ten inches deep.   The latter are in rows about five feet asunder, principally before the north-eastern angle of the building, where the blocks of stone would have been brought by the northern dyke. There is also a remarkable groove, or trench, which, as well as the holes, seems to have been used in the erection of scaffolding, or of machinery when the pyramid was built. The excavation had arrived within a short distance of the centre of the Third Pyramid; and we were in daily ex-pectation of meeting with the granite lining of an apart-ment.   But as it was necessary to enlarge the shaft, little progress was made for some days.   The great depth at which we had now arrived in Campbell's Tomb, made the clearing of the sand very difficult, and laborious.

### March 30th.

Reis, 7.        Men, 135.        Children, 140.

The same works were repeated.

The hole into Wellington's Chamber being practicable, I examined it with Mr. Hill.   The floor was unequal, as it was composed of the reverse of the blocks of granite, that formed the ceiling of Davison's Chamber.   It was entirely empty, excepting one piece of stone thrown into it by blasting.   Not an insect or a bat appeared, nor the traces of any living animal.   There had not been, indeed, any doorway or entrance; and although some of the granite blocks in the southern and northern walls had lugs, or projections, yet the stones composing the roof rested upon them—so that it was impossible that they could have been moved up as a portcullis.   This chamber, in fact, like Davison's and the others afterwards discovered, was merely a vacancy, or chamber of construction, to take off the weight of the building from the King's Chamber. Their dimensions are as follows :— King's Chamber, thirty-four feet three inches, by seventeen feet one inch; Davison's, thirty-eight feet four inches, by seventeen feet one inch; Wellington's, thirty-eight feet six inches, by seventeen feet. In the ceilings alone was any exactness of construction preserved. These were beautifully polished, and had the finest joints, in order most probably to prevent the slightest accumulation of dust or of rubbish. In all other respects, the masonry in these apartments became less perfect as they ascended. The northern and southern walls of Wellington's, and of Davison's Chambers were of granite, the eastern and western of calcareous stone; the ceiling consisted of nine blocks of granite laid from north to south, and were, like those in Davison's apartment, of a sufficient length to extend their bearings beyond the walls of the King's Chamber. The average height of the chamber (which varies, owing to the irregular surface of the floor) was about three feet eight inches. Mr. Perring, in the course of his survey, found that these apartments had been finished from the eastward, and that consequently the western sides were last built.

For a day or two after the chamber had been opened, those who remained in it became blackened as if by a London fog: as this effect gradually disappeared, I conceive it to have been occasioned by blasting, and by the sudden admission of the air. Upon first entering the apartment, a black sediment was found, of the consistence of a hoar-frost, equally distributed over the floor, so that footsteps could be distinctly seen impressed on it, and it had accumulated to some depth in the interstices of the blocks. Some of this sediment, which was sent to the French establishment near Cairo, was said to contain ligneous particles. When analysed in England, it was supposed to consist of the exuviæ of insects; but as the deposition was equally diffused over the floor, and extremely like the substance found on the 25th instant at the Second Pyramid, it was most probably composed of particles of decayed stone. If it had been the remains of rotten wood, or of a quantity of insects that had penetrated through the masonry, it would scarcely have been so equally distributed; and, if caused by the latter, it is difficult to imagine why some of them should not have been found alive when the place was opened evidently for the first time since the pyramid was built.

Having ordered the entrance to be enlarged, I went round the other works. I afterwards wrote to Colonel Campbell, and sent with my letter the idols found in his tomb. Mr. Perring and Mr. Mash having arrived, we went in the evening into Wellington's Chamber, and took various admeasurements, and in doing so we found the quarry marks.

### March 31st.

Reis, 8.    Men, 149.    Children, 187.

Great Pyramid.—Excavation in southern front.
——    Excavation in northern front.
——    Wellington's Chamber.
——    Queen's Chamber.
——    Passage to Queen's Chamber.
——    Northern Air-channel.
——    Large Stone in Great Passage.

Second Pyramid.—Lower Entrance.

Third Pyramid.—Interior.

Campbell's Tomb.

Fourth Pyramid.—Interior.

Rock in centre of northern front of Great Pyramid.

Bridge in southern Dyke.

We discovered the pavement at the base of the Great Pyramid. I still entertained great hopes of finding a sepulchral apartment, and therefore directed that every exertion should be made to get above Wellington's Chamber, for which purpose Daoud was employed. In addition to the other works, the bridge was again cleared out for Mr. Perring's survey. In the afternoon I went with Mr. Hill to Wellington's Chamber, and the Duke's glorious name was inscribed on the southern wall.

Mr. Raven came to see the works. This gentleman, who was afterwards employed, had had the charge of a rice-mill worked by steam at Rosetta. He not only understood the habits and language of the Arabs, but was also a most zealous and active man of business. He got every thing into perfect order, collected and kept in good repair the various tools, boring-rods, &c., and was indefatigable in his exertions during the whole time he remained at the pyramids. He was a friend of Mr. Hill's, to whom I am indebted for his assistance; and I take this opportunity of acknowledging my obligations to Mr. Hill himself, who was always ready to assist me, and was of the greatest possible service.

*April 1st.*

Reis, 7.     Men, 173.     Children, 262.

The same works were continued.

Mr. Perring and Mr. Mash went away, and in the evening I returned to Cairo, with Mr. Hill and Mr. Raven.

*April 2d.*—I remained at Cairo.

### April 3d.

Reis, 8.      Men, 151.      Children, 177.
The same works were continued.

I went with Colonel Campbell to see Ibrahim Pacha, but we were not admitted, as he was indisposed. He had, indeed, returned from Syria on that account. We then called on Mr. Bonfort (his man of business), with whom we sat some time. He wore the Nizam dress, but the room contained books and pictures, and had the air of a European apartment. We afterwards visited Shereef Pacha (the Governor of Syria), to whose assistance I had been so much indebted, when the party, which I accompanied to Palmyra, had been robbed by the Arabs. In alluding to this circumstance, the Pacha mentioned that he had paid the full amount of our losses on that occasion, according to an account sent to him by Mr. Farren; which, he added, could not in justice have been demanded, as he had offered in the first instance a guard, but that Mr. Farren had refused to accept it.

I returned in the evening to the pyramids with Mr. Hill.

### April 4th.

Reis, 8.      Men, 159.      Children, 210.
Great  Pyramid.—Excavation in southern front.
———      Excavation in northern front.
———      Wellington's Chamber.
———      Queen's Chamber.

VOL. I.                                    P

The rubbish on the northern front of the Great Pyramid had been cleared away from the pavement, and, as it was in the form of a step like that at the Second Pyramid, it was considered that a similar entrance might exist; and that it might possibly conduct to the famous tomb mentioned by Herodotus.   The pavement was, therefore, carefully examined, but the stones were found to be laid upon the solid rock.   They had the finest joints, but were perfectly plain, without the slightest indication of sculpture or of painting, or appearance of an entrance.

The large stone in the great passage, and also the excavation of the rock in front of the Great Pyramid, were given up for the reasons before-mentioned.

Having been informed that there was a well of good water in the plain below the tents, which had been cleared by M. Caviglia, and afterwards by Mr. Wilkinson (and, it is to be remarked, regularly filled in again by the Arabs),* I ordered it to be excavated, and walled

* The female figures introduced in this sketch represent the Arab girls employed to supply the workmen with water, of which, as it may be supposed, the heat of the climate, and nature of the work carried on occasioned a great consumption.   The usual dress consists of a blue loose gown, and a large black, or chequered handkerchief thrown over

WELL of SWEET WATER.

Published by J. Fraser, 216 Regent St.

round sufficiently high to prevent the drifted sand from falling into it. The water was excellent, and at about the same depth as that in the well near the palm-trees, but the latter, from some cause or other, was brackish.

the head with which they occasionally cover their faces, as they do not wear the black veil (called boorcko).* Their hair, plaited with black strings, to which brass rings were attached, hangs down their backs; and their heads are bound round by a smaller black handkerchief, with a coloured border: they generally wear a profusion of necklaces, rings, and ear-rings, and are tattoed on the chin and other parts of the face, and also on their arms, and hands, which are often stained with henna. The water jars are of a very picturesque form, and have a slight concavity at the bottom to fit the shape of the head, which is protected by a piece of linen folded in the form of a wreath, or by a corner of the large handkerchief gathered up beneath the jar, which occasions the drapery to fall in square folds over the shoulders with the grace of antient sculpture. Their features are often very handsome, their teeth extremely beautiful, and their eyes naturally fine, although, in many instances, diseased by neglect, and by a constant exposure to the sand, and dust, so that one-eyed persons are frequently met with.

Their figures, when young, are wonderfully graceful, and well formed, and also perfectly erect, although perhaps not inspired with the air of liberty and independence which more properly belongs to their wandering sisters of the desert, notwithstanding that they also pride themselves on being Bedouins.†

The boys are well made, active, and capable of great exertion; several of them are very intelligent, and work extremely well. The children, of five or six years old, are also good-looking, and animated, notwithstanding the hardships and squalid misery to which they are

---

* See Mr. Lane's work on modern Egypt.

† Nothing can be more striking than the majestic figures occasionally seen near the wells at Alexandria. Long flowing robes of dark blue adorn their fine limbs with the most classical drapery, and large silver bracelets and other ornaments call to remembrance the accounts of patriarchal times.

They both appeared to stand nearly at the same level as that in the wells on the cultivated grounds, which seemed to be regulated by the Nile. The comparative levels of these wells, and of the water in the tombs, were taken by Mr. Perring and Mr. Mash, and may be referred to in the Appendix.

I was this morning informed, that a cavity had been discovered below the second tier of stones under the step in the passage leading to the Queen's Chamber; but, upon examination, it was found to be accidental, and full of sand, rubble-work, &c. A similar vacancy occurred at about the same depth under the stone near the niche in the Queen's Chamber, which contained, like the other, fillings in of desert sand, and a quantity of the black particles of decayed stone; they were about three or four feet deep, and evidently did not lead to any concealed communication. The works, therefore, were abandoned. The Arabs recommended that a stone should be removed at the right of the entrance into the Queen's Chamber, where a ledge or grooving at the bottom of the wall had been discontinued. The sparry excrescence on the sides of this chamber gives it an unfinished appearance. The slight projection at the corner of the entrance

exposed, and, with proper management, would become a fine population. But the men, with a few exceptions, are sullen, irrecoverably idle, deceitful, and totally insensible to good treatment, and therefore apparently incapable of amelioration. Their clothing, like that of the Bedouins of the desert, should consist of a red tarbouse, a shirt, a pair of short trowsers, and a white blanket; but most of these people have seldom any other covering than rags, and are generally bare-footed; and it is remarkable with what perfect indifference and ease they pass over the sharp stones and thorns of the desert.

has been made, according to some opinions, to prevent the blocks, with which the passage is supposed to have been closed up, from being forced into the Chamber; the step may also have some relation to these blocks.

I discharged Giachino at his own request,—which I intended to have done on other accounts, for his conduct had lately been far from satisfactory. As he refused to take with him the effects, which had been intrusted to his care by M. Caviglia when he left the pyramids, they were sent to Mr. Hill's hotel, and a list of them signed by Giachino to the British Consulate.

### April 5th.

Reis, 9.　　Men, 227.　　Children, 193.

Great Pyramid.—Excavation on southern front.
―――　　　　Excavation in northern front.
―――　　　　Wellington's Chamber.
―――　　　　Northern Air-channel.
Second Pyramid.—Lower entrance.
Third Pyramid.—Interior.
Campbell's Tomb.
Fourth Pyramid.—Interior.
Bridge in the southern Dyke.
Well.

Osman, the janissary, was obliged to go again into Cairo on account of ophthalmia, occasioned probably by the Kamseen wind, which was extremely violent.

The entrance of the forced passage made by the Caliphs on the exterior of the northern front of the Great Pyramid, was uncovered. It was in the centre, of considerable size, and appeared to have been effected by fire; a quantity of dried forage (Tibni), and of decayed litter were also found near it, as if a number of camels had been employed there. Mr. Perring and Mr. Mash, during their survey, had penetrated from the interior through this passage into a cavity, that had been made by former explorers in the mound of rubbish, with which it had been concealed. Mr. Raven, who came to remain, went round the several works with Mr. Hill in the evening.

### April 6th.

**Reis, 9.     Men, 173.     Children, 174.**
The same works were continued.

Under Mr. Raven's superintendence, the terrace, upon which our tents were pitched, was covered over with a layer of earth, and the sand in the other parts was kept firm by constant watering, which was a great advantage during the intense heat of summer. The tombs, in which we lived, were likewise floored with earth, repaired, and whitewashed. Two Moors were hired, who kept the place in good order, and were better guards than the common Arabs; but we had watchmen from the villages at night, as the Sheiks were accountable for the security of the place.

The lower entrance into the Second Pyramid was opened.

The sand was cleared out from a rough grotto, that was at the bottom of a shaft at the south-eastern corner of Campbell's Tomb, and that also opened into the central excavation. It contained three sarcophagi—one of red, another of white granite, and a third of basalt, crowded together in an extraordinary manner.[3] They appeared to

---

[3] One of the granite sarcophagi found in this tomb has been sent to the British Museum at the suggestion of Lord Prudhoe, on account of

TENTS AT GIZEH.

Printed by C. Hullmandel

Published by James Fraser, Regent-Street

be in their original positions, and must have been deposited with great difficulty. The lids had been removed. They were extremely well-finished, and adorned with rows of hieroglyphics. The one made of basalt, in particular, was of most excellent workmanship, but broken, and entirely ruined. Three hundred and ninety green idols were found near them, but the sarcophagi had been completely ransacked, and nothing was left excepting a quantity of fine gum, attached to the mummy-boards in the one formed of white granite.

Mr. Perring and Mr. Mash arrived, and went round the works.

*April 7th.*

Reis, 9.      Men, 189.      Children, 154.

Great Pyramid.—Excavation in southern front.
————            Excavation in northern front.
————            Wellington's Chamber.
————            Northern Air-channel.
Third Pyramid.—Interior.
Campbell's Tomb.
Fourth Pyramid.—Interior.
Bridge in southern Dyke.
Well.

I sent the idols to Colonel Campbell, and M. Caviglia's goods to Mr. Hill's. Mr. Perring and Mr. Mash returned to Cairo. The sand had been sufficiently cleared out from the bridge in the southern dyke. Mr. Hill came respecting gunpowder, for which I was obliged to apply

the hieroglyphics with which it is inscribed; and a fragment of the one made of basalt has been also sent with it, which is remarkable for the finish and beauty of the workmanship.

through Colonel Campbell to Government, as I had bought all that I could find in Cairo, where it was only allowed to be sold in small quantities.

### April 8th.

Reis, 9.    Men, 182.    Children, 154.

Great Pyramid.—Excavation in southern front.
———    Excavation in northern front.
———    Wellington's Chamber.
———    Northern Air-channel.
Third Pyramid.—Interior.
Campbell's Tomb.
Fourth Pyramid.—Interior.
Well.

Mr. Gates, of the 20th regiment, who had arrived from India, came to the pyramids, and returned in the evening to Cairo with Mr. Raven. Mr. Mushet encamped on the plain near the palm-trees.

Two quarry-men were sent to blast over Wellington's Chamber. The building in the centre of Campbell's Tomb was this day discovered. It extended east and west, and was covered in by a perfect arch. The walls were of white stones, which, although not remarkable in point of size, were well jointed and finished, and, excepting the arch, the masonry had the appearance of Grecian architecture. A passage had been forced into the western end of the upper apartment, and in the centre of the roof there was a circular opening, into which a stone stopper had been fitted, with a small hole in the middle of it lined with coarse pottery, for the circulation of air. The floor of this apartment was flat down the middle, but sloped off on each side to the springing of the arch; and

F. Arundale, del.                                                    Day&Haghe Lithrs to the Queen.

## BUILDING IN CAMPBELL'S TOMB.

This drawing is partly a Section, and the side A does not in reality exist, for the
Arch'd building is connected with the western side of the central excavation by the horizontal passage A. and the regular entrance to it is by a separate perpendicular
shaft excavated through the solid rock, see IV. Fig.5.

Published by J. Fraser, Regent Street.

in its centre, immediately below the hole in the roof was a similar aperture, which had been filled with the same kind of stopper. These stoppers were lying near the apertures; and in the upper apartment fragments of coarse amphoræ were found, with a quantity of desert sand. The lower apartment, or tomb, had a regular entrance at the western end. From the upper apartment, which was about seven or eight feet high, I entered by the air-hole already described into the lower, where an immense stone, supported on each side by masonry, had originally formed a complete covering to a most magnificent sarcophagus placed beneath it. Several rows of hieroglyphics were engraven upon the lower part of this stone, also upon the sarcophagus, and upon the lid. The end of the stone over the head of the sarcophagus had been broken off, and the lid was lifted up about fourteen or fifteen inches. Some broken amphoræ were found upon the large stone on each side of the apartment under the springing of the arch. The place was nearly full of sand, and the smoke of a lamp or candle was visible in various parts. The sarcophagus had been imbedded in very small pieces of white stone, and on each side, near its shoulders, were niches or hollows, in which several tiers of green idols were subsequently found, standing in double rows. They were swathed, after the fashion of mummies, with narrow tape, which had imbibed the colour of the idols, and decomposed on the slightest exposure to the air. At the foot of the sarcophagus was a square pit, about nine feet deep, and lined with masonry; it had two air-channels near the bottom, and a row of charac-

ters, many of which were not hieroglyphics, inscribed on
one of the walls. It was at first supposed to communicate
with a lower tomb, but this was not the case. As the lid
of the sarcophagus had only been raised a few inches, I
thought that part of the mummy might yet remain. I
accordingly wrote to Colonel Campbell, Mr. Perring, and
Mr. Hill, and having ordered the two janissaries, and
some of the reis to watch during the night, I postponed
any further investigation till the following day.

### April 9th.

#### Reis, 7.      Men, 16.

Mr. Hill arrived. We immediately went to the tomb.
Having cleared out a quantity of sand, we found the
sarcophagus entirely empty, excepting a few trifling ornaments of stone. The cartouche of Psammetichus the
Second was not upon the sarcophagus, although it appeared in a line of hieroglyphics inscribed in a hollow
groove round the inside of the central excavation, in
which the building was placed.

Mr. Wilkinson has remarked, that the most antient
stone arch discovered in Egypt is in a tomb on the north-
eastern rocks of Saccara, and that it was constructed
during the reign of Psammetichus the Second about six
hundred years before Christ. It is remarkable that this
building appears to be of the same date. These two instances are therefore the earliest specimens hitherto discovered of this mode of construction in stone. The
Egyptians, however, formed arches with bricks in very
remote times; and it is surprising that the Grecians were
unacquainted with them.

But at the time when the pyramids were built, and for many subsequent years, they do not seem to have been invented, and ceilings appear to have been composed in three ways.

The most simple consisted of horizontal blocks with flat surfaces, like those in the King's, and in the four chambers immediately above it in the Great Pyramid; and in the temples and porticoes in various parts of the country. It is to be remarked, in some instances, as at Abydos, that the lower surface of the horizontal stones was cut into a coved shape.

When additional strength was required, or when the space was of great width, it was covered in by the successive projection of the horizontal courses from the bottom, towards each other; so that the perpendicular ends of the stones formed a notched line, as may be seen in the sections of the Great Gallery, and of the niche in the Queen's Chamber in the Great Pyramid; and likewise in the chambers of the Northern Pyramid at Dashoor. In some other buildings formed in this manner, the ends of the projecting blocks were cut into a curved, or continuous line, which had the appearance of an arch; as may be seen in a building at Thebes; in the Treasury of Atræus, at Mycenæ; in the Mamertine prisons, at Rome; in the gateways at Tiryus, and at Tusculum; and in other Cyclopean buildings.

Another method is equally antient, and has been adopted in the Queen's, and in Campbell's Chambers in the Great Pyramid; in Belzoni's, in the Second; and also in the sepulchral apartment in the Third. In these instances the blocks are inclined, and, meeting at the top, form an angular roof. The imperfection of this arrange-

ments, when the superincumbent weight is considerable,
seems to have been fully understood, by the great depth
to which the blocks have been inserted in the walls; and,
in Campbell's Chamber, where the weight is very great,
and the masonry comes down upon the ceiling, four
apartments, or vacancies, have been contrived as an additional precaution. The roof in the Queen's Chamber is
protected by the Great Gallery; and that in the Third
Pyramid is merely set up in an excavation; but, in the
Second it apparently sustains the whole perpendicular
weight of the building; and, as it is ill calculated for
such a purpose, the rock, of which the sides of the apartment are composed, probably rises above it, and, by some
contrivance, assists in supporting the enormous weight of
the edifice.

The fosse, which surrounds the central excavation,
had been evidently arched over, for some of the stones
remained; but as the surface of the rock, whence these
arches sprung, was not on the same level, there must
have been false joints at every angle. The remains of
stone arches are also to be seen in the apertures of one
or two of the adjacent shafts, so that there can be no
reason for supposing, from the existence of an arch, that
the sepulchral chamber was posterior to the excavation.

But the most extraordinary circumstance is that the
building was found to rest upon a stratum of desert sand,
between two and three feet thick, beneath which sand
was the solid rock without aperture, or shaft of any kind.
People have passed entirely under the building, and rods
and poles have been inserted in every direction. It is,
therefore, to be concluded, that, after the central excavation had been made, it was filled up to the top with sand,

that the tomb was built upon it, and the sarcophagus and the large stone placed over it, possibly on account of the difficulty attending these operations at the bottom of the pit, into which it was afterwards gradually let down by taking out the sand in the same way as the lining of a well is lowered. The building, in its present state, would be soon destroyed by the crumbling away of the substratum from beneath it, did not the sand fall in from the mounds on the top, and continually accumulate around it.

Mr. Maltas and Mr. Mushet called at the tents. In the evening Mr. Perring and Mr. Mash arrived from Cairo, when we again visited Campbell's Tomb.

### April 10th.

Reis, 9.　　　Men, 180.　　　Children, 169.
The same operations were repeated.

Mr. Perring, Mr. Mash, and Mr. Hill went to Cairo. There was a strong Kamseen wind, and consequently blasts of air were felt in the interior of the Fourth Pyramid. In the course of the excavation at the northern front of the Great Pyramid, it was found that not only the lower part of it had been forced in search of an entrance, but that a large hole had been made through the pavement into a deep hollow, which had been filled up with rubble work, pieces of granite, and of other stones, and afterwards closed with large blocks, and effectually concealed by the pavement.[4] The disclosure of it,

---

[4] It will be seen that this hollow was subsequently cleared out to the depth of forty-seven feet, when it became so narrow that the people could not work. A low grotto, and a small channel branched off from it. It seemed to be a natural fissure, and extended along the centre of the northern front, within ten feet of the building.

therefore, could not have been the result of accident, but
of an examination expressly made in search of a subterraneous passage, of which there is not the slightest indication in the interior of the pyramid, but where, on the
contrary, an inclined passage from the regular entrance
three hundred and twenty feet in length leads directly to
a subterraneous chamber more than one hundred feet
below the base.    It is evident, therefore, that in very
remote times some tradition existed of a subterraneous
passage peculiar to this pyramid; for, although the stones
at the base of the Second Pyramid had been forced, yet
the pavement at that place did not appear to have been
attempted notwithstanding that the existence of a lower
entrance must have been manifest to all, who examined
the interior of that building.    These facts coincide with
the account of Herodotus, that the tomb of Cheops was
at so great a depth, that it was surrounded by the water
of the Nile, and differed from any thing to be seen in the
Second Pyramid,—a description the more remarkable, as
it relates to the only pyramid which contains chambers
in the masonry, and cannot apply to any apartment at
present discovered in it.[5]

[5] The level of the river is not inconsistent with this account.  The
base of the pyramid was, in the month of May 1837, one hundred and
forty-six feet five inches above the level of the Nile, and, allowing
twenty or thirty feet for the increased elevation of the bed of the river,
the whole would only amount to about one hundred and seventy-six
feet; and a passage like that at the Second Pyramid, inclining at an
angle of twenty-six degrees, at the distance of forty feet from the base,
would arrive at the depth of two hundred and twenty feet below the
centre of the pyramid.  The step at this pyramid is thirty-three feet six
inches from the base, and one foot nine inches high.  The floor of the

It is difficult to imagine that the Great Pyramid was intended to be the tomb of more than one individual. Indeed the whole structure seems built for the security of the King's Chamber, and for the sarcophagus within it; but if the dread of violation was as strongly felt as antient authors seem to describe, it is possible that the apartments and passages in the masonry were intended as a blind, and that the tomb in this, as in all the other pyramids at Gizeh, was an excavation in the rock at a depth sufficient to elude discovery. Or, on the other hand, if the testimony of Herodotus is to be refused on this point (although it has been found correct in many other instances), we must conclude that Cheops was actually buried in the King's Chamber, and not, according to the usual manner, in an excavation; and that the unfinished subterraneous apartment was intended to deceive, and to support the fictions of the priests, which were communicated to Herodotus.[6] It was my intention to have blasted the rock to a considerable depth, in search of a communication; the discovery of this fissure, therefore, saved me a great deal of trouble and expense; and as much interest was attached to this inquiry, I directed, when I left Egypt in 1837, that a shaft should be sunk in the floor of the subterraneous chamber, to the depth of fifty feet. This operation was attended with

subterraneous chamber, which is now open, is above one hundred feet below the base.

[6] As Cheops and Chephrenes are stated to have been decidedly hostile to the religious institutions of the country, it is not probable that the priests would have felt any great interest in preventing the violation of their tombs.

difficulty, from the want of a free circulation of air; but, in September 1838, it had penetrated thirty-eight feet through the solid rock, without any appearance of a chamber.    An excavation of this kind appeared to be the easiest way of ascertaining the truth, as it is nearly in the centre of the pyramid, and as there is no clue, by which any regular entrance can be found.

As it is evident, in many parts of Egypt, that the desert has been continually encroaching, particularly from the westward, there was probably little or no sand upon the rocks at Gizeh when the pyramids were erected.  It would also appear that they were broken open soon after they were built, and at about the same time; for at the bottom of the mounds, at the northern fronts of the two largest, the strata of undisturbed desert sand are of inconsiderable depth below the lines of rubbish produced by the first aggressions committed upon them; indeed Diodorus Siculus states, that neither the bodies of Cheops nor of Chephrenes were deposited in the pyramids, from an apprehension of the violence to which they might be exposed; and we know that they were open in the time of Herodotus, four hundred and forty-five years before Christ, and in that of Pliny, A.D. 79, as these authors describe their interior construction; nor is it likely that when once the solid masonry was removed from the interior of the passages, they were ever again closed up, excepting by the effects of decay and of dilapidation.  A considerable space of time must have elapsed before the regular entrances were so effectually concealed by the accumulation of stones and rubbish, that even the positions of them were forgotten, which appears to have been the case, when the Caliphs penetrated into the interior through the solid masonry; although, as the Arabian historians relate, they seem to have possessed some knowledge respecting their construction, for in both instances, the excavations have been carried on from the centres of the northern fronts, and have been directed eastwards, at proper levels, so as to intersect the passages with an exactness, that could not have been the effect of chance.

A slanderous paragraph, intended to be inserted in the English newspapers, was this day shewn to me, which accused Colonel Campbell of having improperly laid himself under obligations to the Pacha by obtaining the firmaun; and which implied that the Colonel and myself intended to make our fortunes under the pretence of scientific researches. This absurd accusation is only worthy of notice as affording a specimen of the anonymous attacks to which the Colonel is exposed, from the adventurers who infest Egypt.

### April 11th.

Reis, 9.　　Men, 195.　　Children, 174.

Great Pyramid.—Excavation in southern front.
—— Excavation in northern front.
—— Wellington's Chamber.
—— Northern Air-channel.
Second Pyramid.—Roof in Belzoni's Chamber.
Third Pyramid.—Interior.
Campbell's Tomb.
Fourth Pyramid.—Interior.
Well.

As Mr. Perring was desirous of ascertaining how the roof in Belzoni's Chamber was constructed, an excavation, which in the end cost a good deal of trouble, was begun. I copied the quarry-marks found at the

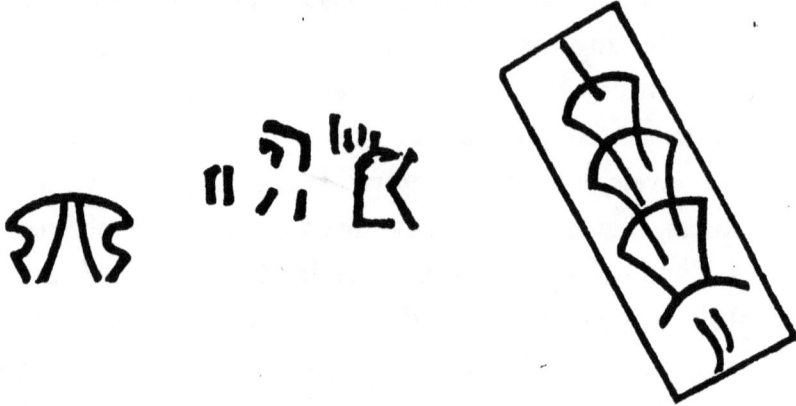

southern front of the Great Pyramid. The broken amphoræ, and green idols, were sent to Colonel Campbell.

### April 12th.

Reis, 9.　　　Men, 205.　　　Children, 219.

The same works were repeated.

Lights were shewn during the night from the top of the Great Pyramid, probably by Mr. Mushet's party. The thermometer was above 90 in the shade, and the Kamseen winds were extremely violent, so that Mr. Mushet's tents upon the plain were overwhelmed with sand, and he was obliged to set out for Cairo.

Several more windlasses and triangles were put up to raise the sand from Campbell's Tomb. The excavation had arrived within nine feet of the centre in the Fourth Pyramid.

I attended in the afternoon at a wedding in the village of Cafr el Batran, but nothing occurred worthy of notice.

*April 13th.*

Reis, 9.    Men, 77.    Children, 150.
The same works were repeated.

The Sheiks, who had assembled to celebrate the wedding, paid me a visit: they galloped, two at a time, brandishing their guns with loud exclamations, across the sandy plain to the bottom of the terrace, and firing, wheeled suddenly round and retired. After repeating this ceremony two or three times, they dismounted, and came up to the tents, where I gave them coffee and gunpowder. They were armed with swords, and very long guns (chiefly German, or French, with a good deal of inlaid work upon the stocks), and wore embroidered pouch-belts, and a kind of red boot, manufactured in Barbary. Their horses were active, but not particularly well-bred, and they had Turkish saddles and bridles. I went down with them into the plain, when they repeated their exercise on horseback. They then dismounted and advanced, either singly or two at a time, shouting, dancing and hopping, with a view, it may be supposed, of alarming the enemy, and of exciting their own courage; when, suddenly stooping down, they fired, and retired in the same way as they had advanced. It was a ridiculous affair, exactly such as might be expected from savages. The Arabs by whom we were attacked in Syria, came on in the same manner, only that they were almost naked, and advanced in two lines, armed with large clubs and stones, as well as fire-arms, followed by a third line, armed with spears and mounted on camels.

A number of idols, &c., were sent to Colonel Campbell. The excavation in Belzoni's Chamber was supposed to have been sufficiently deep for the examination of the roof. Thin pieces of a white stone lining, and some fragments of coarse pottery were found in the excavation at the northern front of the Great Pyramid; and also the bottom of a buff-coloured vase, or jar, of a coarse texture, and lined with a fine green glaize.

### April 14th.

Reis, 9.        Men, 107.        Children, 123.

Great Pyramid.—Excavation in southern front.
———         Excavation in northern front.
———         Wellington's Chamber.
———         Northern Air-channel.
Third Pyramid.—Interior.
Campbell's Tomb.
Fourth Pyramid.—Interior.
The Well.

Colonel Campbell and M. De Laurin (the Austrian Consul-General) came to the Pyramids. They examined the Tomb, Wellington's Chamber, and the different works, and returned to Cairo in the evening. I sent for the Sheiks of Koum el Eswith and Cafr el Batran, that Colonel Campbell might give them directions about the attendance and conduct of their people.

### April 15th.

Reis, 9.        Men, 116.        Children, 129.
The same works were repeated.

More of the buff earthenware was found near the base of the Great Pyramid; in some instances, the glaize was of an extremely brilliant colour, and a perfect vitrifaction. In the evening I returned to Cairo with Mr. Raven.

Colonel Campbell observed yesterday, that many of the people had complaints in their eyes, and desired that they should be sent to Cairo, in order that Nayler Bey might give directions respecting them.  They accordingly received their wages for the day, and went to Colonel Campbell's house, who gave them money, and a good dinner.  Nayler Bey prescribed, and undertook to cure them, but they would neither attend to his advice, nor adopt his remedies, and consequently returned without any benefit.  It is surprising how indifferent the Arabs appear to blindness; several of them employed about the tents were assured, that they would inevitably lose their sight, if they did not wash and foment their eyes; but although fomentations were prepared, they would not make use of them.[1]  Most of the children's eyes are diseased from dust and neglect, and from the irritation produced by swarms of flies allowed to settle upon them; consequently blind and one-eyed persons abound in Egypt, particularly in Cairo, and, I may also add, in Syria.  The inflammation appears generally to commence in the eye-lids, and no doubt with cleanliness, and medical assistance, it might at first be easily cured; but when the eye itself is attacked, the case must be extremely critical.  The periodical visits of a medical man to the villages might be of great benefit, particularly if these indolent people could be prevailed upon to keep

---

[1] One of the people from the villages was totally blind, but he was a very good workman, and had assisted for some days in clearing out the Air-channel on the exterior of the Great Pyramid, before his infirmity was discovered, when, of course, he was employed in a safer position.

themselves clean.    They had generally deep scars near
the eyes, which they had lost; indeed, scarification, and
the application of a fetish, or charm, which consists
generally of a passage in the Koran written by a priest
upon a piece of parchment, and folded up in a triangular
shape, appear to be their only remedies.    The ophthalmia,
that attacked the people at the Pyramids, was extremely
sudden and violent, and was attended with great inflammation, and with severe pain at the temples.

*April* 16*th.* — Colonel Campbell embarked for Alexandria.

I was informed by Mr. Perring, that, in a letter he had
lately received, Mr. Galloway complained of not having
had an answer to an application, which he had some time
before made to me, respecting Mr. Caviglia, who was
anxious to obtain my permission to return to the Pyramids.    I immediately wrote to Mr. Galloway to apologize
for the error I had committed in writing to Mr. Sloane
(the vice-consul at Alexandria), and enclosed a copy of
my letter to that gentleman. — (See March 13*th.*)

### *April* 17*th.*

Reis, 9.        Men, 98.        Children, 119.

The same works were repeated.

Mr. Raven, as usual, returned to the Pyramids by
daybreak.    I settled various affairs at Cairo.    Mr. Perring
sent his drawings of the quarry marks in Wellington's
Chamber.    I returned to Gizeh in the evening.

*April* 18*th.*

Reis, 8.          Men, 166.          Children, 149.

Great   Pyramid. — Excavation in southern front.
———                Excavation in northern front.
———                Wellington's Chamber.
———                Northern Air-channel.
———                Roof in Queen's Chamber.
Third   Pyramid. — Interior.
Campbell's Tomb.
Fourth  Pyramid. — Interior.

There had been a very heavy storm during the night, and there was rain in the morning.  I wrote to Nayler Bey about some people, who had applied to me on account of their eyes, but they were not admitted into his hospital.  An officer paid me a visit, and returned to Cairo.

An excavation was begun for the purpose of ascertaining the manner in which the roof in the Queen's Chamber was constructed.  Mr. Perring and Mr. Mash arrived.

*April* 19*th.*

Reis, 8.          Men, 128.          Children, 133.
The same works were repeated.

Mr. Harris, who was remaining in his boat at Gizeh, paid me a visit.

*April* 20*th.*

Reis, 9.          Men, 114.          Children, 101.

Great   Pyramid. — Excavation in southern front.
———                Excavation in northern front.
———                Wellington's Chamber.
———                Northern Air-channel.
———                Roof in Queen's Chamber.
Second  Pyramid. — Roof in Belzoni's Chamber.
Third   Pyramid. — Interior.
Fourth  Pyramid. — Interior.

The works at Campbell's Tomb were discontinued for want of hands. I wrote to Mr. Hamilton, and sent Mr. Perring's drawings of the quarry-marks, and some of the black dust found in Wellington's Chamber. As the result of the excavation in Belzoni's Chamber was not considered satisfactory, the work was resumed at that place.

*April 21st.*

Reis, 9.    Men, 117.    Children, 146.
The same works were repeated.

The jaw-bone of a sheep and some decayed charcoal were found in the interior of the Fourth Pyramid. These articles were probably brought in by the Arabs;[8] or they would otherwise establish the great antiquity of the charring of wood, and possibly, by inference, of the smelting of metals — the latter process must indeed have been practised before the Pyramids could have been built.

Mr. Perring and Mr. Mash continued the survey; and in the course of it, copied the characters in the pit at the foot of the sarcophagus in Campbell's Tomb. They were inscribed with red paint between double lines, about two inches apart.—(See page 217.)

Captain and Mrs. Mitchell arrived in the morning, and returned after dinner to Cairo.

A quantity of broken pottery was found near the forced entrance on the northern front of the Great Pyramid.

---

[8] When I was employed, in 1832, in an excavation at Bosco Tre Case, near Mount Vesuvius, the same piece of broken pottery was brought up from a shaft five successive times, by way of an inducement to go on with the work.

*April 22d.*

Reis, 9.　　Men, 111.　　Children, 90.

The same works were repeated.

*April 23d.*—A party came to breakfast, including the Count and Countess Odescalchi,[9] and Mr. Piozan — they afterwards went into the Pyramids, examined the different works, and returned to Cairo in the evening. The Count had a house at Saccara, and was desirous that I should undertake some operations at that place; but the firmaun did not extend beyond Gizeh, and I was also fully occupied.

*April 24th.*

Reis, 9.　　Men, 123.　　Children, 118.

Great Pyramid.—Excavation in southern front.
———　Excavation in northern front.
———　Wellington's Chamber.
———　Northern Air-channel.
———　Roof in Queen's Chamber.
Second Pyramid.—Roof in Belzoni's Chamber.
Third Pyramid.—Interior.
Campbell's Tomb.
Fourth Pyramid.—Interior.

The work at Campbell's Tomb was again resumed. As the depth, particularly in the foss, had become very great, and the ropes were much worn, and therefore ill calculated to sustain the weight of the casks, which were secured with iron hooping, I entertained great apprehensions for the safety, not only of the people who worked

[9] An Italian officer, in the Pacha's service, and nephew to the Cardinal of that name.

at the windlasses above, but also of the boys, who were employed below in filling the casks. The greatest care was taken to keep the latter out of the way when the machine was at work, and luckily no serious accident happened; and an application was made to Mr. Piozan, the consul, by which I obtained an order for a rope to be made at the citadel; but, notwithstanding the order proceeded from Habeb Effendi (the governor of Cairo), the people refused to make it, alleging that "a new machine was required to do so," although larger ropes had been made by the same people for Mr. Hill, when he had the care of the steam-engine at the copper works in the citadel. As this application failed, Mr. Hill found in the Pacha's stores some rope, that, by splicing, would have answered the purpose tolerably well. Another order was obtained, and was signed by the governor and by all the different authorities, excepting one person, who, upon being informed that the rope was wanted for the Pyramids, refused to sign it. I was therefore obliged to send to Alexandria (one hundred and forty miles distant), and, in the meantime, to buy up any old cordage of sufficient size that could be met with at Boulac.

### April 25th.

Reis, 9.      Men, 111.      Children, 134.

Great Pyramid.—Excavation in southern front.
—————— Excavation in northern front.
—————— Wellington's Chamber.
—————— Northern Air-channel.
Third Pyramid.—Interior.
Fourth Pyramid.—Interior.

Harvest having commenced, very few able-bodied men came, and the works at Campbell's Tomb, the Queen's, and Belzoni's Chambers, were necessarily discontinued. In the course of the day the chamber, subsequently called Nelson's, was discovered. It was entirely empty, had no regular entrance, and was floored with the reverse of the granite blocks of Wellington's Chamber, which it much resembled, as it had these dimensions, thirty-eight feet nine inches, by sixteen feet eight inches. The ceiling was of polished granite, and resembled those in the other chambers; but the northern and southern sides of the room were not entirely of that material. Several quarry-marks were inscribed in red upon the blocks, particularly on the western side. This apartment was evidently intended for the same purpose as those below it, viz. to carry off the weight of the building from the King's Chamber.

### April 26th.

Reis, 9.        Men, 71.        Children, 72.

Great  Pyramid.—Excavation in northern front.

——              Excavation in southern front.

——              Nelson's Chamber.

——              Northern Air-channel.

Third  Pyramid.—Interior.

Fourth Pyramid.—Interior.

All hopes of an important discovery were not yet given up, and the best quarrymen were employed to get above the roof of Nelson's Chamber. I was sorry to have so few men, but the excuse, viz. the harvest, would not allow of a complaint. I sent an account of our discoveries to Mr. Hamilton.

### April 27th.

Reis, 9.        Men, 50.        Children, 52.

The same works were repeated.

The quarry-marks in Nelson's Chamber were copied. Several Arab Sheiks called. Every evening just before sunset there were strong gusts of wind, chiefly from the north and north-west.

### April 28th.

Reis, 9.  Men, 76.  Children, 59.
The same works were repeated.

Mr. Hill inscribed Nelson's great name in the chamber lately discovered.

### April 29th.

Reis, 9.  Men, 58.  Children, 53.
The same works were repeated.

We had been employed in the interior of the Great Pyramid, and had just come out from the entrance, when Dr. and Mrs. Hardy, and Mr. Andrews came up the side of the building to inspect it.[1] They went into the pyramid, and, after dinner, returned to Cairo with Mr. Hill, and Mr. Raven. Three Arabs ran away during the

---

[1] This view has been taken from a point rather below the floor of the entrance, or the surface of the upper tier of stones, which form the foreground, would have been visible, as they are laid at the same angle as the passage itself, namely, 26·41. The entrance is at some distance from the stones in the foreground.

The large blocks, placed *en décharge* over the entrance, have given rise to many conjectures. Some have imagined that an immense portal existed, in contradiction not only to antient testimony, but to the internal evidence of the building itself, by which it is clear that the entrance was carefully concealed. Others have conceived that a succession of these stones was placed over the passage, in order to sustain the superincumbent weight of the structure; but upon examination, square masonry is found immediately behind them; and it may also be remarked that

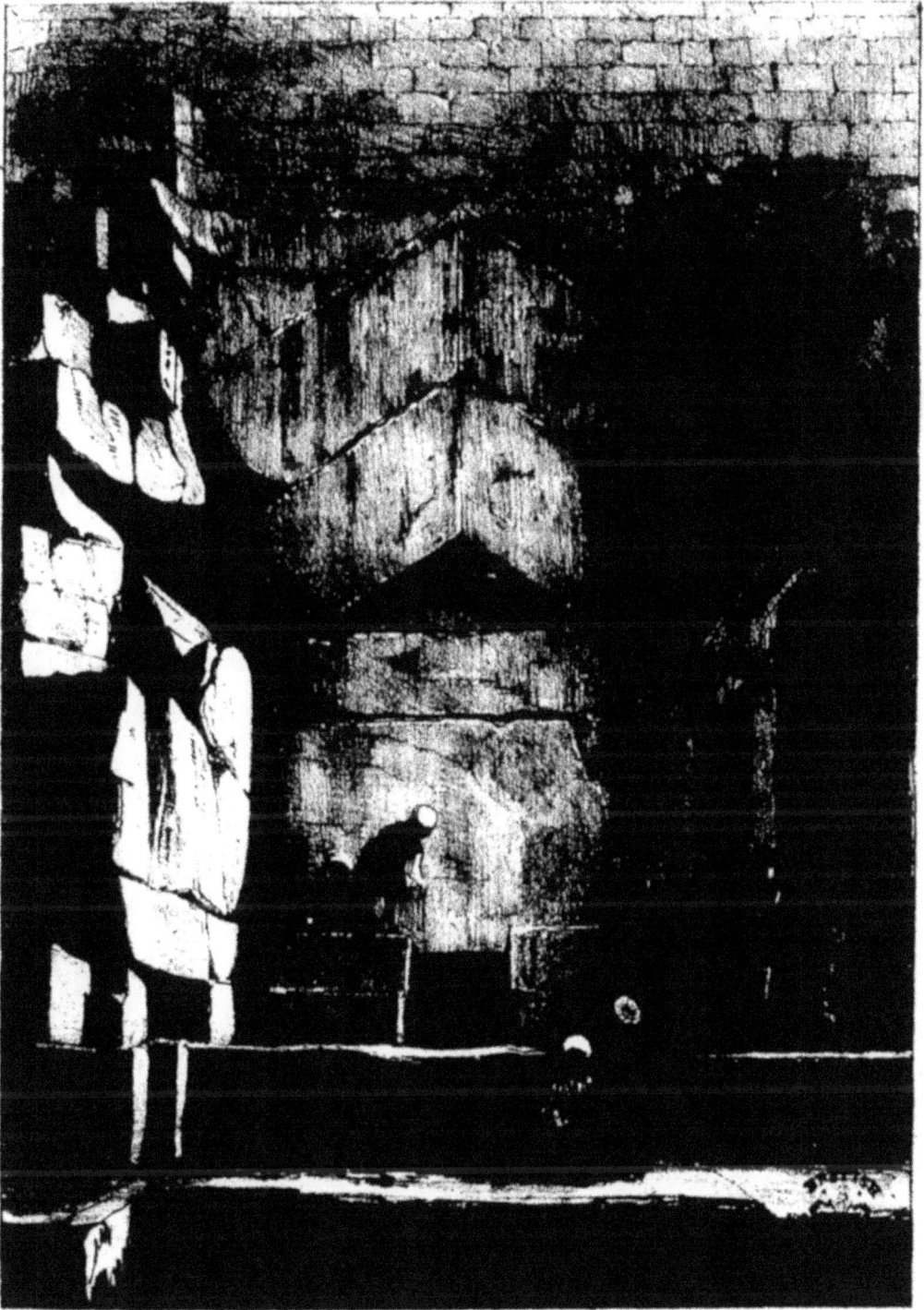

ENTRANCE to the GREAT PYRAMID.

Published by James Fraser, Regent St

night from the Third Pyramid, under pretence of having been ill treated by Jack. I sent the men to their respective villages. Upon inquiry, it appeared that they had totally neglected their work, and had been found fast asleep.

*April 30th.*—I sent for the Sheik of Koum el Eswith, and represented to him the ill conduct of the men on the preceding night. He promised to send a better party; but, in the evening, the same men appeared. He was, therefore, again summoned, and attended at last with a different set.

## May 1st.

Reis, 8.        Men, 74.        Children, 79.

The same works were repeated.

Some men were employed during the night at the excavation near Nelson's Chamber; but it was afterwards determined that a party, at an advanced price of three piastres, should come very early in the morning, and work through the day under the superintendence of Daoud.

I wrote again to Nayler Bey about the sick people.

## May 2d.

Reis, 9.        Men, 107.        Children, 106.

The same works were repeated.

Several Arab chiefs came. Red quarry marks were owing to the form of the pyramid, the upper end of the passage, near the exterior, has no great weight to support.

The courses are inclined near the entrance, but gradually become horizontal, like the rest of the building. The blocks, forming the sides of the passage, are laid perpendicularly to it.

continually found upon the stones, that were removed at the southern front of the Great Pyramid.

### May 3d.

Reis, 9.　　Men, 61.　　Children, 46.

The same works were repeated.

I examined the rocky ground to the westward of the Great Pyramid, and the tombs and buildings to the north of the Second. Foundations might every where be traced under the sands; and shafts lined with unburnt bricks, amongst which probably a cartouche might be found, which would determine the date of the constructions.[*] Portals and sepulchral chambers had been formed in the northern ridge of the mountain. The entrance of one of the largest was supported by square pillars, and contained a mummy-pit. The interior consisted of two ruined chambers, which had formerly been adorned with painted stucco, but were filled with the sands of the desert. A staircase descended from these apartments to a lower range of excavations and shafts, where fragments of mummies, and of embalmed animals were to be found beneath the sand. Part of a large bird, which had been preserved with great care, was brought out. The footsteps of wild beasts, the sole tenants of these deserted sanctuaries, were every where to be seen.

Jack imagined that a stone on a level with the base at the southern front of the Fourth Pyramid concealed an entrance. I thought he was mistaken, but I allowed him to remove it, as the excavation might be of service in

---

[*] Much information might possibly be obtained from the cartouches on the bricks in the various ruins in Egypt.

other respects, and as it would, at all events, shew the level of the building.

Captain Demay, Mr. Mash, and Mr. Perring came; and Sir Robert Arbuthnot brought me a letter of introduction from Colonel Campbell.

### May 4th.

Reis, 9.      Men, 56.      Children, 52.
The same works were repeated.

Captain Demay and Mr. Hill went to Cairo. The stone at the Fourth Pyramid was blasted, but no passage was discovered. I directed that this excavation should be carried on to the centre, for the reasons already mentioned.

I became extremely anxious to finish my operations before the inundation of the Nile, and therefore sent again to the Sheiks of the different villages for more men. My applications were not, however, attended with much success, unless the weather was extremely hot, when the corn could not be safely carried, on account of its shedding. On these occasions a considerable number of people came to work, and the Sheiks took great merit to themselves, and boasted of their exertions in my service.

I did not observe any interference on the part of the Pacha's officers at either of these villages during the harvest; but there was no reason to suppose that they were exempt from the usual contributions in agricultural produce and in cattle.

The Egyptians have remained for many ages in the most abject condition; but it may be doubted whether their situation was at any period more calamitous than it is at present, although they enjoy the inestimable benefit of a strong and efficient government — without which, neither private security, nor public prosperity, can long exist. Unhappily, however, this peculiar advantage is in many instances perverted to their ruin, and together with their own idleness, dishonesty, and ignorance, has plunged them into a state of misery, which Christianity and its attendant blessings can alone effectually relieve. It may, therefore, be worth while to consider how far the Pacha deserves the commendations so lavishly bestowed upon him in this country, in consequence of the innovations, and reforms he has attempted in his own; and whether a power, as extensive as that which was at any time possessed by the Romans in Egypt and in Syria, has been exerted for the welfare of those countries, or for the gratification of his own private ambition.

The schools and manufactories every where established, indicate, as I have already mentioned, the Pacha's anxiety to civilize the people; and the condition of the army and navy, however inferior they may be to European establishments — his success in war — the whole tenour of his memorable life — and, above all, the unexampled extent of his authority, prove the resources and vigorous energy of his mind, and also the rectitude of his intentions, whenever his own personal interests do not interfere. At the same time it is to be observed, that notwithstanding these merits, influenced probably by the prejudices of early life, he appears to be desirous of carrying his improvements into effect on the short-sighted principles of eastern despotism; and to be unable to understand, that the permanent interests of every government are essentially involved in the prosperity of the people: that, for instance, the most effectual manner of increasing his own revenue would be to employ his despotic authority in preventing fraud and oppression, and by a firm administration of justice to establish the foundation of all prosperity — namely, security of person and of property. But the idea of self-interest seems to actuate every arrangement. Instead of holding out an incitement to agriculture, (in which, after all, the real wealth and power of Egypt consist), the Pacha, according to a custom, which has long prevailed in this unfortunate country, has taken possession of the land, and carries on the cultivation by forced labour. A great proportion of produce and of cattle of every description, is periodically taken from the villages ; and, besides the usual duties, taxes are levied upon the palm trees and the sakias — imposts, which inflict great privations upon the people, and directly tend to limit cultivation. With the same interested view monopolies of every kind are established ; the sale even of the necessaries of life is regulated by the Pacha, and the prices vary from time to time as appears most likely to suit his immediate speculations. When to these measures are added the oppression of the Sheiks, and of the other subordinate officers — the spoliation arising from the farming of the taxes — and the rapacity that any appearance of wealth excites — together with the actual poverty occasioned by commercial monopolies and by legal enactments, that have the effect of sumptuary laws — it is not surprising that provisions have risen considerably in price ; that corn is imported for home consumption ; and that the people have acquired such habits of hopeless and dejected indolence, that the common operations of life can scarcely be carried on without coercion, and the dread of corporal punishment. In addition to these evils frequent conscriptions for the military services,

and for the manufactories, have reduced the population to that degree that vast tracts of fertile land are
left uncultivated; and the repeated levies are so repug-
nant to the people, that they frequently put out an eye,
and otherwise mutilate themselves and their children,
or escape to the mountains to secure their freedom. It
has been supposed, that, if the Pacha's independence and
the quiet possession of the territories at present under his
authority were formally guaranteed, his subjects would
experience relief by a considerable diminution of his army
and navy; but even this result is not probable, for like
all other usurpations his power can only be supported by
extensive military establishments, and they will always be
kept up on some pretext or other : such as the expedition
of 10,000 men, which was contemplated in 1838, to take
possession of the gold mines in Kordofan, and in the
adjoining countries.

The war in the Hedj-as has been a principal cause
of these oppressions, and, after all, is likely to prove an
unsuccessful contest. It occasions (as I have already
observed), not only a vast consumption, but also an immense waste of supplies of every description; and so great
a loss of men, that the conscription has not only been
extended with great severity into the upper country,
where people are forcibly carried off by day and by
night; but coffles of slaves have been sent from Suakim,
to repair the vast numbers, who perish by disease, by
famine, and by desultory warfare with an active and
indefatigable enemy.

As the habits of the people in Syria are more domestic
and refined than those of the Arabs, the misery and de-
spair occasioned by conscription are more severely felt in

that country; and there also, in consequence of general insecurity, and of the want of hands, cultivation is much diminished, and provisions are proportionably dear. But, as it was said of the Romans, "ubi solitudinem faciunt pacem appellant," so it must be confessed, that by disarming the country, and by drafting such considerable numbers for military service, before the late disturbances broke out public tranquillity was preserved, and the safety of the traveller ensured to a degree never before experienced.[3] What may now be the situation of that interesting country, and to what an extent the dreadful evils, which the Syrians experienced from their brutal oppressors, may at present be carried, it is painful to consider. No situation, not even that of the Greeks, which excited so much sympathy in Europe, can be more desperate; and the

---

[3] During a tour in Syria, I witnessed many distressing scenes at Jerusalem, Hebron, and at other places. The dread of conscription indeed, was so universal, that the inhabitants of the villages immediately concealed themselves upon the appearance of a traveller, who accidentally approached to obtain information respecting the road, or for any other purpose: and the waste lands about Cæsarea Philippi, and in other parts of the country, were full of unfortunate persons, who, having fled from their homes or from their escorts, found shelter in the woods and thickets, and who must in the end from necessity become banditti. The Emir Bechir was compelled to take his subjects by force, and to confine them in his own palace for the inspection of the Pacha's officers. A considerable number were imprisoned in the buildings that surround the great court at Ebtedin. Some of them escaped; but in March 1835 about fifty-six were inspected by Achmet Bey, and on the morning of the 13th they were brought down into the great court, where they were fastened in parties of ten or twelve by a long rope, with their hands confined in a cleft piece of wood. Their cries and lamentations were dreadful. If they went aside, and knelt down to pray, they were driven back

Syrians have an additional misfortune, in the conviction that their calamities lead to no permanent result, but that they are themselves sacrificed and their country ruined, for the transitory interests of the Pacha and of his son.

Affairs, however, cannot long continue in their present state, either in Egypt or in Syria; European interference must sooner or later take place, and unless the interests of Great Britain be in future better attended to than they are at present, that interference, particularly in the event of the death of the Pacha or of his son Ibrahim, will be French. The influence which that people already possess in these countries must be obvious to every casual observer. Their language is taught in the different seminaries, the European instructors in the military and civil establishments, are almost entirely French, or Italians connected with France; and last, although not least, education and accomplishments are diffused in the different hareems through the same channels.

This nation also, whose interests have always been, and must necessarily be hostile to those of Great Britain, have established a complete system of steam navigation in the Mediterranean precisely at the moment when the communication with India is opened through Egypt, and have

into the crowd by the sticks of the Arab soldiers; and were at length marched off under a strong escort, never to return. A woman dressed in white, with a child in her arms, and with her naked feet swollen and bleeding, followed the party in mournful silence as it proceeded over the rocky mountains.*

---

* Since this was written, Mr. Farren's "Letter to Lord Lindsey" has been published, and fully corroborates these remarks, as far as they relate to Syria.

also formed permanent establishments in Africa, which give them, besides other important advantages, the command of both shores of that sea, and place them within a few hours' sail of Sicily.   They have likewise, a considerable army in the field, and armaments afloat, much superior in numbers to our fleet at Malta; whilst on the other hand, the garrisons at the Ionian Islands, and at Malta are very weak.   The system likewise by which the latter place has hitherto been supplied with grain, is proposed to be given up, notwithstanding that Egypt and Sicily import corn for home consumption, that the supply from Barbary may at any time be prevented by the plague, or, in the present state of affairs by French interference, and that the trade with Odessa is daily becoming more and more precarious.   To complete the whole, a free press is to be established at Malta, which cannot fail of exciting discontent against our own authority, and well-grounded apprehensions in the neighbouring states, as the island will naturally become a receptacle for the turbulent and seditious, whose crimes may occasion their expulsion from other countries.[*]   These matters cannot but excite the apprehension and wonder of those, who consider the importance of Malta, as regards our eastern possessions, and who call to mind the extreme jealousy naturally felt by all former governments at the repeated efforts made by our national enemy from time to time, and particularly during the last war, to secure possession of it, and to extend her power in the Mediterranean as a means of promoting an interest in India similar to that, which it formerly cost this country so much blood and treasure to counteract.

[*] It is to be observed, that the written language of Malta is Italian.

The interests of different nations must ever, according to their relative positions, be conflicting and opposite; and war will inevitably ensue, unless aggression be met with a dignified and timely assertion of right, supported by an adequate power to enforce remonstrance. But what is the case at present? The military establishments of France, and of the whole of Europe are wisely kept up in an efficient state, while those of Great Britain are so reduced that they cannot even preserve tranquillity at home, and in the colonies, much less can they meet the difficulties of the times abroad; and this at a moment when the East Indies are menaced by the power of Russia, and by the defection of the native princes on the one hand, and by the aggrandisement of the French on the other; when, owing to seditious practices both within, and without the walls of parliament, Canada is probably for ever lost, and Ireland scarcely acknowledges obedience to the law. The government in fact under the influence, if not the dictation of a corrupt press, of reformers and dissenters of all sorts and denominations are no longer free agents, but temporise, and fluctuate in order to meet the inflamed and democratic fancies of a senseless, and deluded mob, rather than to promote by a steady, and consistent policy the great and permanent interests of the State. History can scarcely furnish an instance, in which a government in little more than twenty years has so rapidly lost stability at home, and consideration abroad.

The prosperity and power of Great Britain consisted in institutions and principles of government that united in one common interest the different classes of a well-regulated community; and a foreign policy consonant to these monarchical principles maintained the country in security and happiness through years of calamity and of war, and finally advanced her to a summit of unexampled glory. This policy is now entirely discarded, and our former alliances are postponed in favour of a connexion with revolutionary France; who, with a patriotic steadiness well worthy of imitation, is gradually but rapidly advancing her national interests over those of this country.

These matters are not mere assertions, but facts evident in every part of Europe from Russia to the unfortunate Peninsula to any person who will take the trouble to examine them. It is likewise equally manifest that these evils will not only continue, but must rapidly increase as long as republican principles are permitted to infest the country, and to array the different classes of society against each other — as long as corresponding unions for the avowed purpose of rebellion are allowed to exist, and itinerant demagogues to excite the people to insurrection, by a false display of imagined rights, incompatible with any form of civilized society, and utterly subversive of those institutions in Church, and State, upon which the real liberty and welfare of every individual are founded.

These observations may appear irrelevant to the subject of this book; but to what part of the world can an English traveller direct his steps without perceiving with proud exultation the high position which his country has attained among the nations of the earth, and without feeling an ardent and increased desire to perpetuate a constitution and form of government, which, under Providence, have been the sources of such great advantage?

To return, however, to the object more immediately in question — namely, the present state of Egypt — it will appear upon examination, that the manufacturing interests are not in a more prosperous condition than those connected with agriculture.

In consequence of the communication by steam, Egypt will probably again become a great emporium of Eastern commerce; and if encouragement was given to the valuable productions which the country can abundantly supply, and if security of property and freedom of trade were established, an extensive intercourse must take place, that would greatly contribute to the prosperity of the country, and to the civilization of its inhabitants. But, unfortunately, the Pacha, either from an idea of independence or of improving the habits of the people, endeavours to supply the wants of the country by native industry. The home-market is, therefore, stocked with inferior articles; and monopolies are necessary to prevent the importation of those of a better description at a cheaper rate, and at once put a stop to speculation and improvement. The establishments are extensive, and comprehend various branches of manufacture — such as, silk and cotton, cloths, hardware, paper, glass, sugar, &c., the arms and accoutrements for the army, and the stores for the naval arsenals. The machinery is in general excellent; and some of the superintendents are Franks — a few of whom possess knowledge and abilities, that could not fail of leading to a favourable result in the course of time; but from a jealousy of European interference, from intrigue and party motives, or from a mistaken idea of economy, these persons seldom keep their situations for any length of time. Even those appointed by the late Mr. Galloway, who is said to have been an intelligent person and to have had great influence, were discharged in his absence, and replaced by Turks or Arabs, unqualified for the business.

There is also a total want of co-operation between the several departments, which are under the direction of Boards, chiefly composed of worthless adventurers from all nations, who abound in Egypt, and are ready to undertake any speculation by which money can be obtained. The Pacha appears to be aware of their characters, and to employ them merely because he cannot procure better assistance, without being fully sensible of the mischief that results from their mismanagement, of which, amongst many others, the following instance occurred when I was in Egypt:—An instrument belonging to one factory was essentially necessary for the repair of the machinery in another; but, notwithstanding repeated applications, and a written order from what was considered the proper authority, it was never obtained, the repair could not be effected, and the operation of the establishment was consequently impeded. From the same insubordination, and spirit of rivalry, fictitious prices are put upon the manufactures furnished for the Pacha's service, in order to shew the prosperous state of the different establishments, which not only renders it impossible to form an estimate for any undertaking, but gives rise to endless disputes, and altercations between the persons employed and the government.[5] Amongst other causes of failure, an apparent want of steadiness in the Pacha himself may be mentioned, for one project is no sooner begun than it is abandoned for another; and also a total ignorance of the means necessary for the accomplishment of his designs,

[5] Inferior articles of wrought-iron have, in this manner, been valued at four times the price at which the best might have been obtained from England.

which occasions the employment of people in situations for which they are totally unfit; it may likewise be remarked, that either from ignorance, or unaccountable obstinacy, inferior machinery is in many instances made use of when that of a superior kind, and imported at a vast expense, is spoiling through neglect, and is often entirely forgotten, and destroyed. Besides these circumstances, the benefits derived from the division of labour are entirely overlooked, and, in short, so many difficulties arise from the dirty and idle habits of the Arabs, their want of skill and extreme repugnance to labour,[6] from the heat of the climate and the dryness of the air, that it is surprising that the articles produced under such disadvantages are not more imperfect.

[6] The occurrence here stated will shew the manner in which compulsory labour is carried on. An Arab blacksmith, employed by me at Gizeh, was taken up in Cairo, on account of a debt alleged to be due from him to the Pacha, but he was immediately released as being under the protection of the British flag. Upon inquiry, it appeared that the man had been originally taken by conscription, and employed, although ignorant of the trade, to convert a certain weight of iron in a given time into a quantity of nails, which it was found could be effected by a skilful workman. The deficiency that necessarily arose from his inexperience was deducted from his wages, and he was also to be kept to hard labour and imprisoned till the whole was paid: his embarrassments, therefore, could terminate only with his existence, as every stroke with his hammer plunged him deeper into debt. He was also obliged to bribe the person employed in weighing out the iron, who would otherwise have given him short weight. The Pacha is entirely ignorant of these acts of oppression that perpetually occur. He cannot with justice be accused of cruelty; indeed, many instances of his generosity and clemency might be cited; nor did I witness during the time I was in his dominions, any instance of capital punishment, excepting of a woman (for the same offence as that mentioned in Mr. Lane's interesting work, namely, the marrying four husbands at the same time), an execution probably pro-

Egypt, in its present state, is ill-fitted for manufacturing speculations, and the population would derive infinitely more advantage, and also be more effective for military purposes, by employment in agricultural pursuits and in the production of cotton, indigo, sugar, grain, &c., than by forced labour in unwholesome factories.

German and English miners and engineers have explored Mount Lebanon, the neighbourhood of Tarsous, and other parts of the Pacha's dominions, and coal and iron ore have been sent to a blast furnace, lately erected at Cairo; the metal hitherto used has been brought from foreign countries. Iron ordnance is imported, but brass guns are cast in the citadel. They are, however, imperfectly formed, as the metal, from not being properly refined, gives out a quantity of scoriæ; and as the mules have not sufficient power to keep the turning machine

ceeding from Mahomedan laws and customs, with which the Pacha could not well interfere. The gaols, however, are in a most horrible condition; the people are fastened by the neck to a chain, and are crowded together in a most disgusting state, with scarcely any light, air, or food; so that, considering the intense heat of the climate, it is surprising that malignant fevers are not the consequence. The suppression of the dancing girls, who had existed from the earliest periods, as antient sculpture proves, was an extraordinary instance of the Pacha's despotic authority, and of the promptness with which it is put in force. They were simultaneously seized upon at Fouah, Nigeleh, Cairo, and throughout the whole of Egypt. Many of them, married as well as single, were sent to the army in Syria, and the rest confined at Esneh, and at other towns in Upper Egypt. Their performances were entirely prohibited and put a stop to. The duty (about £4000) which they paid as a license in Cairo, was levied upon the rest of the inhabitants; and no disturbance of any kind ensued, although their exhibitions formed a considerable part of the amusements of all classes. With a power so despotic, how much good might be effected!

steadily in motion. The muskets are most injudiciously of both French and English patterns, but together with the rest of the arms are tolerably made according to models. The cutlery is not well finished, and is often decorated after the French fashion, with plated ornaments. Files, at present cannot be manufactured.

The construction of a wet-dock at Alexandria has for many years engaged the Pacha's attention, and people of various qualifications have from time to time been employed upon it, but hitherto with little success. In order to procure materials for this, and for similar undertakings, a railroad has been laid at the western end of the harbour for the conveyance of stone. The quarries, which are immediately accessible by it, have, however, been nearly worked out in forming the road, and a quay at the bottom of a small cove; and the cove itself is approached with risk owing to sunken rocks. Another railway has been lately established near Tourah, between the antient quarries on the Mokattam and the Nile; this is under able direction, and may be of use, but the line was not well chosen, and was adopted by one of the boards contrary to the opinion of the civil engineer employed in conducting the work.

The communication with India by means, of wheel carriages across the desert from Cairo to Suez, and of steam vessels on the Nile, and on the Red Sea, must have the most beneficial effects upon Egypt; it is, therefore, the Pacha's interest to give it every support, and at present he seems inclined to do so. It cannot, however, be considered as an establishment connected with the government.

It is unnecessary to allude to the various canals for

the irrigation of the land, and to other improvements, particularly about Cairo and Alexandria, which have in many instances been attended with success.[7] Of these, perhaps the canal from Alexandria to Atfee is the most remarkable; but the Barrage is worthy of notice, which has for its object, besides the addition to the revenue which its name implies, a considerable increase of the productive ground; although it may be observed that at the time it was begun vast tracks of fertile land were lying waste for want of hands to cultivate them. It is said to have originated from a survey taken when Napoleon was in Egypt; but it can hardly be supposed that he had leisure to attend to such matters, and still less, if an opportunity had occurred, that he would have attempted so extraordinary a project.

It is proposed to stop up the Rosetta and Damietta branches, and to cut a new channel for the river from the northern end of the Delta, and also to construct at that point immense flood-gates, by which the level of the water is to be raised and regulated. The difficulties to be surmounted may be easily imagined. The stream is exceedingly powerful, and varies considerably at every season of the year, and also in one year from another. The present channels are wide and very deep, and, consequently, the formation of a new watercourse of a suffi-

[7] Amongst other undertakings, a company of Greeks were employed in 1837 to weigh up a number of guns in the Bay of Aboukir: many of them are English, and were probably lost in the unfortunate expedition under General Fraser, of which no detailed account was ever published. It was probably thought by the ministry then in power that the result of the expedition to the Dardanelles was sufficient to gratify public curiosity.

cient capacity will be attended with prodigious labour and expense; and it is to be doubted whether, from the nature of the soil, an adequate foundation can be obtained for buildings intended to resist the full force, (even during the inundation,) of a stream at all seasons navigable for one thousand miles by boats of fifty or sixty tons. Neither the expense nor the consequences of such a gigantic undertaking can be calculated; and the desired effect might be obtained by partial means at a much less expense, and without the risk that must attend any great alteration in the channel of such a body of water. To form an opinion of the abilities of the Pacha's advisers, and of their resources for such an undertaking, it is only necessary to mention that it was proposed to take down the Pyramids of Gizeh, Saccara, Dashoor, &c., and to use the materials in stopping up the branches of the river. Fortunately, however, both projects are equally impracticable.

In 1836 an attempt had been made to dig out the foundations, and a few tons of stone had been collected; a range of mills and ovens had also been built for the supply of forty or fifty thousand men, but upon so bad a plan, that a much fewer number would have answered the purpose. The work was soon afterwards discontinued on account, as it was alleged, of a great mortality amongst the labourers, but, in fact, because both money and men were wanting, and also because the projectors found it impossible to proceed.

*May 5th.*

Reis, 9.　　Men, 56.　　Children, 56.
The same works were repeated.

More of the buff earthenware with the green glaize was found near the northern front of the Great Pyramid.

### May 6th.

Reis, 9.      Men, 71.      Children, 80.

The same works were repeated.

I copied some hieroglyphics which Mr. Perring had observed on the ruins of the temple eastward of the

Second Pyramid.[8]   These characters appeared to be upon the inner face of a stone, which must therefore have previously belonged to some other building of extraordinary antiquity; and it is to be remarked that blocks have been discovered in the tombs to the westward of the Great Pyramid inscribed with inverted hieroglyphics on their inward faces.

Whilst I was thus employed, M. Deval, the son of the French consul at Aleppo, introduced himself.   I sent

---

[8] This inscription had been observed and copied by Mr. Salt, and, through the kindness of the Earl of Mountnorris, I am enabled to insert it as it appeared when that gentleman was in Egypt.   Since that time some of the characters have been effaced.

some people with lights to shew him the interior of the pyramids. Soon afterwards I met his father, with M. Massara, the French dragoman, whom I invited to the tents. I then joined Mr. Perring and Mr. Mash, who were employed in surveying the ground between the Great and Second Pyramids. At twelve o'clock M. Deval and his son came to my tent, and, after having taken some refreshment, the former returned to Cairo, and the latter with the dragoman went on to Saccara.

The chamber above Nelson's (afterwards called Lady Arbuthnot's) was opened, and in the course of the afternoon I entered it with Mr. Raven. We found this apartment of the same description, and nearly of the same dimensions as the others below it, being thirty-seven feet four inches by sixteen feet four inches. Like the rest it was quite empty, and built in the same manner, but with less care, and with a greater proportion of calcareous stone on the northern and southern sides. The excavation was continued, in order to get above it.

In the evening I returned to Cairo with Mr. Perring and Mr. Mash.

*May 7th.*—I called on Sir Robert and Lady Arbuthnot at Colonel Campbell's house.

### *May 8th.*

Reis, 9.　　Men, 61.　　Children, 91.

Great Pyramid.—Excavation in southern front.

—— 　　　Excavation in northern front.

—— 　　　Lady Arbuthnot's Chamber.

—— 　　　Northern Air-channel.

Third Pyramid.—Interior.

Fourth Pyramid.—Interior.

I returned in the afternoon with Mr. Hill to the pyramids.

In crossing the Nile I saw a crowd of people on the eastern bank, who, I was informed, were assembled to witness the execution of a woman for having married four husbands.[9]   The criminal soon made her appearance, completely wrapped up, and concealed in an Arab shawl, and was conducted down the bank to a boat, and seated in the bottom.   She was tied round, and probably strangled, with a cord, to the end of which a heavy stone was affixed. The boat was then put off from the shore, and the woman, together with the stone, were suddenly thrown into the deep channel westward of the Mekias, on the Island of Rhoda.   I never afterwards passed the river without an unpleasant recollection of this event.   It was, however, the only execution that I witnessed during the two years I was travelling in the East.

An immense piece of rock of eight or nine tons weight fell during the night from the cliffs above the blacksmith's shop into the plain, but luckily without injury to any one.

### May 9th.

Reis, 9.          Men, 78.          Children, 80.

Great  Pyramid.—Excavation in southern front.
———            Excavation in northern front.
———            Lady Arbuthnot's Chamber.
———            Northern Air-channel.
———            Roof in Queen's Chamber.
Third  Pyramid.—Interior.
Fourth Pyramid.—Interior.

[9] It is remarkable that Mr. Lane, in his account of Egypt, mentions the execution of a woman for a similar offence.

Several pieces of broken pottery, a quantity of red stucco, or mortar composed of pounded granite, and of a red stone (some of which was found near it), were dug out near the base of the northern front of the Great Pyramid. This red stone is still used for the same purpose in Egypt.

A number of blocks which formed part of the casing were likewise discovered. As it was not then ascertained that the pyramid had been cased, these stones were at first supposed, from their angular shape, to have been employed in filling up, and in concealing the cavity near the entrance. They were extremely hard, and remarkably well worked; but contrary to the testimony of Abdallatif, and of other Arabian authors, they did not shew the slightest trace of inscription, or of sculpture. Nor, indeed, was any to be found upon any stone belonging to the pyramid, or near it (with the exception of the quarry-marks already described, of a few lines drawn in red upon a flat stone, apparently intended for a lining), and of part of the cartouche of Suphis, engraved on a

brown stone, six inches long by four broad. This fragment was dug out of the mound at the northern side on June 2d; but it did not appear to have belonged to the pyramid. Mr. Perring states, that he has not observed inscriptions upon stones quarried upon the spot, but only upon those brought from the Mokattam, and that the same red colouring, called moghrah, is now used in the

PANORAMIC VIEW OF THE RIVER, FROM THE TENTS.

quarries. The excavation under the roof of the Queen's Chamber was resumed. Lady Arbuthnot's Chamber was minutely examined, and found to contain a great many quarry-marks. Notwithstanding that the characters in these chambers were surveyed by Mr. Perring upon a reduced scale, I considered that facsimiles in their original size would be desirable, as they were of great importance from their situation, and probably the most antient inscriptions in existence. I requested therefore Mr. Hill to copy them. His drawings were compared with the originals by Sir Robert Arbuthnot, Mr. Brettel (a civil engineer), Mr. Raven, and myself, and are deposited in the British Museum.

Sir Robert and Lady Arbuthnot, and her brother, Mr. Fitzgerald (an officer in the fourth dragoons), arrived.

The weather was exceedingly hot, and the gnats and other insects, particularly the small sand-flies, were very troublesome. A number of Bedouins were continually passing along the sandy plain below the tents, as the proximity of the cultivated land afforded water and other resources for their flocks of sheep and goats, and herds of camels. They had few horses, and those very bad. The camels travelled at the rate of about two and a half miles per hour, in a desultory manner, wandering occasionally from the direct path to crop any prickly herbage that the desert might afford. The women were carried by them in close howdahs, or tents, made of blankets stretched over framework; and were not only exposed, in this confined situation, to the rough and irregular movements of the camels, but to the intense heat of the sun, and of the burning sands,—a mode of conveyance which constant habit could alone make supportable. They feel, however, a pride in being secluded, and thus taken care of. The men, armed with long guns, and shrouded from the rays of the sun by thick blankets, brought up the rear.

### May 10th.

Reis, 9.  Men, 112.  Children, 85.

The same works were repeated.

Mr. Perring, with the assistance of Mr. Hill, surveyed Lady Arbuthnot's Chamber. Sir Robert and Lady Arbuthnot examined the works, as far as the intense heat would allow. They had a long and uncomfortable voyage before them, at a very unfavourable season; as, besides crossing the desert to Suez, they were to make the voyage to Jidda, or to Mocha, in Arab boats, which are kept close to the shore, and are anchored every night; and were to proceed to Bombay in whatever vessel might accidentally be found at either of these ports.

### May 11th.

Reis, 9.  Men, 115.  Children, 106.

The same works were repeated.

### May 12th.

Reis, 9.  Men, 80.  Children, 91.

The same works were repeated.

Sir Robert and Lady Arbuthnot, and Mr. Fitzgerald, were obliged, much to my regret, to return to Cairo, on account of the great heat, which made such accommodation as I could give them very inconvenient, particularly for a lady. The thermometer in the tent in which we sat exceeded, during the day, one hundred and twenty degrees, and in the tombs, during the night, stood above

ninety.  Mr. Perring and Mr. Mash likewise returned to
Cairo.

After having gone round the several works, I was sent
for about two o'clock to the Great Pyramid, as the casing-
stones at the base had been discovered.  The size and
angle of the building could
therefore be exactly determined, and all doubts were
removed respecting a re-
vetment.   Two of the
blocks were in their ori-
ginal position, nearly in the centre of the pyramid;[1] and
those adjoining them to the eastward must have been
covered by the mound of rubbish for a considerable time
before they were removed, as the exact space, which
they had occupied, was left in it, like a perfect model.
Why they were thus taken out sideways, and by what
means, without disturbing any part of the mass above
them, it is difficult to say.

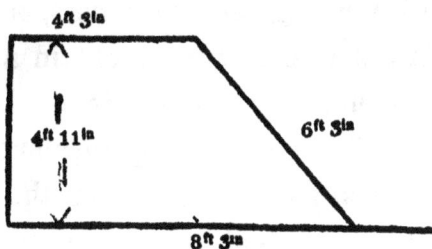

They were quite perfect, had been hewn into the
required angle before they were built in, and had then
been polished down to one uniform surface;[2] the joints
were scarcely perceptible, and not wider than the thickness of silver paper; and such is the tenacity of the
cement with which they are held together,[3] that a frag-

[1] Their dimensions were taken by Mr. Brettel, and the angle was
51·50.

[2] This was proved to have been the case by the excavations afterwards made at the Eighth Pyramid, which, it is remarkable, was supposed to be that of the daughter of Cheops.  See *August 8th*

[3] During a visit to Thebes, I endeavoured to find out the means by
which the blocks composing the columns in the Great Temple at Karnac

ment of one, that has been destroyed, remained firmly fixed in its original alignement, notwithstanding the lapse of time and the violence, to which it had been exposed. The pavement beyond the line of the building was well laid, and beautifully finished; but beneath the edifice it was worked with even greater exactness, and to the most perfect level, in order, probably, to obtain a lasting foundation for the magnificent structure to be built upon it. I consider that the workmanship displayed in the King's Chamber, in this pavement, and in the casing-stones, is perfectly unrivalled; and there is no reason to doubt that the whole exterior of this vast structure was covered with the same excellent masonry.

### May 13th.

Reis, 9.　　　Men, 114.　　　Children, 106.

The same works were repeated.

The Sheiks of Cafr el Batran, and of Harranieh, reported that the men of their respective villages would be sent for to clear out a canal in the neighbourhood. I went accordingly to Cairo in the evening, with Mr. Hill and Mr. Raven, and arranged, with Mr. Piozan, to visit

had been united. It was said that wood had been used for that purpose in the same manner as in the Grecian temples, but I could not discover any of that substance, nor yet of metallic fastenings; in searching, however, between the joints of one of the larger columns, the upper part of which, with its stupendous architrave, had fallen over probably many centuries before, I discovered in a cavity formed at the centre, in the shape of double wedges meeting at the points, a quantity of white cement, which, notwithstanding a long exposure to the extreme heat of the climate, had not been pulverised, but still retained a degree of moisture, and could be cut with a knife.

the Madyr of the district at Mabietta on the following morning at eight o'clock.

*May* 14*th.*—I went with Mr. Perring to Mabietta, but the Madyr had not arrived.   In the afternoon I was taken ill, and did not return to Gizeh till the evening of the 18th.

### *May 15th.*

Reis, 9.        Men, 81.        Children, 67.

The same works were repeated.

I was informed, by a letter from Mr. Raven, that the passage through the northern Air-channel was open, but that a partial obstruction remained, which he proposed to remove by means of the boring-rods.   This was soon effected, and the rods, and also water, passed freely from the top to the bottom, which proved that the Channel did not communicate with any apartment excepting the King's Chamber.   Before Mr. Raven's arrival this difficult operation had been attended to by Mr. Hill; but, in justice to the former gentleman, it is to be remarked, that, although he had at the same time the superintendence of all the other works, he succeeded in clearing ninety feet of the upper part of an inclined channel, only nine inches, by nine and a half inches, wide, and situated more than three hundred feet above the base upon the exterior of the pyramid, from the sand and stones with which it had for centuries been choked up.   For this purpose his Arab servant was constantly on the spot, and he was himself obliged to ascend the pyramid two or three times every day to direct the Arabs how to proceed.

### *May* 16*th*.

Reis, 9.        Men, 79.        Children, 78.
The same works were repeated.

### *May* 17*th*.

Reis, 9.        Men, 91.        Children, 106.
The same works were repeated.

I rode in the evening, with Sir Robert and Lady Arbuthnot, to see the ovens for hatching chickens at Gizeh. The process has been sufficiently described by Mr. Wilkinson, and also by Mr. Lane. The ovens were not in full work, as they can only be employed at particular seasons; but abundance of chickens had been produced. They appeared to have been dwarfed by the process, and, as M. Denon remarks, are sold by measure. The building was extremely dirty and full of vermin; and in order to arrive at the ovens, we were obliged to creep through several low doorways and narrow passages.

### *May* 18*th*.

Reis, 9.        Men, 86.        Children, 99.
The same works were repeated.

Dr. Walne applied, through Mr. Perring, for copies of the characters found in the Great Pyramid, in order to send them to M. Rosellini. I requested Mr. Perring to express my regret that I could not accede to his request, and received from that gentleman a satisfactory and obliging answer.

Mr. Piozan wrote to the Madyr respecting the men of Cafr el Batran, and of Harranieh.

I returned to the pyramids with Mr. Brettel and Sir Robert Arbuthnot, and found every thing in good order under Mr. Raven's superintendence.

The Shereef of Mecca had encamped on the arable land near the northern dyke.

## May 19th.

Reis, 9.          Men, 104.          Children, 96.

The same works were repeated.

Mr. Fitzgerald arrived before breakfast. The Shereef of Mecca having called in the morning, I returned his visit, but I did not see him, as he was at prayers. I received a letter from Mr. Piozan, to say that the Madyr would dine with me on the following Sunday.

We examined the northern Air-channel; and Sir Robert Arbuthnot, Mr. Brettel, Mr. Raven, and myself, compared Mr. Hill's drawings with the quarry-marks in the Great Pyramid; and we afterwards signed an attestation of their accuracy. The two former gentlemen and Mr. Fitzgerald returned at night to Cairo.

In the evening, the people belonging to the Shereef of Mecca exercised their horses with the jereed, in the sandy plain below the tents; several of them were well bred, and very clever, and the men were picturesquely dressed with Wahabee handkerchiefs on their heads, &c., and together with their horses, made a capital show. Their exploits with the jereed were not, however, very excellent, and the deep sand took away from the speed of their horses.

## *May 20th.*

Reis, 9.        Men, 126.        Children, 132.

Great  Pyramid.— Excavation in southern front.
———        Excavation in northern front.
———        Lady Arbuthnot's Chamber.
Second Pyramid.— Roof in Belzoni's Chamber.
Third  Pyramid.— Interior.
Campbell's Tomb.
Fourth Pyramid.— Interior.

Mr. Brettel arrived, and took the dimensions of the casing-stone.

I wrote to Mr. Hamilton.

The excavation at Campbell's tomb was again resumed. Abd el Ardi pointed out a shaft near the brick peribolus, to the northward of the Sphinx; another between that monument and Campbell's Tomb; and a third between Campbell's Tomb and the Second Pyramid, which contained water.[*]  The latter, he said, had been opened about three years before by M. Massara.   I directed, therefore, Mr. Hill to get a pump made, and a hose was sent for from Alexandria, in order to examine them.

Jack had been informed by an old Arab (who had been employed under M. Jemel in former excavations), that there was an underground communication between the southern front of the Third Pyramid and the most eastward of the three smaller to the south of it (which is called the Fifth).   Although I did not imagine that the information could be depended on, a party was set to work in search of it.   The Arab likewise stated, that some years ago four or five Europeans were employed in

---

[*] Marked in the Map, No. 3 ; No. 2 ; and No. 1.

excavating at the pyramids, and that they quarrelled so disgracefully, that the Pacha was obliged to interfere, and to divide the ground between them.

The wedding of a Sheik's son took place in an adjoining village, and in the morning an immense concourse of people came across the plain, no doubt in full expectation of a backshish; they were accompanied by a band of music and dancing; and some of the performers were girls, who, in addition to their usual dress, were covered with a loose drapery composed of shawls and scarfs, which floated in the air, as they moved about with swords in their hands, which they brandished with violent gestures.[5] The bride and her attendants were mounted upon camels; and horsemen fired and skirmished in various directions, and formed an escort, which was, probably, in other times, necessary as a defence. I gave them a few piastres, and a pound of English gunpowder. The Shereef of Mecca returned to Cairo.

*May 21st.*—Mr. Piozan arrived to meet the Madyr, and soon afterwards his dragoman brought us word that that person was engaged, and could not come, which I considered, on his own account a very happy circumstance, as it was extremely hot, and as the tent, which

---

[5] I saw an extraordinary ceremony of this kind at the celebration of a wedding in the Haouran, in which each of the women in turn figured with a sword, and appeared to defend herself with it from the men, who danced hand in hand in a circle around her, and pretended to approach her with the same violent gesticulations and hoarse guttural noises that they use in their religious performances, and, as in those exhibitions, they did not leave off till they were in a state of complete exhaustion. This dance is probably a very antient custom.

was all the accommodation I could offer, was ill calculated for a large party. I had provided cooks from Cairo, and a great Turkish dinner was prepared. In the course of the day, Mr. Hill drew my attention to an Arab, who was employed to turn a spit, upon which a sheep was roasting whole over a large fire; it had been lighted in an angle made by two walls, with the noon-day sun in full force upon it. The only protection which the man had from the rays of the sun was a cotton cap and a thick blanket; and although he appeared to be, upon the whole, better done than the sheep, he was perfectly unconcerned and at his ease. The wedding luckily afforded an opportunity for getting rid of the sheep, and of a variety of greasy dishes, for which, however, I never received any thanks or acknowledgment.

The exact level of the mouth of the northern Air-channel, on the exterior of the pyramid, was carried round to the southern front, the centre of which was also marked, and a reward of one hundred piastres offered to Abd el Ardi if he could find the mouth of the southern Channel. It was soon discovered in the same relative position as the northern.

Mr. Brettel, Mr. Piozan, and the dragoman, in the evening returned to Cairo.

### May 22d.

Reis, 7.     Men, 129.     Children, 154.

Great Pyramid.—Excavation in southern front.
———        Excavation in northern front.
———        Lady Arbuthnot's Chamber.
Second Pyramid.—Roof in Belzoni's Chamber.
Third Pyramid.—Interior.
Fourth Pyramid.—Interior.

Campbell's Tomb.
Excavation between the Third and Fifth Pyramids.
Boring the Sphinx.
Shaft westward of Sphinx.

As the rods were no longer employed at the Air-channel, the boring at the shoulder of the Sphinx was again resumed; and a party was sent to clear out the shaft which contained the water between the Sphinx and Campbell's Tomb.

I went to Cairo, and sent Mr. Perring's drawings, and Mr. Hill's facsimiles of the quarry-marks to Colonel Campbell at Alexandria, to be forwarded to Mr. Hamilton.

### May 23d.

Reis, 7.     Men, 137.     Children, 183.
The same works were repeated.

On returning to the pyramids with Mr. Hill, I called at Gizeh, on the Madyr Mahmoud Effendi. As he was taking his siesta, and was not visible for some time, I was received by the Mamoor. I was at length, however, admitted, and found him in a large airy apartment, fitted up with a divan in the Turkish manner. After the usual ceremony of coffee, pipes, &c., I explained the object of my visit; namely, that he would assist me in procuring more men, and also in insuring their regular attendance. I likewise mentioned, that the Sheiks had informed me that their people would be sent to work at the canal. He replied, that he had heard from Colonel Campbell on the subject, and had written already to the Sheiks, and that he would again send orders to them. I then expressed my regret that I had not the honour of seeing him at the pyramids on Sunday, and my hope that he would name another day for that purpose; he said that he was then about to proceed into Upper Egypt, but that on his return he would pay me a visit.[6]

[6] On this occasion, as on many others, I felt the want of a proper dragoman; and, I may add, that many of the difficulties and quarrels which travellers meet with are owing to the ignorance or dishonesty of their interpreters. Nothing can, indeed, completely supply the place of personal communication; yet a professed dragoman is always more useful than a common man like the Copt employed upon the present occasion, who could neither understand, nor express any complimentary language: and who, in all probability, made ridiculous, and even offensive, what was intended to be obliging and respectful. For instance, when I told the Madyr that one of the chief objects of my visit was to express my regret at not having had the honour of seeing him at the pyramids, and my hope that he would appoint an early day for that purpose, I have reason to believe that Ibrahim told him that I came to know why he had not come according to his engagement, and when I might expect him. The English consulate at Cairo is badly provided in this respect. Other nations, by giving adequate salaries, are served by men, who can be depended upon; in many instances by Franks properly educated and instructed in the language of the country. The miserable pittance afforded by us will not retain a respectable person; and the hinderance and embarrassment in public affairs, and the difficulty and injustice in private transactions where these interpreters are concerned, together with the consequent estrangement and disgust generally felt for consular authority, may be readily imagined. The dragoman of the British consulate, when I left Cairo, was a son of the French interpreter—a circumstance not likely to insure secrecy or despatch, where British interests were concerned. The Turkish and Arab authorities perceive their advantage, and in private matters but too often profit by the ignorance or corruption of these inefficient agents. It may also be observed, that the consuls themselves, however zealous and respectable, are in an awkward and false position in Mahommedan countries, where Europeans are, to a great degree, exempt from the Turkish and Arab authorities, and only amenable to that of their own consulate, which, in the case of the British consul, is exercised on personal responsibility.

In proceeding to the pyramids, the Kamseen wind was extremely violent. Near the village of Cafr el Batran I was met by two men, who stretched out a red ribbon before my donkey, to intimate that I must stop and give a backshish to two sons of a Sheik, who had just been married. I found that it was a usual custom in this part of the country, and I therefore complied with it. The bridegrooms were fine-looking lads; their red caps, and blankets, were new and clean, and their hands were stained red with henna.[7]

The shaft in the centre of the Third Pyramid was fifty feet deep, but had not led to the discovery of any apartment or passage. Some green idols were found in the southern part of the fosse at Campbell's Tomb.

### May 24th.

Reis, 8.        Men, 146.        Children, 168.

Great Pyramid.—Excavation in southern front.
———        Excavation in northern front.

If a Consul abuses his power, he should be deprived of his situation; but in the proper exercise of his authority, he should be supported, and not be liable to such penalties as Mr. Barker has incurred, or with which Mr. Farren had been threatened, in 1836, in consequence of a transaction at Damascus. At all events, some more effectual power than that which now exists should be provided to control the rabble of Maltese, Ionians, and, I may add, of British adventurers, of every class and description, who seek in Egypt, and in the East, for employment, which their crimes and notoriety prevent their attaining in their own countries.

[7] A red dye (said to be composed of minium), was used by the Romans, on joyful and triumphant occasions. Could this custom have been deduced from Egypt? The application of henna, and also of indigo, appears to have been of great antiquity, and to have prevailed formerly amongst the savages that inhabited Europe, as it does at present amongst most others in every part of the world.

Great Pyramid.—Lady Arbuthnot's Chamber.
Second Pyramid.—Roof in Belzoni's Chamber.
Third Pyramid.—Interior.
Excavation between the Third and Fifth Pyramids.
Campbell's Tomb.
Fourth Pyramid.—Interior.
Boring the Sphinx.
Shaft westward of Sphinx.
Shaft between Campbell's Tomb and Second Pyramid.

After much labour, the excavation at the southern front of the Great Pyramid had been carried to the level of the supposed entrance, but without the slightest appearance of a passage. The difficulties encountered in this operation proved how much expense and labour would be necessary to take down one of these great edifices. The stones must be carefully lowered from the top, or they would be broken, and unfit for any useful purpose; and unless extensive causeways were formed, the surrounding ground would soon be encumbered to that degree as to impede all further operations. So wonderfully have these monuments been constructed for duration.

In part of the fosse at Campbell's Tomb the bottom had been found at the depth of seventy-two feet. The shaft westward of the Sphinx was cleared, and a party had begun upon that between Campbell's Tomb and the Second Pyramid. The thermometer was 115° in the shade.

*May 25th.*

Reis, 8.     Men, 150.     Children, 172.

Great Pyramid.—Excavation in southern front.
———         Excavation in northern front.
———         Lady Arbuthnot's Chamber.
———         Southern Air-channel.

Second Pyramid.—Roof in Belzoni's Chamber.
Third Pyramid.—Interior.
Temple eastward of the Great Pyramid.
Excavation between the Third and Fifth Pyramids.
Campbell's Tomb.
Fourth Pyramid.—Interior.
Boring the Sphinx.
Shaft westward of Sphinx.
Shaft between Campbell's Tomb and Second Pyramid.
Shaft north of Sphinx.

An excavation was begun at the foundation (supposed to be that of a temple) to the eastward of the Great Pyramid. A few stones remained in their original position; but we soon found that nothing was to be discovered except by proceeding on a larger scale than at that time was advisable. The building appeared to have been destroyed by fire, as the basalt, which was in considerable quantities near this and the other foundations beyond it, seemed to have been burnt. Several of the blocks had been carried down the side of the mountain into the plain below, apparently for removal. Some men were employed at the shaft north of the Sphinx. Mr. Hill blasted near the mouth of the southern Air-channel, to get sufficient room for the erection of a scaffold to support the boring-rods, as we imagined that this operation would be attended with as much trouble as that on the northern front.

### May 26th.

Reis, 8.        Men, 153.        Children, 163.

Great Pyramid.—Excavation in southern front.
———        Excavation in northern front.
———        Lady Arbuthnot's Chamber.

Great Pyramid.—Southern Air-channel.
Second Pyramid.—Roof in Belzoni's Chamber.
Third Pyramid.—Interior.
Temple eastward of the Great Pyramid.
Excavation between the Third and Fifth Pyramids.
Campbell's Tomb.
Boring the Sphinx.
Shaft westward of Sphinx.
Shaft between Campbell's Tomb and Second Pyramid.
Shaft north of Sphinx.

I examined the shaft to the north of the Sphinx. The tomb was an excavation in the rock, and was entered on the southern side. An outer chamber conducted to two others, one to the north, and the other to the west; both of them contained shafts; and over that in the western chamber a figure, in a sitting posture, had been sculptured in a niche. As our object was to ascertain the level of the water, we only cleared out the shaft in the northern chamber, which was found to contain, at a certain depth, a sarcophagus, in a grotto or recess. The level of the water is given in the Appendix; and the only objects of interest which we met with, consisted of some green idols, a piece of flat stone marked with one or two straight lines, and the fragment of a Sphinx, about eighteen inches long, roughly carved in coarse stone, without inscription or hieroglyphics.

The boring-rods were broken owing to the carelessness of the Arabs, at the depth of twenty-seven feet in the back of the Sphinx. Various attempts were made to get them out, and on the 21st of July gunpowder was used for that purpose; but being unwilling to disfigure this venerable monument, the excavation was given up, and several feet of boring-rods were left in it. During the operation a very beautiful fossil of a reed was discovered, which is now in the British Museum.

The shaft to the westward of the Sphinx, was in a tomb formed in a ledge of rock. It was of considerable depth; and from the bottom of it, apartments had been excavated to the east and west — that to the east contained a sarcophagus of granite covered with hieroglyphics, the lid of which had been removed. Out of this apartment was another to the northward, with a recess on the eastern side, and two passages branched off towards the south. They had been already plundered, and contained only a small quantity of sand, a few large stones, and shallow water, which stood at the depth of four inches within the sarcophagus, and must have been, some time or other, therefore, as high as the top of it, unless it had been placed there by modern explorers. Abd el Ardi told me that the doorway into this tomb had been filled up with masonry, and that he had formerly cleared the sand out of it by a hole, which may still be seen near the entrance. Our researches, as in the other tomb, were confined to the examination of the water.

More fragments of coarse pottery were found in the excavation at the northern front of the Great Pyramid; and Mr. Hill discovered a piece of iron in an inner joint, near the mouth of the southern air-channel, which is probably the oldest piece of wrought iron known.[7] It has

[7] Lord Prudhoe is said to have brought from Egypt an antient iron instrument; and I thought that I had perceived the remains of an iron fastening in the chamber containing the sideboard or shelf in the great temple at Abou Simbel. In fact, stone could not have been quarried

been sent to the British Museum with the following certificates :—

"This is to certify, that the piece of iron found by me near the mouth of the Air-passage, in the southern side of the Great Pyramid at Gizeh, on Friday, May 26th, was taken out by me from an inner joint, after having removed by blasting the two outer tiers of the stones of the present surface of the Pyramid; and that no joint or opening of any sort was connected with the above-mentioned joint, by which the iron could have been placed in it after the original building of the Pyramid. I also shewed the exact spot to Mr. Perring, on Saturday, June 24th.

"J. R. HILL.

"Cairo, June 25th, 1837."

"To the above certificate of Mr. Hill, I can add, that since I saw the spot at the commencement of the blasting, there have been two tiers of stones removed, and that, if the piece of iron was found in the joint, pointed out to me by Mr. Hill, and which was covered by a larger stone partly remaining, it is impossible it could have been placed there since the building of the Pyramid.

"J. S. PERRING, C. E.

"Cairo, June 27th, 1837."

"We hereby certify, that we examined the place whence the iron in question was taken by Mr. Hill, and we are of opinion, that the iron must have been left in the joint during the building of the Pyramid, and that it could not have been inserted afterwards.

"ED. S. ANDREWS,
"JAMES MASH, C. E."

The mouth of this Air-channel had not been forced— it measured 8¼ inches wide by 9¼ inches high — and had

without metal, which must, therefore, have been in use in the earliest times. The smelting of metals seems to have been an antediluvian art, as artificers in iron are mentioned in the Bible; but it is impossible to say in what state metals then were. In M. Rosellini's work, people are represented cutting granite with a yellow instrument.

been effectually screened from the sands of the desert by a projecting stone above it. The northern had probably been constructed in the same manner.

### May 27th.

Reis, 8.     Men, 143.     Children, 174.

Great Pyramid.—Excavation in southern front.
——— Excavation in northern front.
——— Lady Arbuthnot's Chamber.
——— Southern Air-channel.
——— Roof in Queen's Chamber.
——— Temple eastward of Great Pyramid.
Second Pyramid.—Roof in Belzoni's Chamber.
Third Pyramid.—Interior.
Excavation between the Third and Fifth Pyramids.
Campbell's Tomb.
Fourth Pyramid.—Interior.
Shaft westward of Sphinx.
Shaft between Campbell's Tomb and Second Pyramid.
Shaft north of Sphinx.

The excavation near the roof in the Queen's apartment was again resumed. The chamber over Lady Arbuthnot's (subsequently called Campbell's) was opened and minutely examined. The people employed at the mouth of the southern Air-channel could be distinctly heard from it; its length was thirty-seven feet ten inches, and its width twenty feet six inches; it was entirely empty, without door or entrance, and seemed to have been intended for the same purpose as the chambers below it; but appeared to be the last and to complete the series, as it had an inclined roof, like the Queen's and Belzoni's Chambers, composed of eleven slabs of calcareous stone, twelve feet three inches long. They rested upon a low wall about three feet high, which allowed for the inequalities of the floor, composed, as in the other instances, of the reverse of the granite slabs that formed the ceiling of the rooms below it; the stone, by the side of which the entrance was worked up, was six feet six inches in thickness. Holes had been cut in the floor, apparently for the purpose of sustaining temporary supports of wood for the erection of the roof. Excepting the floor, the whole of the chamber was built of calcareous stone. The joints were open, and there were considerable settlements; some of the stones of the roof also were cracked, which was not surprising, considering the immense weight they supported. When we first entered this chamber, the floor was covered with the same deposit of dust which we had observed in the apartments below it, and, in addition, the calcareous stones were covered with an exudation, which had the appearance of white feathers, and resembled that afterwards found in the Third Pyramid. There were many quarrymarks similar to those in the other chambers, and also several red lines crossing each other at right angles, with

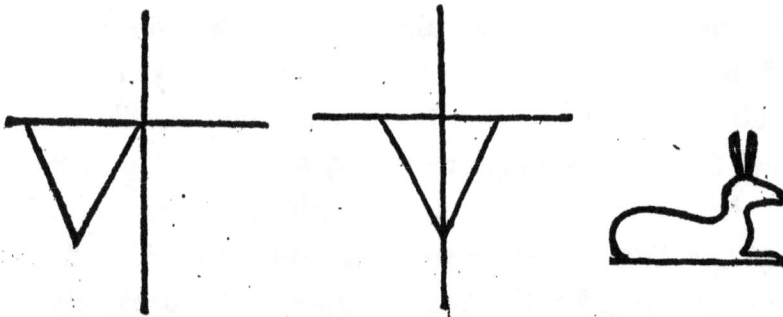

black equilateral triangles described near the intersections, in order probably to obtain a right angle.

* This hieroglyphic was not observed by Mr. Hill.

LINE ON THE SOUTH SIDE.

LINE ON THE NORTH SIDE.

LINE ON THE WEST SIDE.

LINE ON THE EAST SIDE.

CAMPBELL'S TOMB.

HIEROGLYPHICAL INSCRIPTIONS ON THE SIDES.

Scale of

9 Feet

F. Arundale, del.

Day & Haghe Lith. to the Queen.

Published by J. Fraser, Regent Street.

I returned in the evening to Cairo in company with Mr. Raven and Mr. Hill.

The following observations, by Mr. S. Birch of the British Museum, relates generally to the quarry-marks in all the chambers of construction that have been cleared in the Great Pyramid, and specimens of them are given in the annexed plates :—

"The symbols or hieroglyphics, traced in red by the sculptor, or mason, upon the stones in the chambers of the Great Pyramid, are apparently quarry-marks; a supposition strengthened by the fact of their appearance upon the blocks which have been transported from the Mokattam, and of their absence on the stones quarried upon the spot.

"Although not very legible, owing to their having been written in semi-hieratic or linear-hieroglyphic characters, they possess points of considerable interest from the appearance of two royal names, which had already been found in the tombs of functionaries employed by monarchs of that dynasty under which these Pyramids were erected.

"A cartouche, similar to that which first occurs in Wellington's Chamber, had been published by Mr. Wilkinso mater. Hieroglyph. Plate of unplaced King's E; and also by M. Rosellini, tom. i. tav. 1, 3, who reads the phonetic elements of which it is composed "Seneshufo," conjecturing it to be the Sensaophis of Eratosthenes, which name is supposed by Mr. Wilkinson to mean "the Brother of Suphis." Without entering into any discussion as to the etymology of the prefixed SEN, or as to the syllables to which it might be paralleled in Coptic, or in the sacred dialect, it is to be observed that the reading of

Sensaophis is false, owing to an error of the transcriber, which has been adopted by subsequent editors through the want of a proper analysis of the passage. After mentioning the first Saophis, Eratosthenes gives in his catalogue, Θηβαιων ιϛ εβασιλευσαν Σασαωφις : β' where the σω of εβασιλευσαν is affixed to Σαωφις. β'; there being no other Sensaophis in his list (see Eratosthenica, Godfred. Bernhard. 8vo. Berlin, 1822). The whole value of M. Rosellini's reading rests on the supposition that the vase and the animal (the ram) placed after it reads SEN, and signifies a Brother; but it is well known to all occupied in philological researches upon Hieroglyphics, that no such combination has hitherto been found: which fact is alone sufficient to destroy the felicity of M. Rosellini's theory, and has already given rise to considerable doubts as to the general correctness of his reading. The presence of this name, as a quarry-mark, in the Great Pyramid, is an additional embarrassment.

"The other name discovered with it, which he had already observed in an adjacent tomb, and conjectured to be that of Cheops, demonstrates at the same time the value of the phonetic system, and the ingenuity of the learned Italian. It is composed of elements purely phonetic, and is decidedly a name. It has also been published by Mr. Wilkinson, mater. Hieroglyph. unplaced King's; and M. Rosellini, tom. i. tav. 1, 2, and reads Shoufou (Suphis). or Khoufou (Cheops), according to the aspiration given to the initial—a sieve ⊕, which appears in Mr. Wilkinson's work without any distinction from the solar disc. The merit of assigning it to Cheops belongs to M. Rosellini.

"There is, however, no difficulty in dealing with the two names, for ascend to what period we will, the existence of prenomens is unquestionable, and the tombs in the vicinity of the Pyramids bear ample testimony of names at a very early epoch composed of elements equally phonetic with those of the Pharaohs of later dynasties, of the Ptolemies, or of the Cæsars. Without, therefore, any very positive violation of analogy, the two cartouches may perhaps thus form the prenomen and name of one monarch known to the Greeks under the appellations of Suphis, Saôphis, Cheôps, Chemmis, and Chembes. Nor is it the less probable on account of the absence of the solar disc, that this cartouche containing the jug and ram is a prenomen, as several cartouches of early epoch do not commence with that symbol; among others may be particularly specified the twentieth of the upper row of the Tablet of Abydos, where the hawk of Hôr, or Horus, is substituted for the solar disc in the prenomen of Merenre or Merenhôr, and two other prenomens, in which the disc is wanting, are also given by Messrs. Burton, Wilkinson, and Rosellini. It is at all events very probable, notwithstanding the assertion of M. Rosellini, that the jug and ram (not sheep) represent the name of the god Neph, or Nεv, the Chnouphis, Chnêbis, Chnêphis, Knêf, Chnoumis, or Chnêmis, of the Greek writers and inscriptions, one of the types, or avatars of the god Amoun-ra, the eponymous deity of Thebes, and the Jupiter of Egyptian mythology; and who, as Chnouphis, always appeared with the head of a ram, and presided over the inundation of the Nile.

"Mr. Wilkinson supposes the Ithyphallic form of Amoun-ra, the Harsaphes of M. Champollion, to indicate

Khem, Χμ, and Chemmo to mean the city of Pan, or
Panopolis; but it is within the circle of probabilities, that
Chnem or Chem were one and the same deity, and Chemmis is known to have been a large city of the Thebaid, in
which district both types of Amoun were worshipped.
Should this conjecture be right, the names at once subside
into one; Saophis and Cheops are mere dialectical variations of the same differently aspirated, or Grecianized,
and Chemmis is the prenomen transcribed into Diodorus
(lib. i. c. 63), from the name of Chnouphis, or Chnoumis,
replacing the disc of the sun.   This position is, however,
at present hypothetical, inasmuch as the mere presence of
these names in separate parts of such a vast edifice as the
Pyramid does not preclude the possibility that the cartouches indicate the name of Suphis I. and II.[9]

   " The meaning of the hieroglyphics following the prenomen, and written in the same linear hand as the cartouche, is not very obvious.   A reference however to those
on other monuments gives a solution of most of the forms
represented.

   " They consist of a gom or koucoupha sceptre, a
pschent, a curved line, a sword, a peculiar instrument, and
a level, and apparently compose the titles of the monarch,
similar to " Giver of Life, like the Sun for ever," of later
rulers; and the sentence may mean " Mighty in Upper
and Lower Egypt, giver of power."   The third, fourth,
and fifth symbols, indicate some office, the particular

---

[9]   The chambers wherein they were found were altogether in one
part of the building, and connected in one original plan, as chambers
of construction.

function of which is at present unknown. The same title appears on the coffin of the Queen of Amasis in the form of [hieroglyphs]. These inscriptions are peculiar to this period, and to the era of the Saite dynasty, who revived many of the earlier prenomens, titles, and offices.

"The symbols following the name are very indistinct, but apparently titles; other symbols written in characters more nearly the Hieratic also appear, but possess less interest than those previously described. The figure of a bird resembling a swallow, and used to express Шep, "great, chief," &c., is of common occurrence, as is also the symbol of a priest, a man pouring water over his head, but the cartouche of Suphis is followed by a hieroglyphic to which it would be difficult to find a parallel. The symbol also which appears in Wellington's Chamber, and perhaps the fourth to the left in the west end of the same chamber preceding the cartouche (neb Shoufou), are equally difficult of solution; they may possibly replace the figure of the priest; but this is mere conjecture, and far from being proved, and may also be a portion of the standard of Suphis I. and II., which is about to be published by M. Rosellini.

"A curious sequence of symbols occurs upon the blocks of the northern and southern sides of Campbell's Chamber. The mason has marked upon those of the south the symbol [hieroglyph] Hoцpe, "good," or "excellent," perhaps likewise used in these instances as a cipher, for it is accompanied by numerals.  The first instance presents

≡≡⚲ ‘NOFRE, eight,’ where the recurved line indica-

tive of the decimal has probably been rubbed off, since the

block next but two in succession has ꞮꞰꞰꝅ ‘ NOFRE,

21,’ which would make the number of the preceding block
‘ 18.’  After 21, a single unmarked block occurs, then

ꝅꞰꝅ which signifies NOFRE, 2, 3.  No analogy between

NOFRE and South has been as yet discovered.  The blocks
on the opposite quarter are marked with a koucoupha
sceptre, called gom, or tom, apparently with reference to
strength, power, &c., the Coptic Ⲭⲟⲙ.  One block bears
this symbol by itself, and the other with the numerals IV.
gom IV.  At the east end the symbol NOFRE again occurs
with some other marks apparently numerals, but imperfect
and indistinct, and at the joint is a gazelle couchant having
before it a sword, or glaive.

"Hieroglyphics are at present so imperfectly understood, that it is difficult to give an explanation of the whole
of these signs, many of which may after all have been
merely appropriate to masonry;  it is indeed equally so to
assign for what reasons the South should have been considered ‘ the Happy or Gracious,’ and the North, ‘ the
Powerful’ quarter."

*May* 28*th.* — The following articles were sent to the
Consulate for Colonel Campbell — a small image of leaf
gold, found in the fosse of Campbell's Tomb, and a few
trifling ornaments of ivory, found near the Sarcophagus;

three or four green idols, and a fragment of the small Sphinx already described.

It appeared by Mr. Perring's drawings, that the mouth of the southern Air-channel was forty-seven feet higher than the roof of Campbell's Chamber.

I understood that M. Caviglia had been for some days at Cairo, and that he returned soon afterwards to Alexandria. I had no intercourse with him excepting an application through Giachino for the goods which he had left at Gizeh: these were delivered to him by Mr. Hill, according to a list which I had sent to the British Consulate.

In the evening, I arrived at the Pyramids with Mr. Mash and Mr. Hill. It was a very stormy night.

### *May 29th.*

Reis, 10.　　Men, 174.　　Children, 189.

Great Pyramid.—Excavation in southern front.
——　　　　Excavation in northern front.
——　　　　Roof in Queen's Chamber.
——　　　　Southern Air-channel.
Second Pyramid.—Roof in Belzoni's Chamber.
Third Pyramid.—Interior.
Excavation between the Third and Fifth Pyramids.
Campbell's Tomb.
Shaft westward of Sphinx.
Shaft between Campbell's Tomb and Second Pyramid.
Shaft north of Sphinx.

Mr. Hill proceeded with his operations at the southern Air-channel, and about seven feet from the surface of the Pyramid, he found within it a large stone which he was afraid would get fixed further down. He therefore removed it with the utmost caution, which was fortunate for Mr. Perring, who was employed in the King's Chamber, and having contrived to force his head and shoulders at that very moment into the lower part of the channel, would probably have been killed had the stone in question fallen through it. Upon the removal of this block the channel was completely open; an immediate rush of air took place, and we had the satisfaction of finding that the ventilation of the King's Chamber was perfectly restored, and that the air within it was cool and fresh. The channel above the stone was clean, but below it was much blackened with fires made from time to time in the lower part to discover its direction. It was nearly or quite horizontal through the wall of the King's Chamber, and afterwards ascended in one continued line to the opening on the outer side of the Pyramid; but as the King's Chamber is to the southward of the centre of the Pyramid, and as the openings of both the Air-channels are at the same height, the line of the southern is considerably shorter, and more inclined than that of the northern — the length of the southern Air-channel being 174 ft. 3 in., that of the northern, 233 feet. Had not the upper part of the latter channel been forced, and that of the southern filled up with the above-mentioned stone, both of them would in all probability have remained open, and the ventilation of this wonderful structure would have continued as perfect as when it was first built. It is to be remarked, that, as the apartment is to the eastward, the ventilation by the Air-channels, which are in the centre, is oblique.

These channels had probably always excited particular attention; indeed, we are informed by Greaves, that the lower part of the southern had been forced, and was blackened with smoke in 1638. They are noticed by various travellers, and have given rise to many fanciful conjectures by M. Maillet and others; it is therefore surprising that their direction was so long unknown. It is, however, satisfactorily proved by these operations that they were intended to ventilate the King's Chamber, and that they have no communication with any other apartments; and, consequently, it might be inferred that no chambers, or passages, exist in the Pyramid besides those already discovered.

The excavation in search of a southern entrance was therefore given up, which had been carried to a considerable depth without finding the least indication of a passage, either by an inclination in the courses of the stones, or by any other circumstance. The great magnitude of the building, compared with the smallness of the chambers and passages; and also the position of the entrance to the eastward in the northern front, induced a conjecture that an entrance to the westward in the southern front might conduct to passages and apartments constructed in the great space between the three chambers entered from the north. But this does not appear to be the case; and it is to be believed that the King's Chamber is the principal apartment, and the security of the sarcophagus within it the great object for which the Pyramid was erected. Many arguments might be adduced in support of this opinion; amongst others, it may be observed, that the proportions of the passages correspond with the dimensions of the sarcophagus, and that their arrangement seems expressly intended to facilitate the deposition, and to prevent the removal of it. The Queen's Chamber may be considered as an appendage to the

King's, in the same way as the apartments in the sepulchres at Thebes. It may also, like those in David's tomb, mentioned by Josephus, have contained treasures; but, whatever may have been the object, it has evidently been concealed with great care. It is also to be observed that the King's Chamber has been secured by four granite portcullises,[1] and by the solid masonry with which the whole length of the passages have been closed; that the well has been formed to supply with air the people employed in filling from the interior the reascending passage at the bottom of the great gallery, with blocks laid up in the gallery for that purpose; and that it also afforded to them an escape by the lower passage when the work was completed. The entrance passage was probably afterwards filled up from the exterior. The great importance of the King's Chamber is also proved by the air-channels expressly made for its ventilation, and also by the precautions taken to secure even the walls from any superincumbent pressure by the five chambers above it, which are less carefully built, and of worse materials, in proportion to their distance from it; whilst, at the same time, the exquisite finish of the ceilings in the four lower apart-

---

[1] The portcullis consisted of slabs of granite fixed in grooves, which were not, in the first instance, brought down below the top of the passage, till it was necessary to lower the portcullis, when the grooves were cut out to the bottom. One of the portcullises has never been lowered, but remains suspended over the entrance,—a circumstance which might be supposed in some degree to corroborate the assertions of Diodorus Siculus, that the body of the king was not laid in this tomb, had not the other three been lowered, the passages filled up with masonry, and an excavation been carried under the sarcophagus, which could scarcely have been attempted if the tomb had been found empty.

ments prevent any accumulation of rubbish, and it would appear, also, the deposition of the sparry excrescence, which was found only in the upper. Nor should the masonry of the chamber be forgotten, which is probably the finest specimen in the world. It consists entirely of enormous masses of polished granite worked down, and laid with the greatest exactness, and has retained its original perfection for unnumbered centuries, whilst other mighty fabrics, composed of coarse workmanship and materials, have gradually crumbled away into shapeless masses of stones and of rubbish.* In this instance every block is as fresh and as perfect as when taken from the quarry; and such is the ponderous solidity and perfection of their texture, and the labour and science employed in their arrangement, that they seem to set at defiance the effects of time, and the efforts of human violence. It has been remarked that the upper chambers were finished from the east, and the vast blocks of this floor appear to have been closed in by a smaller oblong stone at the north-western corner. This had been removed, no doubt, in very early times, in search of treasures supposed to have been concealed beneath the sarcophagus. The excavation is mentioned by Greaves; and, when it was cleared out for the boring, an opportunity was afforded of observing the great care with which the supports and bedding for the blocks had been constructed,

* It may likewise be observed, that of all the remarkable objects which were formerly considered peculiarly worthy of notice, and therefore termed the "Seven Wonders," the Pyramids alone at present remain.

and the extraordinary manner in which they were worked
and put together. (See page 11.) The custom of de-
positing treasures in mausolea seems to have prevailed
universally in the earliest times, and to have been at once
the cause of the solidity of their construction, and of the
violation to which they have been in all countries subject; for some more powerful motive than mere curiosity
must have caused, in former times, the great labour and
expense attending these researches, particularly at the
pyramids, where it was necessary to cut through and
remove the blocks of granite and solid masonry, which
closed the passages and chambers. It would also appear
that, besides the wealth contained in the chambers, some
object of peculiar interest was supposed to be concealed
in or about the sarcophagi, as all of them in the pyramids
at Gizeh, and many at Thebes, have been broken into,
and various excavations have been made around them;
and it is singular that the only instance in which success
appears to have attended these excavations, is the secret
passage beneath the sarcophagus in Belzoni's Tomb at
Thebes: in none of the others do any cavities, or traces
of a communication appear.

I happened to be employed at Campbell's Tomb when
the southern Air-channel was opened, and I heard with
great satisfaction Mr. Hill's three English cheers on the
occasion, as I fully expected that we should have had as
much trouble with that, as we had with the northern.
Some green idols, broken jugs, coarse red pateræ, cups,
and other pieces of earthenware, together with a small
quantity of leaf-gold, were found in the southern fosse of
Campbell's Tomb. Similar pateræ and cups had been

also found near the Fifth and most of the other pyramids. Mr. Perring and Mr. Mash surveyed Colonel Campbell's Chamber.

### May 30th.

Reis, 10.     Men, 196.     Children, 185.

Great Pyramid.—Excavation in northern front.
—— Roof in Queen's Chamber.
—— Clearing the Chambers and Passages.
Second Pyramid.—Roof in Belzoni's Chamber.
Third Pyramid.—Interior.
Excavation between the Third and Fifth Pyramids.
Campbell's Tomb.
Fourth Pyramid.—Interior.
Shaft westward of Sphinx.
Shaft between Campbell's Tomb and Second Pyramid.
Shaft north of Sphinx.
Bridge in southern Dyke.

Several Arab Sheiks came to the tents.

Mr. Hill copied the hieroglyphics in Campbell's Chamber. The survey was continued, and a party was again sent to the bridge in the southern Dyke. The lid of the sarcophagus in Campbell's Tomb was moved out on wooden rollers, that the hieroglyphics might be copied; and various articles were sent from this place to the consulate. A quantity of bones and pieces of earthenware were found on the buttress at the south-western angle, and in different parts of the fosse. I examined, with Mr. Hill, the chasm at the northern front of the Great Pyramid; it had been cleared to a great depth, and had become so narrow that the works were carried on with difficulty. As the operations were nearly finished in the interior of the Great Pyramid, people were employed to clear away the stones and rubbish from the different chambers and passages. The sand had been taken out of the shaft between Campbell's Tomb and the Second Pyramid, and a grotto was discovered at the bottom of it.

**END OF THE FIRST VOLUME.**

# ERRATA in Vol. I.

Page 11, {3rd from bottom} *for* wet      *read*   red
.. 24, last line,    Sovadee      ..    Souadee
.. 41, line 19,    Abousier      ..    Abouseir, *passim*
.. 42, .. 6,    Darfour      ..    Darfoor, *passim*
.. 47, .. 4,    form      ..    forms
.. — .. 11,    pummels      ..    pommels
.. 48, .. 3,    Kalabsha      ..    Kalabshee
.. 52, .. 19,    Cordofun      ..    Kordovan
.. 60, .. 3,    up on      ..    upon
.. 64, .. 10, *after* desert      *insert*    country
.. 67, .. 18, *for* propylæa      *read*    propylæon
.. 69, .. 3,    Rameses      ..    Remeses
.. — .. 8,    contains      ..    contain
.. 72, .. 16,    nor      ..    or
.. 82, .. 3,    Oisirtesen      ..    Osirtesen
.. 86, .. 22, *before* Government      *insert*    The British
.. — .. 27, *for* this country      *read*    Great Britain
.. 89, {2nd from bottom} .. were      ..    are
.. — last line,    are      ..    were
.. 96, line 14,    Assasseuf      ..    Assasseef
.. 97, .. 19,    Deir      ..    Drah
.. 108, .. 7, *after* is      *insert*    being
.. 112, last line, *for* three      *read*    these
.. 115, line 16, *omit* that
.. 126, .. 6, *for* Faioum      ..    Faiyoum, *passim*
.. — {5th from bottom} .. head, chief, or      ..    head or chief
.. 130, .. 13,    Antinoe      ..    Arsinoe
.. 135, last but one, .. in      ..    on
.. 182, .. 18, *before* be      *dele*    to
.. 219, .. 24, *for* Atræus      *read*    Atreus
.. 220, .. 19,    sprung      ..    sprang
.. 224, .. 2,    thirty-eight      ..    thirty-six
.. 243, {6th from bottom} .. 1835      ..    1836
.. 258, .. 14,    Abdallatif      ..    Abd Allatif, *passim*
.. 275, last line,    Abon Simbal      ..    Abou Simbel
.. 279, .. 4,    relates      ..    relate
.. 284, .. 7,    2, 3      ..    23

## CORRECTIONS MADE BY HAND.

.. 17, line 21,    1780    *instead of*    1786
.. 282, inverted commas at note erased

www.ingramcontent.com/pod-product-compliance
Lightning Source LLC
Chambersburg PA
CBHW062033090426
42740CB00016B/2894